Blackwell Manifestos

In this new series major critics make timely interventions to address important concepts and subjects, including topics as diverse as, for example: Culture, Race, Religion, History, Society, Geography, Literature, Literary Theory, Shakespeare, Cinema, and Modernism. Written accessibly and with verve and spirit, these books follow no uniform prescription but set out to engage and challenge the broadest range of readers, from undergraduates to postgraduates, university teachers and general readers – all those, in short, interested in ongoing debates and controversies in the humanities and social sciences.

Already Published

After Globalization

Eric Cazdyn and Imre Szeman

WILEY-BLACKWELL

A John Wiley & Sons, Ltd., Publication

This edition first published 2011
© 2011 Eric Cazdyn and Imre Szeman

Blackwell Publishing was acquired by John Wiley & Sons in February 2007. Blackwell's publishing program has been merged with Wiley's global Scientific, Technical, and Medical business to form Wiley-Blackwell.

Registered Office
John Wiley & Sons Ltd, The Atrium, Southern Gate, Chichester, West Sussex, PO19 8SQ, United Kingdom

Editorial Offices
350 Main Street, Malden, MA 02148-5020, USA
9600 Garsington Road, Oxford, OX4 2DQ, UK
The Atrium, Southern Gate, Chichester, West Sussex, PO19 8SQ, UK

For details of our global editorial offices, for customer services, and for information about how to apply for permission to reuse the copyright material in this book please see our website at www.wiley.com/wiley-blackwell.

The right of Eric Cazdyn and Imre Szeman to be identified as the authors of this work has been asserted in accordance with the UK Copyright, Designs and Patents Act 1988.

Wiley also publishes its books in a variety of electronic formats. Some content that appears in print may not be available in electronic books.

Designations used by companies to distinguish their products are often claimed as trademarks. All brand names and product names used in this book are trade names, service marks, trademarks or registered trademarks of their respective owners. The publisher is not associated with any product or vendor mentioned in this book. This publication is designed to provide accurate and authoritative information in regard to the subject matter covered. It is sold on the understanding that the publisher is not engaged in rendering professional services. If professional advice or other expert assistance is required, the services of a competent professional should be sought.

Library of Congress Cataloging-in-Publication Data

Cazdyn, Eric M.
 After Globalization / Eric Cazdyn, Imre Szeman.
     p. cm
 Includes bibliographical references and index.
 ISBN 978-1-4051-7794-8 (hardback)
 1. Globalization. 2. Globalization in literature. I. Szeman, Imre, 1968– author. II. Title.
 JZ1318.C39 2011
 303.48'2–dc22

                                                                                                2010049552

A catalogue record for this book is available from the British Library.

This book is published in the following electronic formats: ePDFs ISBN: 9781444396461; Wiley Online Library 9781444396478; ePub ISBN: 9781444396454

Set in 11.5/13.5pt Bembo by Thomson Digital, Noida, India.
Printed and bound in Malaysia by Vivar Printing Sdn Bhd

1   2011

For FRJ

Contents

Contents

Acknowledgments

A book is always the work of more than those who actually sat down to write it. We would like first to thank our research assistants, Nicholas Holm and Frank Castiglione (McMaster University), and Sana Ghani (University of Alberta), for their help on this project, especially the difficult work of transcribing hours of interviews. Justin Sully jumped in to help at the end, just as he has on other projects in which we've been involved; thanks greatly, Justin.

Without the support of colleagues in the countries in which we worked, we would have had a difficult time organizing the student interviews. Thanks to Jaka Primorac (Croatia), Chi-she Li and Tsung-yi Michelle Huang (Taiwan), Eva Boesenberg (Germany), Alexandra Kleschina (Russia), Sára Monok (Hungary), and Gregory Lobo (Colombia). All of these fine scholars contributed to this book through the insights they shared with us and the misadventures in which they involved us while we were visiting the countries in which they work.

The student interviews took place at Central European University (Budapest, Hungary), Humboldt University (Berlin, Germany), Institute for International Relations (Zagreb, Croatia), National Taiwan University (Taipei, Taiwan), Universidad de los Andes (Bogotá, Colombia), and Yekaterinburg State University (Yekaterinburg, Russia). We are grateful, too, to the staff at the Banff Centre for the Arts, where a portion of this book was written in January 2010.

Acknowledgments

Emma Bennett, Caroline Clamp, Caroline Richards, and Ben Thatcher at Wiley-Blackwell helped immensely in translating the manuscript into a book.

This project was made possible by a grant from the Social Sciences and Humanities Research Council of Canada.

A Précis: The Argument

1. Globalization was generally understood to be about transforma-
   tions in economics, politics, and culture – in other words, a change
   in *everything* all at once, a paradigm shift or system change produced
   and/or represented by specific elements (i.e., global markets, a
   24-hour culture, instant communications, increasing levels of
   immigration, etc.), with technology as the key enabling force.
2. Globalization was also, from the very beginning, an ideological
   project – one that served to naturalize capitalism under its name.
   Globalization made capitalism invisible (or as invisible as it ever
   can be) behind a set of changes that were treated as quasi-natural
   phenomena about which little could be done by human beings. All
   of the things that happened as part of globalization were real
   enough. But the big, overarching narrative of globalization into
   which they were placed was a fiction – an effective one, but a
   fiction nevertheless.
3. When capitalism returned following the economic crisis of 2008 (as
   a speakable discourse and an all-too-visible mode of social organization), there was a recognition that globalization's ideological
   project to make capitalism disappear was over. With capitalism
   confronted by its mortality and globalization revealed as a fiction,
   many anticipated a political reawakening on a worldwide scale.
4. But there has not been a serious confrontation with what comes
   after globalization because globalization rested on a more

After Globalization, First Edition. Eric Cazdyn and Imre Szeman.
© 2011 Eric Cazdyn and Imre Szeman. Published 2011 by Blackwell Publishing Ltd.

fundamental ideological project, one unrecognized at the time of its constitution, even though it was essential to its effective operation. *Globalization involves a certain configuration of time – one that cannot imagine an "after."* Modernity could have a post-modernity to follow it. But globalization? Post-globalization sounds like some dystopian coda to everything, not a new phase of human existence.

5. Our project is to understand the construction of this "time limit" that works in the name of globalization even when globalization's over. After establishing seven theses that challenge this ideology of time (theses that negate the standard assumptions about education, morality, nation, future, history, capitalism, and common sense), we examine four popular thinkers (Richard Florida, Thomas Friedman, Paul Krugman, and Naomi Klein) and show how their influential work is dulled by these assumptions. These thinkers not only mobilize these assumptions, but also produce and reproduce them. The overall effect of such assumptions is to preclude the capacity to think an "after" to globalization, and to rely on older narratives of how to deal with capitalism, regardless of the contradictions obviously contained within them.

6. Of course, the ideology of globalization and its time limit is also found outside of the work of such liberal thinkers. We investigate this through conversations with students from around the globe who tend to understand the world differently than the way it is popularly represented, and who seem unconvinced and uninterested in the false promises of the seven assumptions and the "time limit" they sustain.

7. In both cases – that of the liberal popularizers of globalization and the children of globalization – we find that there's "something missing." Something's missing between these two groups, as well as in the way that they both understand that something's missing in the world.

8. It is valuable to understand these limits and gaps, and to consider what they mean for imaginative possibilities. But we also need to be conscious of something else that is missing: a true capacity to think an "after" to globalization. This is the beginning of politics today.

Part I

The Afterlife of Globalization

a.   Nothing Can Save Us

Nothing can save us. Not the schemes of government planning committees. Not the triumphant spread of liberal democracy to the four corners of the world. Neither sudden scientific breakthroughs, nor technological marvels. Neither quick fixes, nor golden bullets. Not the Right turning to the left, the Left turning right, or everyone coming to their senses and occupying an agreed-upon center. Neither vigilantes, nor vanguards. Not the nation. Not NGOs. Not common sense. Not capitalism. Not the future. And certainly not a smart, articulate, young politician able to fuel the hopes of realists and idealists alike.

If nothing can save us, why even wake up in the morning?

To understand that nothing can save us is far from throwing up our hands and closing up shop. Rather, it's the first step in grasping the real limits of where we are and what is required to overcome these limits. At present, we continue to act within these limits, accepting them as the way things are and the way they have to be. We cede to governments the rationale and logics by which our societies are planned and organized. For all manner of impending crises – the end of fossil fuel,

After Globalization, First Edition. Eric Cazdyn and Imre Szeman.
© 2011 Eric Cazdyn and Imre Szeman. Published 2011 by Blackwell Publishing Ltd.

the proliferation of disease, the rise in the earth's temperature – we await the abstract entity called "science" (or the market, or God, or compassion) to save us in the nick of time. We imagine politics as an arena in which a happy (however tortured and difficult to get to) middle ground is reached through intelligent debate among competing parties – or at least, enough of a common position that it manages to allow things to limp along for another day. Even if we still meekly cast ballots, democracy has become associated with the bizarre practice of voting for politicians of different parties with the exact same worldview. We prefer to catch our thieves red-handed, content with discovering the pleasures of exceptions rather than having to confront the hard facts of the rule, so that we can continue to invest in the market and believe in the sanctity of our social systems. We imagine that our families and economies break down not because of how they are structured, but because of covetous, greedy, or weak-willed individuals who cause them to go awry. We continue to mime incredulity and shock in the face of crises and scandals, however much such events are dialectically integrated into how things work.

All of these boundary markers, these limits, are at the very heart of our social imaginings – especially when they function unconsciously. But they are at the center of the political in a direct way, too. For all of the celebration of a new global order, we continually fall back on the nation – that old standby of a political form we once thought we had (or were on the verge of having) successfully outgrown, and yet which remains the awkward jigsaw puzzle of geopolitical space in which most of us are content to live. We know that the nation is a fiction that arbitrarily matches space and belonging. And yet, the nation still structures everything – from our most intimate desires to the armies that defend it. Even the most hopeful dreams of a post-national world – whether we imagine it taking the form of rooted locals or as rootless cosmopolitans – are refracted through the lens of the nation. Globalization was supposed to mark the withering away of the nation; instead, in the twenty-first century we witness nations asserting their identities and fighting over the last scraps of the earth's resources. The struggle to address the problem of climate change – a global problem if there ever was one – has been repeatedly sandbagged by national interests that were supposed to have been transcended. In what was imagined to be the post-national era, the nation is stronger than ever.

What is true of the nation is doubly true of capitalism. Capitalism is now everywhere, which seems to confirm not only its permanence and effectiveness, but also its legitimacy. Without any competing system against which to now measure it, capitalism is no longer up for debate. This doesn't mean that everyone is satisfied with it, or that we can't analyze its problems and failures, but that its reality as a system has disappeared into the background of everyday life. Problems that one might expect would shake its veneer of permanence merely confirm its necessity and power as a social and political (not just economic) system. *As such, capitalism itself now constitutes a very real limit to thought.* When economic crisis produces unemployment, for instance, the longing is no longer for some new system. Rather, the hope is for capitalism to once again start operating "properly" so that everyone can get back to work – that is, get back to what we have come to take as normal life. Perhaps uniquely, capitalism's greatest quality is that it is a system that allows everything except the rigorous consideration of its own logic. It has become impossible to think beyond, even though we know there was a time before capitalism and that there almost certainly will be a time after it – unless we truly are living at the end of human history.

Crisis, the nation, capitalism: it's all so much *common sense* – that same common sense we said above couldn't save us. What do we mean by invoking common sense, this concept that speaks of received wisdom (of the kind that grates on the nerves of youth) and of a pragmatism that imagines itself to occupy a space outside ideology? The ready-to-hand vocabulary of the way things are and the way they should be that we all carry around with us, the accepted narratives that we reach for to explain the nature of things – that's common sense. A theoretical and practical miscellany comprised of (among other things) inherited beliefs about political structures, ideas about how one should spend one's days, and those things for which one should strive and struggle. More often than not our most intimate and unconscious desires are not at odds with common sense, but in perfect coordination with it. Common sense establishes those decisions and acts which are rational and normal, and those that are not. Not mere belief, not something that

7

is an outgrowth of human nature (whatever that is – too often an empty vessel that can be filled with all manner of ideology), it is a product of the social and political systems we inhabit. And, in a reciprocal fashion that should surprise no one, common sense establishes the imaginative limits of these systems, safeguarding their structures in almost territorial fashion in order to perpetuate the sealed logic of common sense and prevent outside ideas from challenging its axioms or principles. Common sense is that paternal voice that stops us in our tracks, reminding us that we've strayed beyond the reasonable and will soon make fools of ourselves if we don't abandon our childish wanderings. It is what we appeal to when we say "It's just human nature" or "It's just how things are," and when we insist that things will always be as they are now (only maybe faster) because they always have been so.

The most stunning contradiction of common sense is not that it doesn't make sense. In fact, common sense *is* perfectly reasonable, rational, and sensible. This is why it is so successful at limiting our imagination. The elegant but brutal contradiction of common sense, rather, is that it does not attend to the *common* at all. It claims a quotidian, empirical. and utilitarian universality, but it delivers benefits for the *few* at the expense of the *many* – even though it is the many who are most comfortable repeating its claims. We want to argue for the other side of common sense. This other side is not the irrational (as one might presume from the standpoint of common sense!), but the rational within a different frame. According to common sense, the political and social configurations within which we currently live are more or less fine. They are adequate to addressing the needs and desires of the common. When and where they are not, all that's needed is some fine-tuning and fixing of broken gears – or at most, when a big and unexpected challenge arises, the addition of some new mechanisms to the old machine. We don't see things this way. The reason we face so many problems and challenges isn't because we haven't been paying sufficient attention to sticky gears and levers already configured in the best possible way; or that so many bad and evil people exploit the machine (if only they would disappear – or be disappeared – then everything would work as it should!). Either way, the whole machine, built piecemeal over centuries, continues to stumble along. But what it creates and produces – its output, if you will – is fated to be as unjust as it has been in centuries past. And yet common sense tells us that time brings with it continual social improvements: we are better now than we have been in the past, and will be better still tomorrow.

Are solutions to our problems to be found in simple ameliorations of an unjust system? To be clear, we don't think that the system is flawed or broken; it works quite successfully, just as its rules and axioms have ingeniously designed it to. The problem is precisely that it *does* work, it continues to work; all of the corruption scandals and temporary system crashes not only fail to invalidate the system, but help to further prove its stability and integrity. Nothing can save us, but only if we adhere to the system of common sense that has brought us to where we are now.

b.   From Globalization to Anti-Americanism

This book began its life as a project examining contemporary expressions of anti-Americanism around the globe. In the summer of 2004, we were teaching a course in São Paolo on the ways in which we understand, theorize, and make culture within the context of globalization. For us, it is important to insist that globalization was not only a vector by which cultural forms and practices were spread around the globe. The most common way of thinking about culture in relation to globalization, even today, is in relation to new hybrid forms of cultural expression that originate out of the mixing and matching of pre-existing local (usually national) forms. Academic and non-academic writing on contemporary culture seemed newly impressed that cultural forms, practices, and expressions come into contact with one another and are reshaped in the process, and that it makes no sense to imagine anything like cultural purity as a result. It does not take much reflection to realize that such cultural sharing is a feature of culture per se: Goethe was already late to the party when he wrote about global literatures in the 1820s.[1] Equally suspect is the initial premise regarding the spatial fixity of cultural forms and practices (again, usually linked to national cultures) which then become uprooted and turned into something else as they travel – a myth of origins if there ever was one. We wanted to push our students to think more deeply about the relation between globalization and culture, but in ways that went beyond the standard narratives that more often than not were content to study the globalization of culture or the culture of globalization. In other words, we wanted them to think seriously about the meaning and significance of the two categories conjoined by the preposition "of," and to question the action of the preposition as well, which in the first instance identifies the result of a process (culture has been globalized) and in the second describes a form of belonging to a moment whose character has been determined in advance.

In the midst of the run-up to the US presidential election later that year, we could not escape the realization that the topic we were teaching felt curiously belated. For us, globalization was never just a way of naming those apparently objective developments which everyone now unthinkingly associates with it – mainly, the ever greater interlocking of national economies with one another through trade and finance – but was a new *narrative* of how the world works that needed itself to be analyzed, assessed, and criticized. Globalization was the name for a novel assertion of economic, cultural, and political power that wanted desperately to hide behind the veil of its claims to have identified, in almost scientific fashion, an actually existing phenomenon. At its core was an extension and expansion of US power – the bringing into being of the "new world order" announced by President George Bush Sr. and most effectively implemented by President Bill Clinton – in order to secure a position of global hegemony which was fast being chewed away by the economic and political rise of countries such as China, India, and Brazil. In São Paolo that summer, it seemed that everyone already knew the lie of globalization, and understood that it was more ideological project than the name for an objective historical process about which, like time itself, one could do nothing. We brought with us complex schemas and offered alternative theorizations to flash the spaces and places where globalization was confusing and complicating things, especially, but not only, with respect to culture. Our Brazilian students and friends had a much simpler way of framing things. Leaving globalization aside, they were offering a challenge to US power and the existing state of the world more generally by being anti-American in the most direct way possible.

Indeed, it seemed that if everyone was not already a full-blown anti-Americanist, then they were quickly becoming one. The war against Iraq was in full swing (Saddam Hussein was on trial for war crimes) and George W. Bush was finding it tricky to assemble a coalition of the willing. The hard truth was out; the United States would go it alone if need be. It was tough to argue with a country that not only possessed the largest military in the world, but spent more on defense than half of the rest of the world combined.[2] Michael Moore's film *Fahrenheit 9/11* had just been released and quickly became the highest grossing documentary film of all time.[3] For all of the interest in *Fahrenheit* in the United States, it was the film's enormous audience abroad that was truly significant. In less than a year, the worldwide sympathy for the United States following the events of 9/11 turned into widely held suspicion, driven by the depressing fact that many Americans (including Bush himself) had trouble distinguishing Saddam Hussein from Osama bin Laden. Anti-Americanism was then there for the taking, and irresistible, like so much low-hanging fruit. The brilliance of Bush is that he didn't seem to care. He was a true believer and was quick to remind anyone who would listen that being President is not a popularity contest – even though the US political structure (with its maudlin candidate advertisements and perfectly staged rallies) is organized exactly on the order of a popularity contest. And it was precisely the popularity of Bush *inside* of the United States that enflamed the anti-Americanism abroad. "How could the citizens of the US be ready to elect him President, *again?*," the world seemed to be asking.

While in Brazil we could not escape *Fahrenheit 9/11*: every conversation was invariably punctuated with a comment about it. And every conversation seemed to turn on what the political effects of the film would – and could – be. Could there be a global movement organized around the criticism of the United States? Would it re-energize the dormant energies against the imperious extension of the global power, an energy witnessed in the worldwide protests against the Iraq War in 2003? Might the film change the course of the war? Or have an impact on the US election? Might an angry yet progressive anti-Americanism actually be more effective at producing global change than so many utopian calls for a new democratic future? Of course, none of this came to pass. Despite catching the mood of the moment and generating an impossible-to-avoid critique of the nature of contemporary politics, Moore's film did not have the force many – including the filmmaker himself – had hoped that it might.[4] This did not surprise us, nor did the growth of the anti-Americanisms around the globe in the wake of the US military involvement in Afghanistan and Iraq. But as scholars interested in globalization, we were intrigued by the nature and character of these sentiments and how they related to the discourses and narratives of globalization, which, for the decade preceding them, formed the bedrock of how people imagined the world.

What was clear to us back then was that anti-Americanism was a symptom of something else. Not only was it not about America or even George W. Bush, but it was not similar in form to past anti-Americanisms, such as the ones that emerged at the time of the Mexican–American War (1846–1848) or those that were a consequence of the Vietnam War. In these instances, too, Americans were frighteningly convinced of their own superiority and moral rectitude, and through the deployment of military power produced similar sentiments of fear, disappointment, hatred, and anxiety toward the US government and the ideologies structuring everyday life in the United States, as well as toward US mass culture (captured by the Coca-Cola which Jean-Luc Godard paired with Marx in *Masculin, feminine* [1966]). It doesn't take much to realize that despite a similarity in sentiment, the contexts in which these various anti-Americanisms were expressed were qualitatively different, thus demanding careful attention to their content and the circumstances in which they operated. Some critics were attentive to this difference.[5] In most studies, however, anti-Americanism was treated as an easily identifiable phenomenon to explain and one equally easy to explain. And so the anthologies, monographs, and op ed pieces began to flow, making connections between current and past expressions of anti-Americanism and (in tune with the need to consider the global frame) paying attention to the distinct forms taken by this latest wave of anti-Americanism in various nations. All were invariably structured by a single question: why do they hate us?[6]

This is where globalization returns. Before 9/11 the growing scholarship on globalization *and* the anti-globalization movements tended to de-emphasize the United States as the primary force of geopolitical power. The United States was an important player and recognized as the most powerful single actor in the world; even so, it was treated as something like a category mistake to focus too directly on the United States at the expense of new networks and systems of power and decision making. Supranational institutions (from the International Monetary Fund and World Bank to transnational corporations) emerged as the key objects of study and, for social movements, of resistance. Michael Hardt and Antonio Negri's influential *Empire* (2000), for example, considered any privileging of the United States as missing the crucial point that there are no longer territorial centers of power and fixed boundaries.[7] It was for this reason that many across the disciplines substituted the adjective "international" for "transnational," a term more suitable to globalization and one which drew attention to the parochialism and paternalism of the nation-state era and the emergence of new non-state actors with considerable power and influence.

Following 9/11 and the subsequent wars in Afghanistan and Iraq, the United States was positioned as once again the most powerful actor in the world. It was the sole superpower. However, it was a superpower in decline. It is this decline that accounted for its actions and its particular impact on the world at the present time. The work of David Harvey, Giovanni Arrighi, and Neil Smith, among others, argued that the shifts in geopolitical power away from the United States were evidenced by the Bush administration's emphasis on political and military solutions to what were fundamentally economic problems of global capitalism.[8] For these thinkers, a superpower financing its solutions to its political problems through unprecedented deficit spending and diplomatic coercion marks a key shift in the history of the dominant powers. They argued that just as the British moment of hegemony gave way to the US one in the twentieth century, the problems arising from superpower overreach in Afghanistan and Iraq

13

were signs of the imminent end of the US imperium and the rise of another hegemonic power (likely China). Writers on the right side of the political spectrum (including Niall Ferguson) differed in their analysis of the current US situation only in their view of the overall desirability of the decline of power of the current global hegemon.[9] However, for these critics, too, when one examines figures such as the US share of global GDP (gross domestic product), one cannot but see a significant shift in power and influence at work.[10]

Since the time of the Vietnam War, scholarly work on anti-Americanism produced both within and outside of the United States has usually coincided with moments of especially egregious US military intervention. There is no doubt that the current explosion of books about anti-Americanism (which themselves participate in the constitution of anti-Americanist discourses in intriguing ways) are linked to the perceived failures of the United States to respond "appropriately" to the challenges of the post-Soviet and post-9/11 era. But rather than explaining anti-Americanism merely by identifying its root causes in the belligerence of a hegemonic power – whether one at the peak of its power, or, still powerful, on the decline – an interrogation of this now near-universal political and cultural discourse can allow us to discover unexpected geographies of the current character of global power.

The current work on anti-Americanism usually comes out of an Area Studies framework that tracks the latest eruption of anti-Americanism in a particular nation or region and moves backward in order to analyze its historical roots.[11] It goes without saying that there will be deep cultural differences between South Korean or Turkish reactions against American foreign policy and Brazilian or Canadian ones. Research that delineates these differences is necessary. But there is always the risk that such research will function to separate and exceptionalize each culture, thus burying precisely those connections we intend to explore. Instead of moving vertically and placing anti-Americanism in a national context, we will move horizontally and place anti-Americanism in a global context that emphasizes similarities across national situations, rather than the differences between them.

Moreover, since anti-Americanism is not our primary object of study (but a means to study the ways by which dominant discourses of globalization limit the contemporary global imaginary), we intend to study anti-Americanism *analytically* rather than to assess it normatively. In fact, we view this general normative bias in work on anti-Americanism – which either condemns anti-Americanism for its naivety and its counter-productivity[12] or celebrates it for its authenticity and courage[13] – as the fatal flaw in much of the recent work on anti-Americanism. Even in the best of the recent books on anti-Americanism, the aim of providing an overview of anti-Americanist discourses is, finally, to offer an explanation to a US reading public of the historical origins of anti-Americanism in all manner of military and political misadventures around the globe – that is, to explain it away by explaining it, and so once again taking these discourses as necessarily an expression of something else. We want, however, to assess and understand the character of this truly *global* discourse, taking anti-Americanism seriously as opposed to concluding whether it is right or wrong. We also want to position contemporary anti-Americanism within and in relation to that other discourse that is supposed to explain the world to us today: globalization. We said earlier that we thought that this anti-Americanism was a symptom of something else. It was: a sign of the confusions of globalization – ideology, narrative, post-national discourse and all the rest – as it started to come to an end without an after.

c. From Anti-Americanism Back to Globalization

It is a surprise that discourses of anti-Americanism returned during the second half of the past decade. What's surprising isn't the reasons for such expressions, or their underlying rationale. It is clear that recent anti-American sentiment was motivated by the aggressive actions taken by the US government in the wake of 9/11. The expressions of sympathy and concern for those directly affected by the attack on the Twin Towers, and for the American people more generally, gave way to worry, fear, and anger when it became clear that the response of the

US government would be to wage war first in Afghanistan and then in Iraq. The ability of the United States to proceed with these attacks (especially the invasion of Iraq) without the sanction of the international community and without fear of upsetting a fragile geopolitical balance (as would have been the case during the Cold War) made the true nature of contemporary power evident to everyone. The collapse of the Soviet bloc left the United States as the sole superpower in 1989; this much was clear. However, even in the wake of the military actions taken by the United States during the Clinton administration (the Iraqi no-fly zone, Somalia, Bosnia-Herzegovina, Haiti, Liberia, Sierra Leone, and so on – though notably not Rwanda), the real consequences of this momentous change in power dynamics only became alarmingly evident with the waging of war on a grand scale and the momentous expansion of the state security through the establishment of the Department of Homeland Security.[14]

So what *does* make today's anti-Americanism surprising? For us the surprise of these most recent anti-Americanisms, expressed by people around the globe, lies less in the "anti" – being against war, against the death of civilians, against the injustices perpetuated via new security measures, and so on – than in the very existence of the "America" to which it is conjoined. For, and at least in a theoretical sense, America was no longer supposed to exist in the new century. Whenever and wherever they are expressed, anti-Americanisms offer a map of global power; they constitute a shorthand of the way things work and how the world is organized. However, as we have said above, historical context is all-important in assessing the how and why of anti-Americanism. The anti-Americanisms of the twenty-first century, like the ones we witnessed in Brazil and heard in the interviews we conducted around the world (discussed in Part III), came in the wake of another shorthand that had come to dominate the public imagination about the nature of contemporary power and the likely direction it would take in the future. This was globalization. One of the key tenets of globalization – something at its very heart as a narrative, assumed as a premise, even if not always directly expressed – was that the nation (if not the state, though perhaps that, too) was coming to an end. The 1980s witnessed a concerted (if belated) critique of the idea of the nation in academic circles from scholars in fields as different as literary criticism and political science.[15] The end of the Cold War seemed to provide the historical circumstances in which, at long last, the demarcation of territory into blocks into which we were herded like cattle, consigned by fate to live out one kind of life over another, allowed to move across the borders which confine us (or not), was going to mercifully come to an end. This new era was globalization and whatever we were supposed to find at its end was certainly not the shameless assertion and defense of the Homeland. But this anachronistic defense of the nation is evident not only when America is endorsed as global hegemon, but also when those in other nations criticize America for compromising their own national interests. It is because of this double jeopardy (that potentially ensnares critics from all ideological sides) that all studies of anti-Americanisms today must begin with a rigorous analysis of globalization itself.

Globalization was and remains a messy concept. Though it is now used without comment in journalism and in academic literature – as if to suggest that it is a term that has accrued a fixed definition about which there is general agreement – it is best to think about it as a concept that conjures up a set of associations. The topics, issues, and themes one associates with globalization are not limited to "real" world developments, systems, and processes, but also include desires, hopes, and beliefs. What are some of the things we have come to associate with globalization? The prospective end of the nation-state is a key one. An invention of the eighteenth century which flourished in the nineteenth and wreaked havoc in the twentieth, the new economic, technological, and political circumstances of the twenty-first century exposed the serious cracks (institutional and conceptual) in the foundations on which nations had been built, and suggested that new forms of political organization might yet come into being.

Shifts in economic systems and technological innovation in recent decades meant that processes and forces that shaped life and experience in any given nation now extended beyond its boundaries and were increasingly outside of its control. Every nation needs to participate actively in international trade to supply itself with goods and services not produced within its borders and to generate income by supplying

17

others with the same – no mystery there. What the term "globalization" meant to draw attention to was a sea change in this process, a new geopolitical paradigm, which rendered the autonomy and sovereignty of existing nation-states increasingly fragile.

The primary driver of this change was thought to be new techno-logical forms that made the world faster and smaller. Various tech-nologies have been assigned a role in effecting this paradigm shift, including air travel (its expansion and democratization), computer technologies, and new media forms such as the internet and mobile phones. These technologies did not respect national barriers and played a significant role in bringing about changes in economic practices. The list here is familiar to anyone who has followed political and economic developments over the past several decades: just-in-time manufactur-ing, global production chains, and labor outsourcing on an interna-tional scale. New technologies not only provided material support for the new economic system, but played a direct role in the economy itself: production, distribution, marketing, and finance. In sum, glob-alization captures political, technological, and economic changes that together generate a historical phase-change, especially with respect to the position of the nation in the geopolitical order.

While there were some expressions of worry about the effects of this change in the status and power of nation-states and its impact on national populations, one of the surprising things about globalization is that, on the whole, this development was greeted *positively*. The transformation of the nation pointed to new possibilities for human communities. The nation-state system was nothing to be celebrated and clung to: its record is of unending war, suffering, and exclusions. The disagreements over and anxieties about globalization lay not in the prospective end of the nation, as much as in the precise character of what was going to take the place of the nation-state system. Those nationalists who opposed globalization did so not out of a deep and abiding love of the national political form, but because they feared that some of the programs and policies enabled and supported by specific national communities – universal health care, environmental protec-tions, universal education, and so on – would be imperiled or brought to an end. Even anti-globalization movements quickly offered a corrective to the name assigned them by journalists after the protests against the World Trade Organization Ministerial Conference in Seattle in 1999. They wanted it known that they weren't against globalization and so in favor of the nation, but rather that they wanted to challenge the political and economic system coming to take the place of the nation-state system (anti-globalization movements are for this reason better described as counter-globalization or alter-globalization – an alternative globalization being at issue, not an end to globalization as such). This was a system of unelected, unrepresentative international organizations and decision-making bodies, largely controlled by rich Western countries, who looked ready to take on the role of de facto government for the entire planet.[16] Globalization was going to happen – it *was* happening – no matter what. It was deemed inevitable. *How* it was going to happen, and what precisely this happening involved, was what was up for scholarly debate and was the subject of political struggle; the reality of this thing called "globalization" itself was not.

Some of the imprecision that has accompanied the concept of globalization has come out of the large number of competing attempts to name the "how" of its happening.[17] The desire to name and define this new thing proved irresistible; attempts to do so extended well beyond economics or politics, and into the realm of culture and identity. This made sense given the significance of culture and identity for the operations of nations. The nation-state produced a national subject; the increasing shakiness of its sovereignty as well as of its physical and cultural borders generated the possibility of hybrid or post-national identities, and on a scale far exceeding earlier experiences of immigration or travel (though these, too, became intriguing subjects of analysis for those who wanted to look at mobility in earlier centuries through the lens of globalization). Analyses of the uncertainty and groundlessness with which contemporary individuals are thought to face life in globalization are built around the assumption of a once stable national subject whose ability to now listen to M.I.A. or reggáeton music, read Orhan Pamuk or Roberto Bolaño, generates new and unexpected individual and communal opportunities. The possibility or impossibility of movements across borders – whether real, imagined, or fantasized – names the way in which the globalization is experienced. A great many academic books and articles devoted themselves to offering increasingly complex analyses of these imaginings, each with its own neologisms and conceptual innovations (as, for instance, Roland Robertson's use of "glocalisation" or the vocabulary of scapes advocated by Arjun Appadurai[18]), each trying to get the "new" of globalization and the "how" of its happening just right, so that we could navigate our way through a life rendered suddenly complex.

Against the backdrop of a world rendered global, anti-Americanism can only seem anachronistic: at best, the crude expression of political dissatisfaction; at worst, a category mistake which doesn't grasp that we are now living in very different times. But it is a mistake to see new anti-Americanisms like the ones we encountered in Brazil in this fashion – as a step back into the comfort of a politics that even at earlier moments was too easy. Anti-Americanism is not a reaction to a world rendered complex by globalization, a throwback to a more transparent view of the way the world is organized. Rather, the sudden reappearance of the nation in anti-American discourse should serve to remind us of a fundamental fact: although globalizing processes and effects exist, *globalization does not exist*.

Of course, many – most! – of the things that have been associated with globalization exist, from cyberspatial communities to transnational trade agreements. But globalization as a system does not exist in the way typically imagined. In fact, globalization as a discourse has come into being and continues to operate today precisely to cover and obscure the system that *does* exist, namely capitalism. There is a conceptual sleight of hand at work whenever globalization is invoked. Like any noun that is meant to name and specify something as complex as a historical period (e.g., modernity) or to capture in a word the character of the *Zeitgeist*, globalization is an assemblage of discrete and distinct actions, processes, effects, and outcomes, bundled together with the aim of producing something legible and intelligible. But in fact this is not what globalization does. Instead of intelligibility, it produces illegibility; it is often represented as a coherent system when it is actually a set of processes and effects across widely different spheres of social life, tossed together for a specific end and effect.

20

Within the academic world, this category mistake is not hard to track and explain. Before the mid-1990s, globalization was not commonly mentioned in academic research. Of course the processes and characteristics later assigned to globalization (compression of time and space, new communications, new forms of financial speculation, etc.) were often invoked, but almost always in the name of something else, such as post-industrial capitalism, transnationalism, late capitalism, post-Fordism, information capitalism, post-modernity, flexible accumulation, global capitalism, and so on. The replacement of these names by "globalization" was not only a semantic matter – a linguistic solution to simplify a confusing set of concepts. Rather, at its core the new dominance of globalization was a way to avoid thinking and speaking about capitalism, and, more profoundly, to avoid the larger question of system altogether.

The effects of globalization were so inclusive, so amorphous, malleable, and chaotic that the very thought of locating its logic or tendencies (as would be the case with any other system) became self-defeating. It was at this point that academics from every discipline crashed the party. Scholars in English literature would write about the globalization of Shakespeare (not just the globalization of Shakespeare studies today, but globalization during Shakespeare's era); anthropologists would track criss-crossed diasporic flows, discovering (eureka!) that we've been globalized throughout our history as a species; epidemiologists would study the global spread of disease; and so on, all the way up to the university administrators who were only too happy to rebrand their universities with the word "global," which soon was a modifier used with any and every noun (global campuses, global undergraduate experience, global curricula, global donors, and so on).

But, and as usual, the historians were the least convinced. When someone would rhapsodize about the newness of globalization – how different everything is and how anyone who does not appreciate these changes are the new flat-earthers – a historian would invariably remind everyone that all of the new characteristics ascribed to globalization have in fact existed for some time. If someone argued that globalization began in the 1970s with the oil crises and the new need for information technologies to make capital more flexible, then a historian would show how many of these same links and networks were at work at the beginning of the century.[19] Or if a political scientist argued for the ways in which the autonomy of the national territory was being undermined within globalization, then a historian would correct everyone by showing how Paleolithic trade routes also undermined local auton- omy. Such naysayers, however, were not only going after those in the social sciences. If a literary scholar appealed to how the new flexibility of globalization related to the formal inventions of the contemporary novel (as decentered, fragmented, and lacking a stable narrative voice), then a historian of the classics would disabuse everyone by showing how all of those techniques already existed in Homer.

The debate over globalization in the university, therefore, turned into a debate over how to periodize this new thing. When did "it" begin? How does "it" relate to what came before it? And, in response to the orthodox historians, might the same phenomenon function differently at different historical moments? These questions regarding periodization necessarily included the question of how to narrate globalization, how to tell the story of globalization. The point here is that the moment globalization became dominant (usurping capitalism and the problem of system itself) was the moment that all attempts to *explain* it were abandoned. All that was left to do at this point was to *describe* globalization – now both a name for a temporal period and a real, existing, irresistible world-historical force – in all its utopian glory or dystopian menace. The struggle over whether globalization was something qualitatively new or simply business- as-usual – a struggle that invariably took place on the level of description – crowded out from the debate a crucial consideration: when might globalization *end*?

It is impossible to ask this question within the dominant discourse of globalization, precisely because when globalization is understood solely on a descriptive level (for instance, as a stylistic category: it's faster, it's more flexible, it's less centralized) then one cannot imagine a different system coming into being. Globalization is simply the name for the here and now, *and* the future as far as the eye can see. As a temporal category, globalization had a very different quality than other descriptions of periods in human history. Even at its peak, it was never imagined that the Cold War would last forever. Something had to give, whether through the victory of one or another of the sides in the war, the occupation of some ideological middle ground, or the destruction of the species through nuclear conflict.

The coming into being of a system whose characteristic elements were such that it could not end was a key to lending globalization its aura of inevitability. This operates especially effectively in the deliberate confusion produced by the term, its seamless combination of empirical elements with ideological ones. Globalization is technological progress. Well, surely computer technologies will only get smaller, faster, and play an ever more ubiquitous role in daily life! Globalization points to production at dispersed sites around the world. Well, of course: could it ever make sense to create something in a single national space again? Why would one ever want to become less productive and efficient? And wasn't this in any case a way to increase GDP for everyone, helping to raise all boats until everyone could experience the same level of economic success? The economic flattening of the world was perhaps the one thing imagined as taking time, as being necessarily slow in a world otherwise characterized by the deranging intensity of speed and scale. Globalization could not come to an end; to suggest it might meant appealing to disaster scenarios, or implying or evoking laughable scenarios of temporal Luddism (appeals to ways of life unmediated by technology, such as organic farming, etc.). The category shift from the structure of capitalism to the effects of globalization, from explanation to description, therefore, snuffed out the possibility of thinking an alternative to globalization. Even if it became increasingly difficult to imagine such scenarios, capitalism was something that could fail or be replaced by some other economic system. But globalization? Social democracies such as Norway and Sweden, or states with economic principles even more distant from capitalism, such as Bolivia, Cuba, or Venezuela, might be seen as standing slightly to the side of capitalism; all, however, participated in globalization. How could it be otherwise? For globalization had no border and no end: it could only get faster, more integrated or divided, more deeply and extensively saturated into the daily life of everyone, everywhere.

With the financial meltdown at the end of 2008, however, the power of globalization has begun to lose its force. Despite everything, its end *has* unexpectedly come. The anti-Americanism that arose during the Bush years were the first signs of some of the difficulties which globalization was having in capturing the planet's imagination as the new common sense for how things were to operate. The component elements of globalization – say, the impact of technology on lived experience, or the movement of peoples across borders, or the on-the-ground effects of historically high levels of international trade – have not suddenly ground to a halt. But the ideological work performed by globalization cannot help but be shaken, finally and thoroughly exposed by a system crash. Instead of globalization – which remember, was supposed to be the name for the present as such – it has now become possible to talk directly about capitalism, whose force, ferocity, and very existence was obscured and mystified by the narrative of globalization that emerged after the Cold War. The reappearance of capitalism can be witnessed in the numerous references to "the system" that have emerged today in attempts to describe the circumstances we now face. "The system did not work." "The system is in crisis." "The system must be substantially reformed." *Who* is saying such things matters a great deal. For some on the left, the possibility of naming the system – capitalism – directly, outside the obscuring blend of concepts, forces, and processes connected with globalization, marks a moment of genuine political possibility. For those initially involved in articulating the ideology of globalization, the mea culpa that one might expect to find in discussions of the need to reform the system are almost nowhere to be found. And when they are, as in Alan Greenspan's mea culpa in October 2008 (right when the bankruptcies and bailouts began to flow), they effectively ascribe the problems to their own short-sightedness (in typical narcissistic fashion) rather than to the systemic logic itself.

One of the earliest, most pointed, and (it has to be said) most criticized descriptions of globalization is Francis Fukuyama's claim that with the end of the Cold War the world is at "the end of history." This claim is not really about time or history, though its evocation of a timeless end-of-times captures the atemporality that would become essential to the apparent inevitability and unavoidability of globalization. It is, rather, a claim about ideology and change, specifically with respect to political and economic structures. For Fukuyama, with the fall of the Berlin Wall,

> What we may be witnessing is not just the end of the Cold War, or the passing of a particular period of post-war history, but the end of history as such . . . That is, the end point of mankind's ideological evolution and the universalization of Western liberal democracy as the final form of human government.[20]

This is not – could not – be a description of an already empirically given possibility; and even if one were to believe in Fukuyama's idea of historical evolution in the strongest sense possible, such a claim would still need to bear the test of time. But in any case, this is neither description nor philosophy, but a call to arms for a political project, one whose aim is to bring about the conditions of the "end of history" announced here. The name for this project was, of course, globalization.

One might expect the system crash through which we are living to have brought an end to such self-confident talk of the "end of history." And it has. The title of Robert Kagan's book on the end of globalization says it all: *The Return of History and the End of Dreams*.[21] But the admission that history has come back – not that it was there all along, hidden or obscured, but gone (for the two decades of globalization) and then returned (the present moment) – does not bring with it an admission that anything of great significance has changed with respect to the momentum or movement of history. To be clear: for Fukuyama, the end of history means that humanity has matured to the point where Western liberal democracy is the only game in town; for Kagan, Western liberal democracy is also the only legitimate, mature political form. The difference is that, for Kagan, the movement of history on its own does not confer the legitimacy that comes with political and ideological maturity. If it was once imagined that history had come to an end with the establishment of a "new kind of international order, with nation-states growing together or disappearing, ideological conflicts melting away, cultures intermingling, and increasing free commerce and communications,"[22] history has now returned in the form of the international competition amongst nation-states. We've gone back to the future – back to the end of the Cold War and an older form of geopolitics, if in a new context. The developments of the past 20 years have proven wrong the assumption that economic liberalization leads to political liberalization, as well as the "abiding belief in the inevitability of human progress, the belief that history moves in only one direction."[23] Even though commerce has been fully globalized, the world is witnessing a revival of competition between democracies and autocracies (Russia, China, Iran), and the creation of "geopolitical fault lines where the ambitions of great powers overlap and conflict."[24] The lesson? "The world's democracies need to begin thinking about how they can protect their interests and defend their principles in a world in which these are once again powerfully challenged."[25] The principles remain the same, despite everything. What has changed, however, is simply the nature of the political project through which these principles might be actualized.

Easy appeals, by political commentators and authors of books on current affairs, to the forward flow and political and economic efficacy of globalization are disappearing. There is a sense that the world faces all manner of challenges that require both serious reflection and action, and a major change in the way things operate. Even so, as the example of Kagan's book shows, there is remarkably little difference between the ideas and values – indeed, the very nature of the system – with which we are expected to confront these problems; there is even less sense that these problems might be an outgrowth of the very system that is now imagined as the only path to resolve them. The animating political ideal of globalization was to see electoral democracy and capitalism joined at the hip across the world. There were two principles driving the political project of globalization. First, without naming it directly, globalization was a way of maintaining and managing the dominant position of the United States in the globe. It did so through the ceaseless articulation of the inevitability and desirability of all of the processes and forces associated with globalization – the production and circulation of the values of liberal democratic capitalism not as an ideology about which one might have an opinion or with which one might disagree, but as a form of common sense, and further, a common sense not directly connected with the United States. Second, this development was, in any case, historically inevitable; it was where nations and individuals would find themselves at some point; resistance was futile – not just because of the force of existing institutions but due to the movement of time itself.

And *after*-globalization, when history has returned? The global spread of liberal democracy and capitalism are treated surprisingly as no less inevitable. There is now, however, once again the necessity of a struggle to bring this state of affairs into existence; this is a struggle that involves the nation-state. The reappearance of the nation in politics might suggest that there is an entirely new actor, suddenly awoken from its slumbers, on the global political scene. In truth, globalization always involved the nation-state, especially the United States. (We can also think of China, a country whose successful integration into the global economy required a strong nation-state, or equally the involvement of the governments of Russia, Brazil, India ... in fact, every nation's state involvement in making globalization happen.) Globalization was a form through which the United States articulated the rationality of the values and ideas – their common sense – claimed on behalf of capitalism and democracy. After globalization, the *form* by which this common sense is articulated has had to change: with the system crash of 2008, the absolute givenness of globalization, its fixity and finality, has come to an end. One form it has taken is the admission of a post-American moment – a concession to the anti-Americanism of the past several years – though one which, as we shall see, is intended to maintain the hegemonic position of the United States as much as globalization. The *content* of this common sense has changed far less. Under the guise of another paradigm shift (first globalization, then its end) requiring concerted analysis, the common sense animating the discourse of globalization is trotted out, if in a new guise.

Almost everything we have written thus far about globalization and its aftermath suggests that it was little more than an ideological screen, a false promise – at best, a social-scientific category that turned out (in the end) to have less explanatory value than hoped for; at worst, a form through which consent was generated for liberal democratic capitalism in a fashion that proved difficult to question or resist. However, this would be to mischaracterize the ways in which globalization was understood and experienced. Globalization was a particularly effective figure/concept in extending US hegemony in the wake of the Cold War, a moment in which there might well have been wariness and resistance to the ideas and ideals of the world's lone superpower on the part of other nations. It is important to remember that globalization was also a moment of possibility and promise. The end of nation-states and the promise of cosmopolitanism; the opening up of borders and opportunities for travel; new forms of communication and human interrelation; a planet-wide rise in living standards; innovative technologies and the novel experiences that accompanied their use – these were developments connected with globalization that stretched the horizons of the social, cultural, and political experience. This is not to suggest that these possibilities were wholly realized, without their dark side, or even wholly new: the exclusions and violence of nation-states did not disappear, borders and mobility remained limited and confined to a small minority, new forms of communication and technology brought with them expanded forms of surveillance, labor exploitation, and so on; and for every new burgher added in China and India, a new disenfranchised slum dweller was added to the world as well. Nonetheless, one cannot discount the way in which the "one world" narrative of globalization generated energies for an economics and politics other than the status quo of capitalism and liberal democracy that we now witness. With the end of globalization comes the collapse not just of an ideological project, but hopes to enact a very different kind of politics on a global scale.

With the financial crisis of 2008, globalization comes to an end. Good riddance, one might say. For at that very same moment, for many the deferred promises of globalization are liberated. The election of Barack Obama in the wake of the financial meltdown resolves in an instant the seething anti-Americanism expressed around the world during George W. Bush's second term in office. It points to new political horizons and suggests that the political struggle announced by

Kagan will take a different form than he might have expected. Or so it might seem.

d. "I face the World as it is": On Obama

Thinking about anti-Americanism brought us back to globalization, but to a globalization operating on a different terrain than before: weakened in its self-certainties and the strengths of its fictions. Anti-Americanism, too, seemed to have been wiped out in an instant with the victory of Barack Obama. Even for those suspicious of claims about abrupt shifts in geopolitics due to singular events, his victory seemed to herald something new on the political and social horizon.

Obama's campaign was never just a national political event, just as his victory over John McCain was not just a national victory. There has never been a moment in modern history when non-citizens were so interested and instrumental in a national electoral race. Everyone the world over knew that what happened in the US election would profoundly affect their everyday lives – perhaps even more profoundly than their own local and national elections. In fact, the largest crowd of Obama's campaign came not in Chicago or California, but in Germany, as over 200 000 people crammed around Berlin's Victory Column to hear Obama on July 24, 2008. Obama began his speech, "A World That Stands as One," by making it clear that he spoke not as a presidential candidate, but as a citizen of the United States and as a citizen of the world.[26]

Part of the attraction to Obama was his background and his unlikely ascension to the top of the US political structure. But, and especially for those outside of the United States, most impressive was his intelligence and respect for fair and critical scrutiny of history and cultural difference in particular. Of course, Obama's appeal was in response to the growing antipathy toward George W. Bush, the leader who ridiculed intellectuals as quickly as he dismissed analytic work. Bush's favor for a folksy gut feeling and his explicit reliance on religious conviction to guide political decision making might work fine in the United States, but rarely for those abroad on the receiving end of its reductions and cartoon-like representations. Whereas a common-sense-driven anti-intellectualism is highly effective in almost any national context, it does not travel well, because common sense necessarily rejects analysis as it strategically mobilizes the national mythology. The most important expression of Obama's intelligence as it operated abroad (as against Bush's anti-intelligence), however, occurred not in relation to a particular policy or electoral promise, but over his parsing of a single sentence: "the war on terror."

Obama, like a good English professor, asked how there could be a war on a noun. There could be a war on a certain country that encourages terrorist acts (like Afghanistan) or even on a certain terrorist (like Osama bin Laden – in fact, Bill Clinton fired over 70 Tomahawk missiles at bin Laden in 1998), but terror is not an enemy in its own right. Unlike Bill Clinton's parsing of another sentence ("I did not have sexual relations with that woman" that was about evasion and the gratuitous use of his intellect to obscure and defend himself against an act that was as clear as day), Obama conducted his parsing in an attempt to return to what was at stake following 9/11. Indeed, if Clinton would have used his legal, rhetorical, and philosophical acumen to argue for why it wasn't the worst crime in the world to have an affair with Monica Lewinski (and that the obsession with the affair is a symptom of a US culture not only saturated by a sensationalized media but also by hypocritical moral positions), one wonders if the anti-intellectualism (and perhaps even the anti-Americanism) that proliferated during the Bush era would have been so strong. At any rate, more than any of his positions on defense policy or geopolitics, Obama's close reading of Bush and Cheney's "war on terror" was what most impressed those looking at the presidential race from abroad.

This desire for Obama to return care and consideration to decision making went a long way. So far, in fact, that many held their tongues when Obama brought into his administration Clinton-era favorites, such as Lawrence Summers as his leading economic advisor (not to mention Hillary Clinton as Secretary of State), and retained key Bush appointee Robert Gates as Secretary of Defense. Even the aftermath of the financial crisis (and the support for financial bailouts) that dom-inated Obama's first year in office did not significantly undercut his popularity at home or abroad. It took over a year, with the combination of the return of Wall Street – Goldman Sachs registering record profits and administering huge bonuses in spite of receiving funds from the Troubled Asset Relief Program (TARP) – and his decision to crank up military operations in Afghanistan, to kill the Obama fantasy.

A fantasy functions by turning Loss into a lost object – so that something that is structurally significant and informing but does not exist in any concrete way (such as the absent presence of Loss) is given positive form. In this sense Loss represents something that is impossible to possess (like having the super-rich without a poor majority within capitalism), while the lost object represents that thing that, or person who, can miraculously resolve this irresolvable contradiction. Indeed, the fantasy of Obama was the fantasy that a national leader could act in a way that exceeded the particular interests of his or her own country. This is the fantasy that was most spectacularly exploded in Oslo on December 10, 2009, when Obama accepted the Nobel Peace Prize.[27]

Only nine days earlier, Obama spoke to the US military academy at West Point to announce his new policy in Afghanistan.[28] Calling for a surge of over 30 000 new troops to be deployed in Afghanistan (for an additional cost of over $30 billion in 2010 alone), Obama refocused the United State's military priorities. Iraq would be wound down (a jab at Bush's failed policy and confusion of priorities), while the war in Afghanistan would be intensified. This decision, which came after months of consideration and debate (with the top US military commanders [Generals McKiernan and Patraeus] in favor, but the US ambassador to Afghanistan, retired Army General Karl Eikenberry, along with Colin Powell and Vice President Biden, resistant), would have to be engaged head on in his Nobel speech. Now Obama had two circles to square: first, how to respect the spirit of the Peace Prize, while having just committed to a major new military offensive (one under dispute even within his own administration); and second, how to accept this prize that represented global hopes and aspirations for the United States on the part of so many of the world's citizens, while not compromising his responsibility to US interests.

31

Acknowledging the Swedish royalty and then the Nobel committee before making a direct reference to the citizens of America (highly aware of how things would play back home), Obama mentioned Afghanistan almost immediately. He knew that Mahatma Gandhi and Martin Luther King (the two other Nobel Peace Prize winners whom he recognized most frequently in the speech) would disagree with his decision to escalate the war in Afghanistan. "But as a head of state sworn to protect and defend my nation," Obama argued in opposition to Gandhi and King, "I cannot be guided by their examples alone. I face the world as it is, and cannot stand idle in the face of threats to the American people." It is the sentence-starting "But" that is most striking. If Obama was not a head of state, he seemed to suggest, then he would be guided by the examples set by Gandhi and King. In other words, Gandhi and King were global leaders (and/or local leaders), while Obama is a national one – and these two different types of leadership cannot be reconciled.

The irreconcilability of national and global leaders is most profoundly expressed in relation to the environment. In his 37-minute Nobel speech, Obama mentioned climate change only once, and, even in this single utterance, environmental concerns were inextricably linked to military interests. Obama stated, "For this reason, it is not merely scientists and environmental activists who call for swift and forceful action – it's military leaders in my own country and others who understand our common security hangs in the balance." The conflation of environmental concerns with military ones is particularly significant given that at the very same time that Obama was speaking in Oslo, the most important summit on climate change (United Nations Climate Change Conference, or COP 15, with 192 nations gathered together, along with NGOs, civil society, and demonstrators from around the world, to seek a new treaty, agreement, or even consensus for how to manage global warming) had begun in Copenhagen, at which Obama was scheduled to give a major address.

The talks in Copenhagen were in free fall from the beginning. Targets, enforcement, and transparency were the buzzwords, with the different players unable to agree on benchmarks and how enforcement and transparency might even be possible on a global scale. For example, the United States hesitated on targets. Washington announced that it would cut greenhouse gas emissions 17 percent below 2005 levels by 2020; this, however, only amounted to a 4 percent decrease based on the 1990 benchmark used by most other nations. China cited sovereignty concerns as it hesitated on enforcement, while India and Brazil questioned why they should be held to the same targets as those of the United States and the European Union given the uneven history of global industrial development; the Group of 77 (an organization of 130 developing countries) argued that cuts in CO_2 emissions should not come at the expense of their development; and the African Union (a 50-member bloc of mostly poor nations) demanded much sharper cuts in emissions, as did small island states (a 39-member group, notably represented by the charismatic Prime Minister of the Maldives, Mohamed Nasheed), without which their very nations will become uninhabitable due to sea-level rise. And then there was the Organization of Petroleum Exporting Countries (OPEC, asking for financial compensation for any decrease in oil prices resulting from the climate negotiations), rainforest coalitions, former Soviet republics, and the suspiciously quiet "yes" countries, such as Canada and Japan.

By the time Obama arrived on the penultimate day, all of the weaker players had been sidelined. The struggle was between the United States and China, with Brazil, India, and South Africa along for the ride. In fact, what became known as the Copenhagen Accord was reached between these five nations (more a commitment to take climate change seriously than anything concrete), and begrudgingly supported by the other member nations who feared not being able to access funds from richer nations to help adapt to climate change. In the mainstream US media, Obama was represented as holding firm against China and coming off as the key figure to save the talks. But for the great majority of participating nations and the various leaders of NGOs and activists looking on, Obama was a terrible disappointment and the event as a whole little more than a sham.

Many of the international hopes and desires that had previously been invested in Obama were quickly drying up – but something seemed different. Instead of blaming the power play on a short-sighted and merciless leader – the way George W. Bush would have been excoriated, for example – many started to blame the larger system of decision making. The process itself was called into question – the process of how national leaders engage supranational problems. The executive director of Greenpeace UK stated that "The City of Copenhagen is a crime scene tonight ... It is now evident that beating global warming will require a radically different model of politics than the one on display here in Copenhagen." Even centrists began to describe the summit as an "abject failure," calling the whole diplomatic structure a farce and singling out Obama's bullying as the factor most responsible for forcing the rest of the member nations to sign a "death warrant."

What became clear in Copenhagen, and what was already on display in Obama's Nobel speech in Oslo, is that there could not be a serious commitment to manage climate change while the United States continued to wage wars in Iraq and Afghanistan. The over $3 trillion price tag for the US wars conservatively calculated by Joseph Stiglitz and Linda Blimes cannot be squared with what is required on the climate front.[29] For all of Obama's erudite allusions to political theory in order to argue for the legitimacy of waging a "just war," it is the economic argument that falls flat. On the streets of Copenhagen and across the world the central contradiction could finally be spoken: in order to finance the wars, the United States would need to keep producing wealth (driven by the limitless expansion and consumption of commodities, especially military weaponry) at a rate that will destroy the species and perhaps even the planet. Obama was backed into a corner, which is why in his Nobel speech he resorted to the final fantasy: "For make no mistake," Obama intoned, sounding more Bush and bin Laden than King or Gandhi, "Evil does exist in the world." *Plus ça change* ...

e. *Of* and *After*: Two Narratives of the Global

What we plan to do in this book is to make sense of what we have here termed "common sense." The common sense we will explore and examine is that which has been developed and articulated with particular force from the end of the Cold War to the end of globalization – from the enthusiasms of Fukuyama to the disappointments of Obama. We are as interested in the common sense *of* globalization as we are in the shape common sense is taking *after* it. Of course, the axioms, tropes, and figures that comprise common sense have not been invented ex nihilo over the past 20 years: they draw on a whole array of beliefs, practices, and relations that have been developed over the past century, and even longer. The widely held belief, for instance, that history is constituted through measurable progress has roots that extend back into the Enlightenment; the belief that this progress is best evidenced by a specific kind of technological development (e.g., the miniaturization of computer technologies) and the social effects to which it is related (e.g., bringing people together through the collapse of space) has a more recent origin. We want to argue that there is today a shared global common sense that constitutes the frame within which we operate; this frame produces a critical limit to our capacity to address problems new and old, from our impact on the environment to the effects and outcomes of our economic systems. It is a limit that may well not itself be all that new, but it is one whose consequences grow more serious by the day.

Why not use a different term? Why common sense? Why not ideology? Or hegemony? In the way we are using it, common sense is certainly related to these. Though hegemony is a concept to which critics don't appeal as much as they once did, having moved on to other, more stylish concepts in the marketplace of ideas, it remains important for grasping how contemporary societies operate. Hegemony names the way in which consent is produced, managed, and reproduced. The consent named here is the consent to be ruled, to participate in an unjust system, and to engage in a mode of life that for the vast majority is far less than it could be – an empirical point and not mere utopian imagining. Hegemony identifies the way in which virtually every aspect of social life is structured to legitimate a social system that benefits certain social interests over others. The components of hegemony include everything, from the social and political "givens" one learns during one's education to everyday norms of behavior; from the character and nature of social relations to the legitimating structure of political systems; from the constituent elements of the family to the expected narrative trajectory of an individual life. Hegemony is not the lie of the system – a trick, knowingly pulled by those whose wealth allows them to miraculously exceed the epistemological limits of the social and so orchestrate things from the outside (the crude way of understanding ideology). It is the truth of the system, what, in a very fundamental way, the system "is."

Common sense is related to hegemony: it points to the same deep social assumptions that structure privilege and generate disadvantage. While evoking hegemony, we see it as doing a different kind of work. The ready-to-hand intelligibility of common sense – the distracted *content* of the social which passes for *form* or *system* – is at the heart of the operations of hegemony; it is where power takes on the innocence of tradition or the apparent scientific certainty that lurks in sociobiology: "it has always been thus." Moving from the depths of hegemony to its surface, common sense appears as a figure when the operations of hegemony are most in doubt, at their shakiest, anxious about their capacity to enact their marvelous capacity to reproduce the present into the future with that fragment of difference needed to offset the fatal rigidity of social stasis. The common sense we are examining is something given, a set of assumptions, facts, and presumed logics. In the circumstances we are exploring, common sense betrays its origins as a social invention because it needs to be insisted on, repeated, pronounced (with varying degrees of confidence and commitment) as a solution to impending crises. It doesn't get to do what it likes to do best: lie dormant, a bear in its winter cave, and just as dangerous when disturbed.

As we have already suggested, in the period from the end of the Cold War (that dreamy period of ossified common sense!) to the end of globalization there are two contexts in which common sense is forced to *argue for its legitimacy by means of the legitimacy of its own arguments*. The first arises out of the expansion of a hegemony (that of the United States) from nation to planet, a process full of danger given the wildly different contexts, histories, and temporalities it would of necessity

Our examination of today's common sense takes place at two sites. First, we look in depth at the arguments put forward about the shape and character of the present in a number of texts written both during globalization and in its aftermaths, that is, when globalization is asserted as all powerful, and then when its guiding ideas are asserted even more strongly to address the crisis of its end. We look to what we take to be especially significant sites at which the common sense we are pointing to is engendered and regenerated, produced and reproduced. Our focus is, first, on those whom Richard Florida has named the "thought leadership of modern society: nonfiction writers, editors, cultural figures, think-tank researchers, analysts and other opinion-makers."[30] The reason for looking at the ways in which common sense appears in the work of some of today's global "thought leaders" is not to overstate the influence of these particular authors. By choosing authors with distinct perspectives, who operate within different fields of knowledge (international relations, sociology, economics, social activism, entertainment), we want to capture the various modalities of common sense in order to produce a map of its worldviews, and to understand its limits. In understanding the operation of hegemony, it is essential to remember that though it works to benefit elites, it is not directly and knowingly produced by them, but rather produces them, too. The work that we will look at is significant not because it contains the beliefs of some of today's most popular thinkers and those on behalf of whom they speak. Rather, they are works in which the author presumes to speak on behalf of the common (sometimes a national common, at other times a global one), first through an explication of the constitutive elements and driving imperatives of existing social and political systems, and second by offering guidance about and advice on what comes next. Each of the authors we look at attempts to explicate a sociohistorical paradigm shift that demands of us a different mode of being; the limits imposed by common sense appear in the way that this shift is characterized, the form taken by their assessments and arguments, and the nature of the difference for which they argue.

In Part II, we examine the constitution of the common sense of globalization by examining texts by Richard Florida, Thomas Friedman, Paul Krugman, and Naomi Klein as well as looking at the rendering of globalization into film, through an assessment of a single film (*Michael Clayton*) starring the actor George Clooney. The texts that we assess include some of the foundational arguments for how we should understand the new geopolitical system – globalization (Friedman) and its aftermath; descriptions of the new character of work and cities (Florida) as well as the economics of the global era (Florida, Krugman, and Klein); critical assessments of the politics and culture of globalization (Clooney, Klein); and a ferocious re-narration of globalization intended to make us see it with new eyes (Klein). Our aim in taking up these texts is not to take them to task for getting things wrong, nor to pick winners and losers amongst them whose views and insights we can thus either jettison or champion. To repeat: the aim is to generate a map of what we have termed common sense and its operations, especially with respect to how it understands the future. Something is missing in the work of each and every one of these authors; something is missing, too, even if they are taken together in the hope that the gaps and flaws of one might be filled out by the smarts and insights of the others.

Florida, Friedman, Krugman, Klein: it might seem as if we are paying particular attention to journalism as a form in which knowledge of the world is rendered (if we add Clooney to the mix, one could say that it is the media more generally that concerns us). There are reasons for this. This book is not primarily intended as an investigation of the limits of journalism in comparison to other ways we narrate the world to ourselves. Nonetheless, journalism plays an undeniable role in constituting our sense of which events are important to the common, as well as how we are supposed to understand the larger significance of these events. Indeed, the latter function of journalism is already contained in the blunt act of reportage. The events that demand the attention of journalists do not, as is still commonly assumed, constitute a pre-existing reality which is then reported on. Rather, these events are picked out of the ebb and flow of social life by means of the logic contained within journalism regarding the significance of this or that event. Journalism thus has an effect at an almost ontological level, offering up to view some component elements of reality, and, by not taking up other elements or aspects of our reality, ensuring that they

39

don't exist. In the end, what we are typically presented with in newspaper or on the television news is the world in the form of a "variety show. . . a litany of events with no beginning and no real end, thrown together only because they happened on the same day."[31] But this does not mean that a larger logic does not work to hold all of these events in place. Even in the obituaries one can find evidence of the organizing common sense of the day. In his analysis of the obituaries in the *New York Times*, Franco Moretti discovers what constitutes the story of an individual life in today's world. It is a narrative that takes a specific form: a slow, steady forward march, with individual lives each contributing in small ways to an already determined historical direction – from rags to riches, a celebration (by virtue of being in the *Times*) of success in the world. This is an example of the larger logic by and through which the world is given: "no changes of direction, but myriad regular steps along a well-worn path . . . a quantitative and orderly march: without confusion, and certainly without catastrophes."[32]

The texts we are examining are not by reporters, but by commentators who frequently offer insights on the op-ed pages. Though the op-ed pages began as the space of opinion in a medium otherwise comprised of fact (the very admission of perspective and partiality in one part of the newspaper functioning to render the rest impartial through the logic of difference), it has come to serve a different purpose. Since the news focuses on "breaking" events and tries to capture audience interest by focusing on new stories and situations, journalism can lend itself to a form of cultural amnesia. Events seem to have no antecedents or consequences, no links to larger and more persistent histories and structures. Things happen, and seem to happen out of the blue: journalism operates in perpetual crisis mode, swinging its attention from one thing to another. There is nothing more disturbing than watching old TV news footage, filled with fearless "expert" predictions and projections of the dire consequences that might unfold from breaking stories that we now either cannot remember or cannot imagine as ever having been of much importance.

Though imperfectly, the op-ed pages try to offer perspectives that put events in relation to other events, as well as in relation to broader cultural narratives that can be called up in short form to stand in for organizing principles and forces behind these events, and which also point to their larger significance. Such renderings of system effects are nevertheless still lost in the short spaces and ephemeral nature of the daily news. And so we get the book-length works that we are probing here – works that are explicit in their desire to paint the big picture of both how the world works and how it *should* work. This makes such texts ideal sites to capture the dominant ethos and epistemology of globalization. Since each of these texts is also didactic – intended to fill in gaps in understanding and offer lessons as to what individuals and nations should believe and how they should behave – we get an unfolding of the common sense about the deepest elements of our reality: its epistemology, ontology, ethics, politics and view about the present and the future. Our analysis would be missing something essential if we did not also include some consideration of the manner in which popular cinema plays a role in this same kind of analysis and didacticism, which is why we end Part II by looking at a film about the present that embodies the limits and fantasies in the common sense we live.

Our claim is that the production of the common sense we find expressed in the texts we examine in Part II forms an essential element of the political project of globalization, and, indeed, is at the basis of emerging narratives of what comes after. Globalization was the process by which the same common sense – the same touchstones, the same general assumptions, the same beliefs in the character of geopolitics – was reproduced *everywhere*. This can be most clearly seen in the global belief in the necessity of capitalist economic systems: with few exceptions, we are all capitalists now. But it extends beyond economics, into all of the registers in which hegemony is expressed. *Of* and *after*.

Globalization is finished, but lives on, even if it is now possible to (for instance) focus on the role of US power within the world, or to fearlessly name capitalism as a system (that is, as a choice) rather than as fate. This is, at least, our contention. To establish this claim and to render clear the depth of its significance, we felt that it was important to go beyond the analysis of symptomatic expressions of common sense such as those found in these texts. In our choice of writers who might be seen as occupying the center or center-left of the political spectrum, our aim was to offer a less partisan and more complex examination of common sense than would be the case if we had singled out conservatives writing in favor of great-power politics and against any substantive change in the world. The authors we chose to focus on view the future as full of problems and in need of change; they do not cling to the way things are, but understand themselves as progressives who are offering ideas that will enable us to address the challenges we collectively face in a manner that will produce a better future. Even though this creates a more compelling site at which to probe the common sense of the global present and its aftermath, it does not fill in the whole picture that we want to paint.

The third part of this book stretches beyond the theoretical positions we develop in Part I and the textual narratives we examine in Part II. Is there a common sense about the present and the future that is now shared globally? If so, what are its claims and assumptions? Its political and cultural implications? In order to address these questions, we conducted a series of interviews with university students over three years (2006–2009). We carried out these interviews at sites around the world in an effort to grasp the similarities and differences in varied local and national contexts. Using the same set of questions in each case, we asked students (ages 18–30) enrolled in a range of undergraduate and graduate programs to tell us about social and political problems faced by their country and the world, the role of education in the world, their sense of the meaning of politics, capitalism, and democracy, their sense of the United States as a global actor, the role of global popular culture and their own culture, and their sense of what promises or threats the future held. For the students we spoke to, the Cold War was at best a dim memory. These students were truly the product of the era of globalization and its common sense – the first global generation, who viewed the world not just from the perspective of their own nations, but with a feeling for the fact that culture and politics operate at a global level, with serious implications for how they live and act locally and globally.

The interviews took place in many nations not usually included in wide studies of anti-Americanism and globalization, and certainly not typically placed in the same study together, in an effort to capture as best as possible the kinds of social framings that we were interested in understanding better. We spoke with students in the new capitalist democracies of Central Europe (Croatia and Hungary), in old European powers (Germany and Russia), and in nations that, each in its own complex way, have a relationship to the United States that is both friendly and filled with tension (Taiwan and Colombia). In the end, we spoke with 60 students in total, in interviews lasting approximately one hour each. Our intention was not simply to confirm the operations of a global common sense by looking for any and every trace of it in the perspectives and beliefs of these students. Nor were we looking for some simple antithesis of the positions and ideologies in the texts examined in Part II. Rather, we wanted to understand the points at which the ideas of this global generation and those of the thinkers in Part II converge and diverge, to see what preoccupations and expectations were present and absent in the outlook of each. We did not take the views of the students as a single bloc and oppose them to those who we took to be writing globalization into existence. As the third part will make clear, we were careful to be attentive to national and historical differences.

We were nevertheless struck strongly by how similar the views of the students were on almost every topic we spoke to them about. Without anticipating too much, what was surprising to us was their almost uniformly insightful and nuanced understanding of the nature of global power. But this was an insight that offered no sense of an ability to act to change the nature of a system which they saw as troubled, unjust, and out of balance. Perhaps the biggest gap between the common sense shared by the students and that articulated by the writers in Part II is a sense of a capacity for action in the world. The writing of the "thought leaders" is meant to generate change, even if they view the present as more or less fine as it is; the students, on the other hand, see a troubled world in need of fundamental change, but the very scale and scope of what would be required to set things aright means that all that they expect is a continuation of the status quo. After all, even if globalization (as ideology) might be seen as teetering, globalization (as the name for a period) has no end. And if there is no end, why should one imagine the future being any different than the present?

We'll leave the significance of this interpretive gap between thinkers and students for later in the book. This book draws attention to what current narratives of globalization and its aftermath offer us, and what they fail to. Our analysis is organized around a view of limits, gaps, and failures in these narratives. The writers we examine and the students we interview also point to limits and gaps, and the need to imagine new futures and to break with old habits of thinking and doing. It is critical for the analysis that follows that we establish clearly that our sense of how to understand what it means to speak of limits – to say, with Jimmy in Bertolt Brecht and Kurt Weil's *The Rise and Fall of the City of Mahagonny*, "something's missing" – is very different than that found in these two groups, and importantly so. The intervention that we wish to make in understanding globalization and its aftermath is captured in the seven theses that follow. Taken together, these point to a different way of imagining a gap in or limit to a system, a theoretical point we articulate in the final section of this first part.

f. Seven Theses after Globalization

Whether one wants to change it or leave it the same, writing about the present and its problems always seems to come equipped with solutions. The structure of a typical book marked "current affairs" on the back cover is: (1) introduce a major change/development/discovery that necessitates the writing of the book (if possible, described through a neologism or catchphrase that might find its way on to the lips of writers for *Foreign Policy* or into the papers of students sitting in seminar rooms in the John F. Kennedy School of Government); (2) describe the theme of the book in some detail, making recourse to the assumptions and theories of common sense to push the narrative along; and (3) conclude with a discussion of what needs to be done to address the change/development/discovery in an appropriate fashion, that is, typically in a manner beneficial to the national community to which the author belongs (e.g., if [nation y] doesn't do [x], it will fall behind the rest of the world, especially competitors [a, b, and c]). The discovery in (1) is implicitly taken to affect the entire world; the solution in (3) is meant only for individual nations, or perhaps for a small group of friends. In every case, there is something that can be done to either take advantage of (1) or to mitigate its effects – that is, to save us.

The better way to think about the world? Think: nothing can save us.

Thesis 1: Education will not save us

Learning and knowledge are imagined to necessarily solve problems. The troubles of the world are explained as the result of ignorance or inadequate understanding. How to resolve these problems? Through education. Education is thought to be the process by which a void of knowledge is filled, only to be followed by new voids that will be filled, and so on, ad infinitum. But education's blind spot is not ignorance; rather it is what goes missing precisely when ignorance is overcome.

Even when education reflects upon its own limits, it fails to reflect upon how it participates in reproducing the very logic that structures these limits. Thus, dominant educational forms invariably understand themselves to be disinterested and neutral. In this role as disinterested interpreter, education is not addressed to a demand for knowledge, but rather to a demand to rationalize the nastiest excesses – from colonialism to environmental destruction to all of the "just wars" underwritten by academic expertise. With the best of intentions, education finds ever-ingenious ways to justify these excesses, to justify injustice (always in the name of knowledge, in the name of neutrality). For every time education questions crime and corruption, it just as surely provides their most perfect rationales. Genocide, war, and the disregard for our fellow human beings are as much a product of education as ignorance. Producing justifications for violence in the name of education constitutes citizens who are internally split and perilously self-alienated. The dissimulated truth of education is power; and power dissimulated is more neurotic and dangerous than power acknowledged.

Knowing and *doing* are not one. To know about a problem, to understand why and how it works, does not necessarily produce an active response. Knowing and *change* are not one. To know about a

45

problem, to understand why and how it works, does not necessarily produce an alteration of present circumstances – and many times this desire and accumulation of knowledge functions to reinforce and harden the very problem under examination. The limits of knowing can only be overcome by acting. Likewise, the limits of acting can only be overcome by knowing. But even this axiom does not go far enough. For the very recognition of this problem of praxis is still shaped by the dominant forms of education.

Standard university education only produces rigor within the confines of the academic disciplines. The university usually produces either a disciplined rigor (the very straight and solid scholarship within the disciplines); an unrigorous discipline (a weak scholarship that coasts on an already established disciplinary tradition); or an unrigorous undiscipline (the worst kind of academic amateurism that often hides behind the moniker "interdisciplinary"). And these three types of knowledge production are driven by the growth of the corporate form of the university (everything valued by quantitative results – "excellence" equaling the number of articles published, students placed, dollars raised) as well as the ideology of neutrality. The gap that separates knowing and doing, doing and changing, theory and practice, criticism and excellence, interest and disinterest, however, can only be engaged by a rigor that resists an education system dominated by the academic disciplines. We call this an *undisciplined rigor*, a mode of thought that necessarily challenges education. Education will not save us.

Thesis 2: Morality will not save us

The most common way of naming the causes of the errors and problems of the world is through moral categories. Right or wrong, good or evil: if something has come undone or gone badly astray, or, on the contrary, if things have worked out or some uncommon valor has been displayed, these are the concepts we trot out (as Obama said: "Evil does exist in the world"). Whether we use "wrong" or "evil" in a given situation depends on the degree of the misdeed or perhaps the rhetorical force with which we want to insist on morality. When

Google claims it will "do no evil," we know it does not mean to hold off inquisitions or to keep demons at bay, but that despite its financial power it will act as a good corporate citizen.

While virtue or vice might be a common evaluative taxonomy, it should never be the place where one begins – or ends. Moral categories are intelligible only in relation to a pre-established code of conduct. To speak of "good" or "evil" is to affirm the existence and legitimacy of this code. What it cannot do is pass judgment on the system itself, nor engender an analysis of its axioms and formulae. Google can avoid doing evil *as* a corporate citizen. Whether the system that allows an abstract entity like a corporation to be a citizen is productive or destructive vis-à-vis the social whole is entirely left out of its calculations. One can do nothing but good, and still be bad.

But isn't it nevertheless meaningful to point to the egregious and immoral behavior of specific individuals? To say: everything would be fine, if only for the corporate thieves, the bad apples, the tax cheats? Such name calling points to a longing for justice, even as it indefinitely defers the possibility of justice. These isolated moral failings of the system confirm its force all the more strongly: when we call some individuals "evil" it must mean the system itself is "good." A better solution is not to imagine the system itself as always already evil, but to push beyond such moralizing to an analysis of its operations. Morality will not save us. It wasn't hypocrisy that transformed religious good into the evil of the Crusades, but a satisfaction with a system of naming that affirms rather than questions.

Consider a thought experiment. What if every person in the world, every day and in every way, acted according to the dictates of morality? We would have the good teacher, the good doctor, the good lawyer, the good policeman, the good politician. Would the result of all this goodness be a "good" system, one free of poverty, injustice, and pollution? Remember: "good" is not the same as "equal." If the presumption is that the good politician would be one who upholds the existing laws to the best of their ability, then the answer is "no." If one imagines that the good politician would change these laws in order to produce equality, then the real issue isn't morality at all.

47

Thesis 3: The nation will not save us

Contrary to what one might expect at a time when economic and financial borders have disappeared, nations and nationalisms are being taken out of the closet, dusted off, and once again worn about proudly and without embarrassment – despite being somewhat tattered and badly out of fashion. The twenty-first century was supposed to be an era when borders were lowered and the lines demarcating nations were erased, both on our maps and in our imaginations. And yet here nations are, proud as can be, standing at the ready to defend the values of Enlightenment civilization against the Islamic hordes or to insist that immigrants absorb their ideas and ideals. "Every nation is one people," Johann Gottfried von Herder wrote, "having its own national form, as well as its own language."[33] Evidently some nonsense manages not only to stand the test of time, but to become even more popular as the years pass by.

We are first born as human beings before we become subjects of nations, even if we tend to learn this the other way around. As human beings, we are one; as national subjects, we are necessarily separate, divided, and at each other's throats. It is hardly a surprise, then, that nations cannot, separately or together, deal with problems that are of importance to the human instead of to their citizens. Despite all of the knowledge generated as to "what is to be done" with respect to the environment, scientific fact that even national leaders take as true, there is little or no substantive action on a threat to our collective futures. The political form of the nation blocks the way forward on a path that we all know we have to take.

Some radicals might disagree with this. Many see political possibilities in the policies and plans of their own individual nations. Isn't it worth using the frame of the nation to create and defend policies – for instance, universal health care – given that such plans are in jeopardy in many parts of the world? Maybe. But this can't be the final step. "Universal" doesn't mean one nation – it means everyone. Health care in one nation is just as limited and just as much of a problem as "socialism in one country." Such schemes will not save us.

Let us be blunt. *We* don't need the nation – capital does. Without such political divisions, *especially* at a moment when economic transactions are borderless, there would be no differential zones of labor, no spaces to realize profit through the dumping of overproduction, no way to patrol surly populations who might want to resist capitalism, no release valve for speculative excess. The basic functions of nations make them perfect objects around which to organize the globe politically. The establishment of zones of inclusion and exclusion, control over the legal status of citizen-subjects, practices of demographic accounting and management, and the mobilization of bodies for use in territorial expansion and war – what could be better for capital? And what has been more disastrous for humanity as a whole?

Theodor Adorno writes: "The formation of national collectivities ... common in the detestable jargon of war that speaks of the Russian, the American, surely also of the German, obeys a reifying consciousness that is no longer really capable of experience. It confines itself within precisely those stereotypes that thinking should dissolve."[34] We say: exactly! In episodes of the *Star Trek* TV series, each time the *Enterprise* encounters a new world it finds on it a single planet-wide community of beings. How disappointed such aliens must be to meet up with humans, who have carried their national differences with them even into the future, even into the final frontier.

Thesis 4: The future will not save us

The future is colonized by the present. The very name and fantasy of the future is contained by the imaginative limits of the present. We pretend that we do not know what the future will bring and this somehow brings us relief, but this, too, is a way of containing the future. The most radical position to take in relation to the future is to not expect that it will come. And, yet, we continue to believe that the future has always come – that every past has been solved by the future. But we only think this as a way to justify our present, to make the present rational.

The present won't save us either. Without the future, the present is only something to be managed, to be sustained, to be tinkered with around its edges. To what else could the defeatist name "sustainable development" possibly refer? To live in a present that is not disturbed and troubled by a different future (even the radically different future of no future) is to submit to the limits of the present. We require not a different present and future, therefore, but a different way of understanding and living these temporal categories we call the present and the future.

The paradigmatic condition that flashes this different mode of being is that of the medical patient who has received a terminal diagnosis of a life-threatening disease only to live through medical advances that then turn the terminal illness into a chronic one. Now the disease remains life threatening, still incurable, however much the illness is managed and controlled into the future, perhaps indefinitely − a sort of sustainable development of the dying. One has been killed, but has yet to die and is now afforded a meantime that functions like a hole in time, an escape route to somewhere else and a trap door to where we began.

This way in which the formerly terminal live on as the "already dead" provides a model for social and ecological challenges. Think about some of the ecological forecasts that predict an already-too-late scenario of our environmental future, or any other it-is-only-a-matter-of-time situations in which the end is foretold, however long it might take to reach. Perhaps it is death itself that has always represented such a limit, a limit that turns the tables on us and returns to time its ultimate freedom.

The most radical field within medicine is palliative care, precisely because it has revalued the temporal field. The dying were generally given the lowest priority as death was understood as a medical defeat or statistical embarrassment. Why spend resources on someone who only has weeks to live? Why value something that will not give us enough return on our investment? Because the moment we stop deferring the future or hoping for another one is the moment something shifts in the present. But, and again, this shift is not a present or future with alternative content, but an alternative presentness and futurity to the reality of both the present and future.

This palliative model does not only relate to the dying patient. History, too, is dying. And so is the species. And the planet. What would a palliative ward for these soon-to-be deaths look like? Like the dying patient, what if we understood the planet, the species, and history as needing a different type of care, a different way of relating to the present and to the future that was not shaped by instrumentality or the miraculous? How to care for something, for someone, knowing that it or they will end soon? What does it mean to act in the face of this end?

True, this relationship to the end might open up new ways of deferring or avoiding it. But we cannot know this in advance. Such a strategy would compromise the alternative attitude to the end that is required to transform it. Unless we think it differently, the future will not save us.

Thesis 5: History will not save us

Human nature does not exist. "Since time immemorial" is the most insidious excuse for human violence and "always" always betrays a fantasy for simplicity. When we appeal to a flattened past to justify the present we are invariably confusing two different modes. For example, "war has always existed and will continue to exist." "Poverty has always existed and will always exist." "Peace has always followed war and will always follow war." These three trivially true statements are profoundly false. Of course, we can point to wars since the beginning of humankind, but the context of war, the logic of war (the very category of war) is something qualitatively different at different moments in history. Yes, there is something called poverty that fills the historical record, but how poverty is constructed and structured as well as what it means and feels like to be poor in the feudal period is incomparable to what that condition and experience is at the contemporary moment. Fixing these categories and pretending that they persist from one historical moment to the next always functions to repress or explain away our deepest fears – not to mention the possibilities of alternative ways of living and organizing ourselves.

History does not contain the hidden secret that we missed the first time around. Yes, secrets are hidden in history, but once they are uncovered they lose their autonomy and thus their significance – they are immediately recuperated and plotted on a straight line to the present. History is important in order to remind us that the very category of history means something different to us today than it did in the past.

The appeal to past evil (personified by Hitler) is always a mistake. If there is evil, then it is always singular. It can never be defined by a set of criteria or repeated, only and always produced anew, making it incommensurable with what evil was before. And before that. To appeal to evil, therefore, invariably functions to falsely straighten and stretch history. Linear history manages evil by representing it as an unfortunate, however temporary slip, on the forward march of history. But not content with that, appeals to linear history go to the end: to justify evil. By appealing to the "eternal" and "continual" presence of evil, linear history assures the presence of evil in the present; in the process, it thus assures the lack of awareness about the historically contingent production of value.

The supposed transhistorical value of evil shapes and is shaped by the supposed transhistorical value of wealth. It should come as no surprise that the wealthy must obscure the historical origins of their wealth. But there is a catch. If immense wealth is not explained historically then it appears fraudulent, but when it is explained historically it comes dangerously close to revealing itself as theft. The arts collective REPOhistory investigates and recontextualizes historical representation through site-specific public art works in New York City. They might produce a sign of a corporate building (seamlessly fitted into the décor of the city) explaining how the building was acquired and any shady and aggressive practices that led to its founding. REPOhistory's guerrilla interventions want to draw attention to the forgotten or suppressed narratives of wealth, while "revealing the spatial relationships inherent in power, usage and memory." The appeal to space is important: by re-mapping history at the same time that it re-narrates it, REPOhistory temporarily resolves the inescapable problem of doing history: how to narrate both its continuities and discontinuities.[35]

History exists. And we have access to the historical archive to prove it. But the continuous history of history does not exist without so many breaks and ruptures, which in turn separate us from the past so absolutely that we can only face it (and remember it) the way we do a dream. And we have access to the historical archive to prove that as well.

Thesis 6: Capitalism will not save us

Capitalism is a system of human design and invention. It did not fall like manna from heaven, offered up by the gods to help us traverse the desert of the social. It is not akin to other systems that form a part of the natural order of things, such as the Krebs cycle (the process by which cells use oxygen in respiration) or the cardio-pulmonary (circulatory) system. Like any human social system, it is of necessity fallible, full of holes and problems that do not allow it to work according to the schemas worked out by economists. The *Homo economicus* that are meant to inhabit the ecosystem of capitalism are supposed to make rational decisions all the time. Even economists recognize that these rare beasts are guided more by what John Maynard Keynes called "animal spirits," and less by that (no-less-invented) capacity named "reason."[36] One might then expect a little humility from a system whose champions expect it to carry us forward into the future.

Let's hold in abeyance for a moment the question of whether the thing we call capitalism properly constitutes a system, even if this is how we are apt to talk about it. If capitalism is necessarily incomplete, if it doesn't constitute the best of all possible worlds, why the need to insist that it does? Capitalism has played a significant role in technological development. Economies have grown around the world over the past century, and even more so over the past two decades, improving living standards for people almost everywhere. Capitalism generates a cornucopia of new products. All well and good.

But does it come as a surprise to anyone that everything about our economic system isn't all that great? The freedom that is often associated with capitalism is experienced by the vast majority of the world's population as servitude: the repetitive boredom of a workaday world that one has no hope of escaping. From shockingly unequal levels of wealth distribution (the top 10 percent in the United States receiving 50 percent of its income share in 2006)[37] to deep financial insecurity for most of us, there are problems aplenty with the regular,

53

systemic operations of capitalism. The operations of financial capitalism benefit only the very rich; it's hard to defend the social good of the abstract production of money by money. Capitalism develops wealth, sure. But where does this wealth originate? Is it like a magician pulling a rabbit from a hat – presto! Absolutely: for as with magic, there is no real magic there, only a sleight of hand that distracts us from seeing that the work of many is for the benefit of the few.

Capitalism has flaws, some very deep ones. It is foolish to imagine that this system, a creature of a specific historical moment, can overcome every limit in a way that benefits the common. It is no one's panacea. Why, then, does one find it defended so strongly? Like a bit of scripture one cannot argue against for fear of blasphemy?

Those who want to insist on the irrefutable necessity of capitalism are repeating (without knowing it) Gottfried Leibniz's argument about the nature of the world. God created the world; if this world of ours is the world that God chose to stick with (after trying out other combinations, one must suppose), it must be the best of all possible worlds. Sure, there is evil and suffering, but this is part of the optimum mix to make the whole what it is, or to make it possible at all. Evil is necessary and can't be done away with; suffering is productive because it incites humans to action. Sounds a lot like the kind of argument that the rich make on behalf of the necessity of the fears and terrors produced by capitalism: it gets the lazy poor to the workhouse. Voltaire's *Candide* famously ridiculed this view of the world. Dr Pangloss's misplaced and irrational optimism in the fundamental good of the way things are seems to be repeated by the many who want to insist that there is nothing but capitalism. It exists – it thus must be part of God's plan! Like Candide, the rest of us know better.

Thesis 7: Common sense will not save us

This is the easiest point to grasp, and yet the hardest one to explain so that it is grasped correctly. Common sense will not save us. We face too many challenges, threats, and problems to rely on old ways of doing things. Who could disagree? Writers of every political stripe who wish to direct their energies toward these problems exhort us to "think outside the box," or demand that we come up with alternative ways of seeing things. In other words, like the famous ad says, almost everyone is imploring everyone else to "think different."

Common sense is a matter of form more than content. Common sense is universal, in the sense that it is a feature of every human society. Within a certain context, common sense takes a specific content. The content of our common sense – a common sense now rendered global – includes the six theses listed above. These theses do not exhaust our common sense – hardly! What they do identify are the social axioms that we imagine will save us from ourselves. In other words, these are the elements of common sense that we typically draw upon to save us from the problems produced by our common sense.

Ah, what philosophical puzzle building! A necessary system of ideas that folds inescapably in on itself! It is perfectly fair to ask: what is it that allows us to see common sense as other than what it is? Is not our own critical perspective just more common sense?

Common sense is what everybody knows. It is all manner of assumed knowledge, from the banal to the erudite. It presumes to already offer the answers to all questions, even if some work needs to be done to re-combine some of its tenets or to extend some of its insights a little further. Such new insights are a form of "thinking outside the box" that congratulates itself for its innovation and radicality, but in fact stays within the range of what is deemed sensible. To give an example: the need for more energy and the problems of global warming might lead to the invention of various forms of green energy. However, a hard look at the question of "need" in this case – a need fueled by a system for which a decrease in economic growth is simply not an option – remains an unthinkable limit. Common sense always impedes the imagination of limits. The imperative to "think outside the box" serves mainly to reaffirm the legitimacy and value of the box.

When we say that common sense is what everybody knows we do not mean to invoke ideology in the usual sense of this term. It isn't that we are blocked from seeing the "bad" aspects of the systems, prohibited (for some reason, by someone) from understanding how things work. Indeed,

> Everybody knows that the dice are loaded
> Everybody rolls with their fingers crossed
> Everybody knows that the war is over
> Everybody knows that the good guys lost
> Everybody knows the fight was fixed
> The poor stay poor, the rich get rich
> That's how it goes
> Everybody knows[38]

What is missing is not knowledge, but a figuration of its systematicity.

Let us be clear. Common sense is not properly understood as an error in our way of seeing things, if by "error" we mean that there is a solution to common sense that takes the shape either of some position completely outside and beyond it (the epistemic fantasy par excellence), or that its "mistakes" can somehow be corrected – for instance, by rendering the lyricism of poetry into the certainty of mathematics, as in Yevgeny Zamyatin's *We*.[39] We make no affirmation of something beyond common sense. But this is not the same as to say we are fated to what already is. The six previous theses are rendered in the negative. The aim of these negations is neither to pass judgment on nor to eliminate the propositions they disclose in a direct and simple way. Rather, what they do is render the limits of thought more transparent to itself than it might otherwise be. It is only at this point that critique can begin – again, to be clear, not from outside of common sense, but from a position *within it* that recognizes that neither its positive content nor its guiding imperatives and axioms exhaust the whole field of thought. *The limits we are pointing to are limits produced by common sense, which common sense insists can only be addressed by those processes which generated the limits.* One need not play fancy games of ontology or epistemology to recognize a space in which critique can originate.

When we say that common sense cannot save us, we are in fact making a positive claim. What we need is critique that addresses itself to analyzing and changing society as a whole. The theoretical insights of common sense aim at explanation and understanding, but never at change at the level of the whole. This, however, is the challenge that is necessary for thought to undertake today.

g. Something's Missing

So, all of these somethings (education, morality, nation, future, history, capitalism, common sense) will not save us. Nothing will save us. What is this *nothing* that will save us? Indeed, this "nothing" can be understood as "something" (and not merely due to the trick of grammar that makes nothing a noun). But first things first: nothing is the very thing that structures these somethings. There is always something missing in these somethings – which is nothing. This nothing is the thing without which something would not exist. Constellations are the nothing that holds the stars together. The space in between the branches is the nothing that holds the tree together. Capitalism is the nothing that holds capital together.

Capitalism is nothing. It's nowhere to be found. One cannot hold it and measure it and prove it. But the stuff of capitalism is everywhere and readily accessible to study. All of the commodities, the bank notes, the heavy lifting, the extreme consumer desire, the prized philanthropic acts, the neuroses (from hypersensitivity to disassociation), the carbon emissions, the floods and fires and other socially generated "natural disasters," the digital ones and zeroes that instantaneously transmit our communications, entertainment, and money around the world, are not capitalism – they are the effects of capitalism. Capitalism is nothing.

The first meaning of "something's missing," therefore, is that *this nothing that is capitalism and that is something, is missing*. Since nothing's missing even though it exists, nothing becomes a matter of belief. We must believe that nothing exists even though we have no positive evidence to prove it. It is for this reason that capitalism is a matter of belief. And today, more and more people are beginning to believe again. Born again. Not necessarily as Leftists or Rightists, but as believers in the system called capitalism – or, more to the point, in the existence of the very category of "system."

This belief in system today returns only after globalization discourse no longer conceals capitalism. During the heyday of globalization, no one believed in the system of capitalism – not only was it nowhere to be found, but it was constantly being concealed. It was out of sight, out of sense, out of our capacity to believe in it. It existed not as system, but as everything – and everything without nothing only exists as fantasy. Now the relations that exist between things, between nations, between past and present, rich and poor, ally and enemy (and a relation is the perfect figure for nothing!) are in the process of being deconcealed. What comes after globalization? The deconcealment of the absent relations that make up, and are made by, our lives – the deconcealment of nothing.

These nothing spaces that come between everything have been the most crucial markets for capital. Our urban spaces are saturated with advertisements, not just on billboards but on our bodies and in our dreams. Every crack is filled with slogans, every piece of available space is occupied like enemy territory. Likewise, time is also saturated, every second filled with jingles and naked bodies, and more slogans – even slogans imploring us to stop looking at slogans. Go to a sporting event and try to focus on the event. There is not a moment that is not occupied – there is no in-between time, no time-outs, not a single instant that is not controlled in advance. Any counter-insurgency of time is immediately snuffed out. Any counter-effect is stillborn without the time to grow and live. Even the future is filled. What is personal and national debt but an occupation of future time?

This is also to say that nothing might not change, but our relationship to nothing can. The way we understand, represent, believe, and experience it changes from one historical moment to the next. In fact, we might even narrate a modern history of our relationship to nothing. As industrial capitalism heated up in the nineteenth century, *nothing* was more readily experienced. Being displaced from the country to the city, to shift one's dependence from the land to factory wages, made it easier to represent and believe in the relations that structured everyday life. The relations of imperialism, with its

58

unambiguous and rigid organization of metropolis and colony, colonizer and colonized, were impossible to miss. And following the 1920s and 1930s, the stark realities of what was on the other side of capitalism (from bread lines to fascist rallies, all the way to the concentration camps) put the relations (the nothing) of the system on display again. The same goes for the Cold War: everything was organized and understood in terms of bipolarity, different systems organized by the space (the space of ideology, the space of production, the space of cultural value) that separated them.

But with the oil crises of the 1970s, the integrity of the two systems of the Cold War began to come apart, and the globalization of one of the systems (capitalism) usurped the other system. By the time the Berlin Wall fell, the usurpation was complete and the space that existed between the two systems disappeared. But when there is only one predominant system, everything changes. In particular, the experience, understanding, and representation of the system itself. This is the moment of full-blown globalization. The system of capitalism went missing as the blowhards for everything (from all sides of the political spectrum) became louder. Something went missing. And that something was the system of nothing, or nothing as system. With the mortgage crisis cum worldwide financial meltdown in 2008, we are beginning to miss something again. *The system has returned and, therefore, something's missing.*

One way to imagine this return of something's missing is as the return of the imagination of something's missing. To believe in system again is to believe in other systems, not only failed or defeated systems of the past, but in future systems. We are not interested in offering up a specific blueprint of a future system. Rather we want to argue for the necessity of imagining alternative systems. All types of systems: absurd ones and dangerous ones and impossible ones and unthinkable ones. To propose and take seriously other systems is not only about inspiring analyses of these alternatives. It also exercises our powers to imagine system as such. Science fiction dystopias, for example, represent miserable societies and disastrous systems, but the very act of imagining such a dystopia is a utopian act – an act that believes in the integrity of a system and how such systems come into being and go out of being.

59

The "end of history" comes to an end when we can start to imagine the beginning and end of systems.

After Globalization, therefore, makes three key claims: (1) following the global economic crisis of 2008, the belief in, and consciousness of, what presently structures the world (the nothing that is capitalism) has returned; (2) this return of belief enables and inspires the desire for another nothing –another system into which capitalism can mutate; and (3) this desire for another nothing, for something else, shakes up what is possible. "Something's missing" is both the *nothing* to which we are alive again and the radical future that we *miss* despite being unable to expressly prescribe, imagine, or desire it. "Something's missing" opens up to what comes *after globalization* – an opening that promises a little more peace and a little more equality than the bag of goods we are once again being sold.

Notes

1. For examples of Johann Wolfgang von Goethe's comments on world literature (*Weltliteratur*) see "Some Passages Pertaining to the Concept of World Literature," in *Comparative Literature: The Early Years: An Anthology of Essays*, ed. H-J. Schulz and P. Rhein (Chapel Hill, NC: University of North Carolina Press, 1973), 1–11.
2. For most recent figures on comparative levels of military expenditure around the world, see figures compiled by the Stockholm International Peace Research Institute (SIPRI), which are available on its website: http://milexdata.sipri.org/ (accessed October 15, 2010). In 2009, US military spending measured as a percentage of global spending was 43 percent.
3. The figure usually cited for box office receipts for *Fahrenheit 9/11* is US$119.2 million. See note in Michael Cieply, "Muscular 'Expendables' Enlivens Battle for Studio," *New York Times*, August 16, 2010. Available at: http://dealbook.blogs.nytimes.com/2010/08/16/muscular-expendables-enlivens-battle-for-studio/ (accessed October 15, 2010).
4. Moore told the media on several occasions that he hoped that the film would influence the outcome of the 2004 US presidential election.

See, for instance, Martin Kasindorf and Judy Keen's interview with Moore, "*Fahrenheit 9/11*: Will It Change Any Voter's Mind?" *USA Today*, June 24, 2004. Available at: www.usatoday.com/news/politic-selections/nation/president/2004-06-24-fahrenheit-cover_x.htm (accessed October 15, 2010).

5. See for example Brendon O'Connor and Martin Griffiths, eds, *The Rise of Anti-Americanism* (New York: Routledge, 2005), and Brendon O'Connor, ed., *Anti-Americanism* (Oxford: Greenwood, 2007), a four-volume set collecting academic writing as well as original source material on anti-Americanism. Other examples of such texts are discussed in Part III.

6. In the wake of 9/11, an enormous number of books have been written assessing the status of US power – its decline, continuation, or rise, or its legitimacy or illegitimacy – with respect to competitor regions or nations. In English alone, a full list would run in the hundreds – enough to create a new genre of books that cut across political science, international relations, advice manuals for foreign policy makers, and pop-psychology at a national level. This includes titles such as: Robert Cooper, *The Breaking of Nations: Order and Chaos in the Twenty-first Century* (New York: Atlantic Books, 2004); Richard Crockatt, *After 9/11: Cultural Dimensions of American Global Power* (New York: Routledge, 2007); Robert Kagan, *The Return of History and the End of Dreams* (New York: Knopf, 2008); Ken Booth and Tim Dunne, eds, *Worlds in Collision: Terror and the Future of Global Order* (Basingstoke, UK: Palgrave, 2002); Ivo Daalder and James D. Lindsay, *America Unbound: The Bush Revolution in Foreign Policy* (Washington, DC: Brookings Institution Press, 2003); Nina Hachigian and Mona Sutphen, *The Next American Century: How the U.S. Can Thrive as Other Powers Rise* (New York: Simon & Schuster, 2008); Stefan Halper and Jonathan Clarke, *America Alone: The Neo-Conservatives and the Global Order* (Cambridge: Cambridge University Press, 2004); Robert Harvey, *Global Disorder: America and the Threat of World Conflict* (New York: Carroll & Graf, 2003); Michael Hirsh, *At War with Ourselves: Why America Is Squandering Its Chance to Build a Better World* (Oxford: Oxford University Press, 2003); Michael H. Hunt, *The American Ascendancy: How the United States Gained and Wielded Global Dominance* (Chapel Hill: University of North Carolina Press, 2007); G. John Ikenberry, ed., *America Unrivaled: The Future of the Balance of Power* (Ithaca, NY: Cornell

University Press, 2002); Andrew Kohut and Bruce Stokes, *America against the World: How We Are Different and Why We Are Disliked* (New York: Times Books, 2006); Charles Kupchan, *The End of the American Era: U.S. Foreign Policy and the Geopolitics of the Twenty-first Century* (New York: Knopf, 2002); Anatol Lieven and John Hulsman, *Ethical Realism: A Vision for America's Role in the World* (New York: Pantheon, 2006); Kishore Mahbubani, *Beyond the Age of Innocence: Rebuilding Trust Between America and the World* (New York: Public Affairs, 2005); Robert W. Merry, *Sands of Empire: Missionary Zeal, American Foreign Policy, and the Hazards of Global Ambition* (New York: Simon & Schuster, 2005); Cullen Murphy, *Are We Rome?: The Fall of an Empire and the Fate of America* (Boston: Houghton Mifflin Co., 2007); Ralph Peters, *New Glory: Expanding America's Global Supremacy* (New York: Penguin, 2005); Jeremy Rifkin, *The European Dream: How Europe's Vision of the Future Is Quietly Eclipsing the American Dream* (New York: Penguin, 2004); Dennis Ross, *Statecraft: And How to Restore America's Standing in the World* (New York: Farrar, Strauss & Giroux, 2007); Rockwell A. Schnabel and Francis X. Rocca, *The Next Superpower?: The Rise of Europe and Its Challenge to the United States* (New York: Rowman and Littlefield, 2007); Nancy Soderberg, *The Superpower Myth: The Use and Misuse of American Might* (New York: John Wiley & Sons, 2005); and Stephen M. Walt, *Taming American Power: The Global Response to U.S. Primacy* (New York: Norton, 2005).

7. Michael Hardt and Antonio Negri, *Empire* (Cambridge, MA: Harvard University Press, 2000).

8. See Giovanni Arrighi, "Hegemony Unravelling," *New Left Review* 32 (2005): 23–80 and *New Left Review* 33 (2005): 83–116; David Harvey, *The New Imperialism* (Oxford: Oxford University Press, 2003); and Neil Smith, *The Endgame of Globalization* (New York: Routledge, 2005).

9. See Niall Ferguson, *Empire: The Rise and Demise of the British World Order and the Lessons of Global Power* (New York: Basic Books, 2003) and *Colossus: The Price of America's Empire* (New York: Penguin Press, 2004).

10. The US share of global GDP declined to 27.7 percent in 2006 from 30.8 percent in 2000. See www.data360.org for figures (accessed October 15, 2010).

11. In addition to those texts listed in note 6 above, see Dan Diner and Sander L. Gilman, *America in the Eyes of the Germans: An Essay on*

Anti-Americanism, trans. Allison Brown (Princeton: Markus Wiener, 1996); J.L. Granatstein, *Yankee Go Home? Canadians and Anti-Americanism* (Toronto: HarperCollins, 1996); Denis Lacorne, Jacques Rupnik, and Marie-France Toine, eds, *The Rise and Fall of Anti-Americanism: A Century of French Perception* (New York: Palgrave Macmillan, 1990); and "What We Think of America," special edition of *Granta* 77 (Spring 2002), which includes articles by Ariel Dorfman, Michael Ignatieff, Ivan Klíma, Doris Lessing, Orhan Pamuk, Harold Pinter, J.M. Coetzee, and others.

12. See Russell A. Berman, *Anti-Americanism in Europe: A Cultural Problem* (New York: Hoover Institution Press, 2004); and Ian Buruma and Avishai Margalit, *Occidentalism: The West in the Eyes of Its Enemies* (New York: Penguin, 2004).

13. For example, see Christopher Connery, "On the Continuing Necessity of Anti-Americanism," *Inter-Asia Cultural Studies* 2.3 (2001): 399–405; and Andrew Ross and Kristin Ross, *Anti-Americanism* (New York: New York University Press, 2004).

14. The 2011 Budget Request for the US Office of Homeland Security is $54.7 billion. To track the growth in expenditures, see the documents collected on Whitehouse's Office of Management and Budget website: www.whitehouse.gov/omb/budget/Historicals/ (accessed October 27, 2010).

15. For example, such influential texts as Benedict Anderson, *Imagined Communities: Reflections on the Origin and Spread of Nationalism* (New York: Verso, 1983; rev. edn, 1991); Ernest Gellner, *Nations and Nationalism* (Ithaca, NY: Cornell University Press, 1983); Eric Hobsbawm, *Nations and Nationalism since 1780: Programme, Myth, Reality* (New York: Cambridge University Press, 1990); and Anthony D. Smith, *The Ethnic Origin of Nations* (Oxford: Basil Blackwell, 1986).

16. Daniele Archibugi has made an argument for a "cosmopolitical democracy" that would maintain the existing system of states while creating a new global democratic structure in which the planet's populace could cast ballots and elect those who control the supranational functions currently carried out by organizations such as the World Bank or the World Trade Organization. See Archibugi, "Cosmopolitical Democracy," in Archibugi, ed., *Debating Cosmopolitics* (New York: Verso, 2003), 1–15.

17. For an overview of theories of globalization, see Imre Szeman, "Globalization," *Encyclopedia of Postcolonial Studies*, ed. John Hawley (Westport, CT: Greenwood Press, 2001), 209–217; and "Globalization," *The Johns Hopkins Guide to Literary Theory and Criticism*, ed. Michael Groden, Martin Kreiswirth, and Imre Szeman (Baltimore: The Johns Hopkins University Press, 2005), 458–465.

18. Roland Robertson, *Globalization: Social Theory and Global Culture* (London: Sage, 1992); and Arjun Appadurai, *Modernity at Large: Cultural Dimensions in Globalization* (Minneapolis: University of Minnesota Press, 1996).

19. Amongst the most powerful of these deflationary accounts of the claims of globalization – especially with respect to the idea of a global economy – is Paul Hirst and Graeme Thompson, *Globalization in Question* (Cambridge: Polity Press, 1999).

20. Francis Fukuyama, *The End of History and the Last Man* (New York: Free Press, 1992), 4.

21. Robert Kagan, *The Return of History and the End of Dreams* (New York: Knopf, 2008).

22. Kagan, *Return of History*, 3.

23. Ibid., 5.

24. Ibid., 12.

25. Ibid., 97.

26. Text and video of Obama's Berlin speech can be found on-line at http://my.barackobama.com/page/content/berlinvideo/ (accessed October 28, 2010).

27. Barack Obama, "The Nobel Peace Prize 2009 – Presentation Speech." Nobelprize.org. 13 Sep 2010. Available at: http://nobelprize.org/nobel_prizes/peace/laureates/2009/presentation-speech.html (accessed October 28, 2010).

28. The full transcript of Obama's speech at the West Point Military Academy on December 1, 2009, can be found at: www.stripes.com/news/transcript-of-president-obama-s-speech-at-west-point-1.96961 (accessed October 28, 2010).

29. Joseph Stiglitz and Linda Blimes, "The Three Trillion Dollar War," *London Times*, February 23, 2008. Available at: www.timesonline.co.uk/tol/comment/columnists/guest_contributors/article3419840.ece

30. Richard Florida, *The Rise of the Creative Class* (New York: Basic Books, 2002), 69.

31. Pierre Bourdieu, *On Television* (New York: New Press, 1999), 6.
32. Franco Moretti, "*New York Times* Obituaries," *New Left Review* 2 (2000): 105.
33. J.H. von Herder, *Outlines of a Philosophy of the History of Man*, trans. T. Churchill (London, 1800), 166.
34. Theodor Adorno, "On the Question: 'What is German?,'" *Critical Models: Interventions and Catchwords*, trans. H.W. Pickford (New York: Columbia University Press), 205.
35. For information on its activities, see www.repohistory.org (accessed October 28, 2010).
36. See two recent additions to an ever-expanding field of books: George A. Akerlof and Robert J. Shiller, *Animal Spirits: How Human Psychology Drives the Economy, and Why It Matters for Global Capitalism* (Princeton, NJ: Princeton University Press, 2009); and Justin Fox, *The Myth of The Rational Market* (New York: Collins Business, 2009).
37. See Emmanul Saez, "Striking It Richer: Evolution of Top Incomes in the United States." Available at: http://elsa.berkeley.edu/~saez/saez-UStopincomes-2006prel.pdf (accessed October 28, 2010). Saez has written a number of influential papers on this topic with Thomas Piketty.
38. Leonard Cohen, "Everybody Knows," *I'm Your Man*. Columbia, 1988.
39. Yevgeny Zamyatin, *We*, trans. Natasha Randall (New York: Modern Library, 2006). The reference is to the activities of R-13, a poet in One State, and his method of approaching his craft.

Part II

The Limits of Liberalism

term this mode of apprehending and acting on the world as "neoliberalism" – a term which more accurately captures the ideological dynamics of geopolitical maneuvering over the past several decades and exposes the ideological function played by the concept of globalization. Globalization as neoliberalism was not characterized fundamentally by the shift of all relations to a global scale, to the increasing presence of communications technologies in the everyday, or to a change in human consciousness or awareness of the international character of late twentieth-century life – or any of the other developments typically connected with the global – but by the ferocious extension and dissemination of market values to every social institution and social action. As Wendy Brown puts it, neoliberalism means that human beings are "configured exhaustively as *homo oeconomicus*, [and] all dimensions of human life are cast in terms of a market rationality."[1] In his book *First as Tragedy, Then as Farce*, Slavoj Žižek writes that "Fukuyama's utopia of the 1990s had to die twice, since the collapse of the liberal–democratic political utopia on 9/11 did not affect the economic utopia of global market capitalism; if the 2008 financial meltdown has a historical meaning then, it is as a sign of the end of the economic face of Fukuyama's dream."[2] Though some might have hoped that the 2008 financial crisis would have brought an end to neoliberalism's dominant and defining political rationality, this hasn't been the case. One need only look to the lack of widespread protests by citizens at the actions of their governments to shore up the financial system, or at the decisions made – or not made – by governments to try to address fiscal deficits: it is apparently now impossible to ever again increase taxes, so the only actions which can be taken are to cut or restrict services, sometimes severely. What *has* come to an end, however, is the ideological function of globalization as a justification and screen for governmental decision making. Žižek isn't the only one proclaiming the definitive end of the fantasy of the end of history. No less a figure than Robert Kagan, senior associate at the Carnegie Endowment, columnist for the *Washington Post*, and a member of the State Department during Ronald Reagan's second term in office, has declared (with explicit reference to Fukuyama) that history has *returned*, and that, accordingly, a new way of thinking about the world has for academics to make use of articles and commentary by the authors in question, but mainly as a way of pointing to the limits and problems of the views articulated by writers such as these. What academics have not done is to seriously examine the positions these popular writers advocate, both in order to assess their own merits and faults, and to map out their relation to what we have been describing as the common sense of the global era, including the common sense of globalization itself. Our approach to the work of the authors we look at in this section – Richard Florida, Thomas Friedman, Paul Krugman, and Naomi Klein – will be critical. We intend to try to make sense of their positions in an effort to capture the logic of the arguments they advocate and to understand the narratives they offer of the present and future. These best-selling authors all produce frankly didactic books whose aim is to puncture the presumptions of others and to offer new solutions to the pressing problems they have identified. In light of the positions we've articulated in Part I, especially the series of negative theses with which we end, our aim is to grasp the common sense of the *progressive* possibilities on offer. We should emphasize: these four authors are not generally viewed as (nor view themselves as) con-servatives who want to keep the world as it is, or who would deny that the world faces significant challenges that need to be addressed. On the contrary: to varying degrees (and, in fact, sometimes in opposition to one another), these authors all want to help us move past the limits that we currently face. It is through an assessment of their framing of the problems and possibilities of the present that we hope to show that something's missing – something's missing in the way we have tended to configure our sense of the present and what awaits us in the future.

The authors we look at – and the film we end with – are all, to one degree or another, liberals. In the wake of the neoliberalism of globalization, they all wish to advocate for the return of a different social ethos, one that had been displaced by globalization, but which in the new space of the twenty-first century can now operate on a global level as opposed to a merely national one. If conservatives (i.e., neoliberals) focused on one part of the political equation of the present – the *capitalist* part of liberal-democratic capitalism – these writers want to revive and restore the liberal-democratic part as a way to think about the prospects of the world after the brutal economic games with which globalization became identified. However, a revived liberalism, and one with global ambitions, has to take into account a world transformed by the tenets of neoliberalism. Or at least it *should* take this into account. As often as not, these writers cast a glance backward at post-World War II US middle-class society as a source of inspiration for the world they would like to bring into being; the intervening years seem simply like history gone off the tracks, an error in which nothing new is created socially or politically, and which is best forgotten. But this is a problematic move, to say the least. One of the many developments that have occurred which allow for the possibility of liberalism taking over from neoliberalism is the fact that the world after globalization is one that has been rendered *American* through and through. It is an American style of liberalism that we hear voiced by these writers, a politics which affirms the centrality of capitalism even as it critiques it through arguments for the necessity of a good state to deal with its social outcomes in ameliorative fashion. History repeats itself: for these authors, just as the excesses of the first Gilded Age in the United States led to the New Deal after the Great Depression, the crash of 2008 and the fraught experience of the past two decades of globalization open up the possibility for a new New Deal to emerge. The drama undergone in the United States at the beginning of the twentieth century is repeated on a global scale at the beginning of the twenty-first, and if the earlier depression offers lessons for the whole globe it is because there is a way in which now there is an assumption that we are all Americans.

What could we possibly mean by this? This sense of the world after globalization being an American one is expressed most directly and unapologetically by Fareed Zakaria in a book whose title seems to suggest the *opposite* of what we are claiming here. Zakaria is former managing editor of *Foreign Affairs* and current editor of *Newsweek International*, and his book *The Post-American World* has played a major role in public discussions of what comes after globalization. For Zakaria, "post-American" is not a term framed by political or ideo-logical hopes, but simply one of analytic convenience: "The hybrid international system – more democratic, more dynamic, more open, more connected – is one we are likely to live with for several decades. It is easier to define what it is not than what it is, easier to describe the era it is moving away from than the era it is moving toward – hence *the post-American world*."[5]

Following an introduction and a chapter that lauds the economic and political successes of the global era, Zakaria devotes his long third chapter ("A Non-Western World?") to an investigation of Western-ization, modernity, and Americanization. He writes: "The world is moving from anger to indifference, from anti-Americanism to post-Americanism."[6] A change has taken place that has left the world indifferent to Westernization. In part, this is because Western modes of being and behaving have been successful. "There was coercion behind the spread of Western ideas," Zakaria writes, "but there were also many non-Westerners eager to learn the ways of the West. The reason for this was simple. They wanted to succeed, and people always tend to copy those who have succeeded."[7] He reaches back into history to offer numerous examples: Peter the Great, Kemal Atatürk, Fukuzawa Yukichi (theorist of the Meiji Restoration), India's Jawaharlal Nehru, Egypt's Gamal Abdel Nasser. If the latter also had disagreements and disputes with the West, Zakaria reminds us that Marxists in the developing world, too, "were simply borrowing from the radical traditions of the West." The world has already been made modern, de facto Westernized: "walk down a street anywhere in the industri-alized world today, and you see variations on the same themes – bank machines, coffeehouses, clothing stores with their seasonal sales, immigrant communities, popular culture and music."[8] This is not cause for alarm, but a reason for celebration. If traditions are being eroded around the world, it is because of

the rise of a mass public, empowered by capitalism and democracy. This is often associated with Westernization because what replaces the old – the new dominant culture – looks Western, and specifically American. McDonald's, blue jeans, and rock music have become universal, crowding out older, more distinctive forms of eating, dressing, and singing. But the story here is about catering to a much larger public than the small elite who used to define a country's mores. It looks American because America, the country that invented mass capitalism and

74

consumerism, got there first. The impact of mass capitalism is now universal.[9]

Modernization or Westernization is figured as part of an historical development with a certain degree of inevitability. In the concluding chapter of his book ("American Purpose"), it is clear that Zakaria sees these developments as benefiting the United States: "The world is going America's way. Countries are becoming more open, market friendly, and democratic. As long as we keep the forces of modernization, global interaction, and trade growing, good governance, human rights, and democracy all move forward."[10] Whether or not the United States remains the sole global power, or its share of global GDP continues to decline, it has already won because the values and organizing principles of the planet are the same as its own.

Lest one think this way of framing things is unique to Zakaria, consider a similar set of claims in Kagan's *The Return of History*:

All the world's rich and powerful nations have more or less embraced the economic, technological, and even social aspects of modernization and globalization. All have embraced, albeit with varying degree of complaint and resistance, the free flow of goods, finances, and services, and the intermingling of cultures and lifestyles that characterize the modern world. Increasingly, their people watch the same television shows, listen to the same music, and go to the same movies. Along with this dominant modern culture, they have accepted, even as they may also deplore, the essential characteristics of a modern morality and aesthetics. Modernity means, among other things, the sexual as well as political and economic liberation of women, the weakening of church authority and the strengthening, the existence of what used to be called the counterculture, and free expression in the arts (if not in politics), which includes the freedom to commit blasphemy and to lampoon symbols of faith, authority and morality. These are the consequences of liberalism and capitalism unleashed and unchecked by the constraining hand of tradition, a powerful church, or a moralistic and domineering government.[11]

Zakaria has no problem with modernity taking different cultural guises – that is, if by culture one means the kinds of dress one might

75

wear to work, the food one eats, or the stories one reads; Kagan, too, encourages countercultures and free artistic expressions. Each is open to difference – even encouraging of it – as long as a more fundamental social rationality or common sense is accepted, and without comment: at no point is liberal democracy or capitalism *ever* placed into question, nor the nature of work explored, nor levels of economic inequality and social suffering pondered. But then again, an exploration of such issues would not help make the case for the perpetuation of US power, which is ensured at some deep level by the fact that there is no longer any need to fight to establish consent to a basic social rationality which is now global; they name this "modernization," misidentifying (if not deliberately) this complex historical process with what is actually on display here: the cultural logic of neoliberalism, behind which hides the intensification of market rationality identified above by Wendy Brown.

Globalization qua US dominance of the post-Cold War world comes to an end, but advantageously the United States retains a leading position in the world by virtue of the fact that the planet has been remade in its image, without apologies. The narratives of Zakaria and Kagan exhibit the features of a discursive form that Sarika Chandra has perceptively named "dislocalism."[12] For Chandra, dislocalism appears to reach out to the world, but only as a way to domesticate the globe in order to make it safe for the projects of the United States and the ideology of Americanism. Dislocalism *is* Americanism disguised as globalization – the apparent dissolution of national presumptions and ideologies that in fact all the more powerfully extends American power – or at least its possibility – on a global scale. Even if such power is being challenged at multiple levels – political, social, and economic – it is not being challenged culturally, which means that US elites find a world open to them, and find other elites to *be* them, even though they might physically inhabit other countries and nations.

In her analysis of the phenomenon of dislocalism, Chandra looks at the surprising use of cultural theory and literary fiction in contemporary management theory; the apparent opening of American Studies to a post-national configuration that is nevertheless framed around a hidden Americanism; the continued political dynamics of travel writing after the end of travel as the possibility of encountering

76

(however problematically) the new and the exotic; and new forms of tourism organized around food cultures – the last remnant of difference which plays beautifully into a global mode of bourgeois distinction and taste. In each case, there is an incomplete or suspect attempt to shed national identifications in an effort to display theoretical sophistication or contemporary relevance – take, for instance, the decade-long struggle for American Studies to take on global theories or thematics while remaining resolutely focused on the (US) American. Something slightly different is going on in these texts like Zakaria's. What is happening on the level of the global is taken not only as confirming the power of national ideology, but as revealing the global to be an ideologically safe space even after globalization – an appropriate level at which to construct narratives that can confidently name the end of US power even while confirming its continued status and function. After globalization, nothing changes because the world has been changed by globalization, which means that a text whose intention is to tell the United States what to do in a post-American world ends up telling it to do what it has already been doing.

Ideologically and politically, the authors that we look at in the analyses which follow imagine themselves to occupy a very different position than Zakaria, and certainly than Kagan. But like them, their liberalism, too, operates in a post-American world that has been rendered safe for America and its ideas even after globalization. This underwrites the confidence with which they promote the values of liberal-democracy in opposition to neoliberalism, and with which they appeal to older ideas of liberal-democratic capitalism to map out the future. And yet: the world *does* seem less certain. The analyses below trace the limits of liberalism after globalization – the limits of a form of common sense that refuses even at its most radical forms (here, the work of Naomi Klein) to part with capitalism, whatever problems and traumas it induces.

b.   Neoliberals Dressed in Black: Richard Florida[13]

In communist society, where nobody has one exclusive sphere of activity but each can become accomplished in any branch he wishes, society

77

regulates the general production and thus makes it possible for me to do one thing today and another tomorrow, to hunt in the morning, fish in the afternoon, rear cattle in the evening, criticise after dinner, just as I have a mind, without ever becoming hunter, fisherman, herdsman or critic.

Karl Marx, *The German Ideology*[14]

It's hard to tell an espresso-sipping professor from a cappuccino-gulping banker.

David Brooks, *Bobos in Paradise*[15]

With the publication of *The Rise of the Creative Class* (*RCC*) in 2002, Richard Florida almost instantly became an influential figure across a range of fields and disciplines. An academic by training, over the past decade his ideas have shaped discussions of current affairs and decisions made by business and government. Though he did not invent the term "Creative Class," his thorough analysis and description of the characteristics and function of what he sees as this newly hegemonic socioeconomic group guaranteed that he would be identified as its progenitor and primary spokesperson. Florida has remained a staunch defender and advocate of the Creative Class and its related concepts (creative cities and creative economies) over a series of follow-up books that answer criticisms and provide further nuance to the central ideas developed in *RCC*.[16] Nevertheless, it is the first book that remains the most significant, both in terms of the articulation of the concepts and ideas he continues to advance, the attention and criticism it has generated, and its lasting impact on the language in which contemporary economic and urban planning decisions are framed.

In Canada (his new home base), Florida's ideas have generated more praise than criticism, more acceptance than dismissal. His appointment in 2007 at the University of Toronto's Rotman School of Management as Professor of Business and Creativity and as Academic Director of the newly established Prosperity Institute was celebrated by local and national media alike. Here was an example of just the kind of Creative Class migration that Florida himself writes about, with the bonus being that his move from Washington, DC to Toronto seemed to confirm the latter's growing importance as a creative city. Even before his physical arrival in Toronto, the discourse of creative cities had been taken up fervently by city governments in Canada, who were anxious to find an urban planning narrative to match the challenges and expectations of a neoliberal age. If organizations such as the Creative City Network of Canada (CCNC) or the series of Creative Places + Spaces conference organized by the non-profit group Artscape are any indication, the idea that creativity is essential to economic growth has been swallowed whole by urban governments across Canada – in big cities such as Vancouver and Montreal, but also in smaller places from Moncton to Moose Jaw.[17] In an effort to create urban environs attractive to members of the Creative Class, local, regional, and national governments around the world have endeavored to create new programs to support and encourage culture. Instead of being a drain on economies, the arts and culture sector is now seen as a potential financial boon, a segment of the economy in which it is necessary to invest.[18]

Is there anything wrong with this interest in the economic spin-offs of creativity? Even if only strategically – focusing on the outcome as opposed to the concepts, arguments, and theories employed by Florida and others championing creativity today – doesn't this development represent a productive and positive situation for the arts and culture, areas in which we expect and hope to find new ways of imagining, thinking, and believing? If the language of creative cities and the Creative Class generates more money for museums and increases in grants for artists and cultural workers, expands government sponsorship of festivals, and so on, what could possibly be wrong with it? And does it even have any connection to the drama of globalization and its aftermath that we have been discussing?

We want to argue that the redefinition of the arts as *one of many* creative practices making up the twenty-first-century economy *is* a problem. The expansion of discourses of creativity into the economy at large represents a loss in how we understand the politics of art – a shift from a practice with a certain degree of autonomy (however questionable, however problematic at a theoretical level) to one without

79

any. Perhaps even more significantly, it constitutes a fundamental reimagination of the operations of labor under global capitalism that pushes aside anxieties about outsourcing, exploited factory labor, downsizing and all the rest.

In what follows, we offer a detailed analysis of Florida's *RCC* to show what work the discourse of *creativity* does in his understanding of globalization. There have now been numerous criticisms made of Florida's ideas, primarily by urban geographers and economists who question his claims about the nature of the Creative Class and the spaces it inhabits. What has not been directly addressed is the very idea of creativity on which it all hinges – a concept that has been increasingly called upon to do important conceptual and political work on both right and left. To fully grasp the implications of Florida's way of conceptualizing creativity – an idea of creativity which threatens to become common sense, if it isn't in fact already so – it is essential to work through his claims in some detail.

As is to be expected from a contemporary, popular, non-fiction text addressing social issues, the core promise and attraction of Richard Florida's *RCC* is its presentation of a new social phenomenon that its author has uncovered; the significance of this phenomenon is figured as being essential to an understanding of the nature of contemporary global society, as well as its coming future. The rhetorical form of the book is that of the explorer's tale: the breathless recounting of the discovery of a paradigm shift that reorganizes our very sense of the operations of the social world. Florida aims to convince us that the Creative Class is the one primarily responsible for the bulk of economic development, and that its influence on and importance for the economy will only grow in the coming decades. The emphasis on a specific class in relation to its economic function is significant. Although Florida presumes to offer a wide-ranging analysis of contemporary society – he positions himself as heir to the work of sociologists such as William H. Whyte, C. Wright Mills, and Jane Jacobs – at its heart this is a labor management book. In the context of a variety of social changes and developments, especially the coming-to-be of the technological society, *RCC* analyzes the characteristics of the Creative Class – their motivations, pleasures, habits, tendencies, goals, likes, and dislikes – in order to give companies the conceptual tools to better capture the fruits of their creativity. It is also a book designed to offer economic advice to city councils and urban planners (less so state or national governments; as for Saskia Sassen, for Florida, the city is the primary unit of the contemporary era).[19] Florida makes it abundantly clear that it is not enough to change the work environment of the Creative Class. The energies of the Creative Class can be harnessed only in urban environments in which this class finds it appealing to live. The book offers guidelines for the character and nature of the cultural amenities and urban characteristics that provide the preconditions for the creativity so essential to economies today.

It is this aspect of the book that has received most of the critical and media attention directed Florida's way. The long fourth section, "Community," offers an account of what constitutes Creative Centers and an overview of the various statistical procedures he and his colleagues have used to map out the new urban geography of class in the United States. Florida explores the logic of the growing gap between those cities with large numbers of the Creative Class and those without; this division correlates directly with the current financial status of the cities in question. The main question that organizes his examination of urban economics is why members of the Creative Class choose to live in some cities more than in others. A clarification of which characteristics make those cities high on the Creative Cities index – San Francisco, Austin, Seattle, Boston – so attractive to the Creative Class is intended to assist those at the bottom of the list – Memphis, Norfolk, Buffalo, Louisville – to develop programs and policies to improve their economies.

One can understand why criticism would be directed here. First, local media seized on Florida's book to either trumpet the standing of their cities or dispute it (are Buffalo or Memphis really such terrible places to live? Can such places really make themselves attractive to software engineers and financiers?). Second, challenges were made to the veracity and utility of the new indices Florida utilized to generate his rankings. In addition to indices such as innovation (measured by patents per capita) and high-tech ranking (the Milken Institute's Tech

Pole Index), he also made use of two even more controversial measurements: the Gay index and the Bohemian index. It is the politics many felt to be hidden in these measures that produced controversy. For Florida, the Gay index – the number of gay people in a city or a region – indicates a region's tolerance, while the Bohemian index – "the number of writers, designers, musicians, actors and directors, painters and sculptors, photographers and dancers"[20] – identifies the cultural amenities in a region – less such things, it should be noted, as symphonies and concert halls (for which there are other indices) and more the cutting-edge, indie vibe of a place. What do these factors have to do with urban economies? Florida claims that "artists, musicians, gay people and the members of the Creative Class in general prefer places that are open and diverse."[21] He identifies a high correlation between these various indices, the population of Creative Class in an area, and economic success. For reasons that will become clear momentarily, members of the Creative Class are thought to value lifestyle, social interaction, diversity, authenticity, and identity. Cities didn't like being deemed uncool (Memphis, Detroit) or intolerant (St. Louis, and poor Memphis again); further, the breakdown of creative cities as opposed to uncreative ones along party lines – with creative cities tending to be blue (that is, Democrat) and uncreative ones red (Republican) – made many on the political right in the United States suspicious of the true intentions of Florida's study.

The claims and arguments made in the latter part of Florida's book about the relationship between cities and creativity have generated criticism; the earlier, more substantive part far less so. The first three sections – "The Creative Age," "Work," and "Life and Leisure" – offer a detailed examination of the character of the Creative Class. It is here, in other words, that he identifies what makes this class meaningfully a class at all. As the preferences for tolerance, diversity, and openness to ideas already named above might suggest, this is not a class in any objective sense of the term, whether understood in the terms of classical economics (the division of the world into quartiles or quintiles based on income) or in the Marxist sense of those who sell their labor as opposed to those who purchase it. The Creative Class is first and foremost treated as an economic class. It is an economic class that is brought together, however, not just by the fact that its members occupy certain professions, but because they adopt a common *style de vie*, an outlook on life that cuts across and ties together the different registers of work, leisure, self-actualization, and social goods. If one had to capture this mode of being in a word, it is in the adjective that Florida gives to this class: creative. One might then expect a clear definition, or even an attempt at one, given the very looseness and indefiniteness of the social meanings of the term, which can at times act as little more than an empty approbative: to label something creative is to offer approval or praise. Startlingly, none is given. Nevertheless, there *is* a core significance and function for "creative" (adjective) and "creativity" (noun) that emerges in Florida's book. To understand the work that the concept of creativity does for his understanding of the social – and indeed, the work it does more generally today – one has to consider the significance of the multiple identifications and associations he proposes throughout the book.

Though many of Florida's descriptions of creativity appear to operate in the same register (that is, they point to the same noun, the same thing, even if they do so with slight variations), looking at the claims and assumptions made in each case is essential. There are (at least) *seven* forms or modes of creativity identified in *RCC*:

(a) Creativity is an innate characteristic of the human mind or brain. "The creative impulse – the attribute that distinguishes us as humans from other species."[22] It is an attribute that distinguishes the human *as such*, though it is also described as "a capacity inherent to varying degrees in virtually all people."[23]

(b) It is a cultural or social characteristic and/or good. Just as with individuals, societies can be more or less creative; they can be organized to be conducive to creativity, to limit or prohibit it. The text stands as a warning to the United States to be careful about losing its creative edge to countries such as the UK, Germany, and the Netherlands, which are doing a better job of being creative.

(c) Creativity is the subversion or breaking of rules. "It disrupts existing patterns of thought and life. It can feel subversive and unsettling even to the creator."[24] Creativity as subversion is especially important in Florida's re-narration of the social drama of the 1960s and its central place in the constitution of the ethos of Silicon Valley and in technological industries more generally.[25]

(d) It constitutes the key element of certain kinds of work, which cuts across the spectrum of previous definitions and distinctions of labor (i.e., white collar, blue collar, executive class, working class). There can be white-collar creative jobs just as there can be blue-collar ones, which is why for Florida it is better to speak of a Creative Class instead of depending on these older, Fordist categories. Creative jobs are challenging and involve problem solving. There is an innate pleasure to this kind of work – it wouldn't even be work except for the fact that you are paid (bonus!). Creative people are attracted to their jobs because of the intrinsic rewards offered by the character of their jobs. Such work allows one to exercise the innate impulse identified in (a).

(e) Creativity is used as a stand-in term for acts that produce the "new": new ideas, new concepts, or new products. In other words, novelty is creativity (and vice versa).

(f) Creativity is strongly linked to technology. One measure of creativity is the number of patents issued per capita; another is the amount of spending on research and development. Florida identifies Nokia cell phones and the film series *The Lord of the Rings* as creative products. Though he identifies other fields of endeavor and other products as creative, there is no doubt that he sees the field of contemporary high technology as a place where it is especially in force.

(g) Finally, creativity is repeatedly identified as a characteristic of work in the arts – those whose activities are named by the Bohemian index. This is an element of the arts that has now expanded to cover other forms of human endeavor as a result of social change, technological development, or simply insight into the productive process: in hindsight, many forms of work were always already creative. "Writing a book, producing a work of art or developing new software requires long periods of con-centration."[26] When creativity is described by Florida, the arts are always in the pole position: "[Prosperity] requires increasing

84

investments in the multidimensional and varied forms of creativity – arts, music, culture, design and related fields – because all
are linked and flourish together."[27]

At times these varied appeals to creativity stand alone; more often,
creativity is described and discussed by linking two or more of these
different ideas of creativity together. The chain of associations through
which Florida runs these work something like this:

technology *(f)* is creative because
it is full of people who are allowed to be subversive *(c)* and so
create new things *(e)*,
all as a result of a new social setting *(b)*
that enables companies to *(d)* create working conditions to permit this
  to happen.

Working in a high-tech company and being able to be creative in this
fashion is the best of all possible worlds, but is nonetheless at heart:

(a) an expression of an innate human impulse which the economic
  world has hitherto squashed underfoot.

Unsurprisingly, the circulation of these multiple ideas of creativity
generates an increasing number of tautologies and inconsistencies as
the book progresses. Creativity is described as an essential aspect of
human beings[28] and yet we are also repeatedly told that there are
"creative people" (and so presumably less creative ones, too), and
a distinct Class whose creativity must therefore be the function of
something other than simply being human.

The seventh definition of creativity (g) is without question the most
important one in Florida's view of it. His most substantive definition
of the Creative Class identifies its key characteristic to be "that its
members engage in work whose function is to 'create meaningful new
forms.'"[29] A broad definition, to be sure; the nature of these forms
and their function is clarified in his elaboration of the kinds of work
that constitute the Creative Class. Drawing on categories from the

Occupational Employment Survey of the US Bureau of Labor Statistics, he divides the Creative Class into two component elements: the Super-Creative Core and the Creative Class more generally. The first group includes workers across a wide field of employment categories:

> scientists and engineers, university professors, poets and novelists, artists, entertainers, actors, designers and architects, as well as the thought leadership of modern society: nonfiction writers, editors, cultural figures, think-tank researchers, analysts and other opinion-makers ... I define the highest order of creative work as producing new forms or designs that are readily transferable and widely useful – such as designing a product that can be widely made, sold and used.[30]

The Super-Creative Core is paid to engage in the production of new forms that are transferable and useful. By contrast, while the rest of the Creative Class might at times produce new forms, it is not a fundamental aspect of their jobs; they have to think on their own, but in doing so, they do not necessarily generate new forms. The second group is just as broad and includes knowledge-intensive workers such as legal and health professionals, financial services workers, lawyers, and those who work in the high-tech industry. Should any of these workers have the opportunity to engage in the creation of new forms in their jobs – everything from new products to new job opportunities – they have the chance to move up to the Super-Creative level, where generating usable and transferable new forms becomes the main purpose of their labor.

Like commodities, such as oil or coal, or the work of laborers in tax-free zones or maquiladoras, for Florida creativity is an economic good. But it is not just any good. As he states directly in the Preface to the paperback edition, and repeats throughout the book, "Human creativity is the ultimate economic resource."[31] Many might imagine creativity to be a quality or characteristic with intrinsic value – a value that isn't established by markets, or through its utility or transferability. Florida sees things differently. For him, creativity is at the core of "new technologies, new industries, new wealth" and so has to be encouraged, since all "good economic things flow from it."[32] The contribution made by *The Rise of the Creative Class* is thus twofold. First, Florida plays the role of a lobbyist on behalf of creativity to government, business, and the general public, working tirelessly to get them to recognize the importance of creativity to the economy. And second, in his role as a social scientist, he develops numerous theoretical and empirical schemes to better understand the creative-economic systems that have, until now, evolved on their own. His aim is to help encourage and harness creativity, so that with the knowledge provided by social science these systems can operate even better, which will equally benefit nation-states and the lives of those workers whose creativity is currently being wasted in jobs that fall outside of the Creative Class.

A utopian vision, is it not? Who could be against more creativity in the world? Or the outcomes that creativity seems to produce: more diverse and tolerant societies, better jobs, and wealth for all?[33] Florida's view of the significance of the Creative Class for our collective futures is unambiguous: "We have evolved economic and social systems that tap human creativity and make use of it as never before. This in turn creates an unparalleled opportunity to raise our living standards, build a more humane and sustainable economy, and make our lives more complete."[34] This opportunity has not yet been taken up. Luckily, for this extraordinary future to be realized all that is needed is a completion of the "transformation to a society that taps and rewards our full creative potential."[35] A proud member of the thought leadership of "our" society, Florida is prepared to help light the path to a better future (and to make a fortune through his consultancy firm along the way).

Despite his enthusiasm for the project of rendering the world safer for creativity, Florida's view of a social and economic system nearing perfection functions only to the degree that it fails to address or account for a number of issues that – given his subject matter and the concepts he employs – he cannot leave by the wayside. We can get a sense of these gaps and elisions by looking at the few moments in which he raises concerns or questions about the picture of the present he paints. In a 400-page book that sometimes seems intent on addressing almost everything (Jimi Hendrix and the rise of agriculture, Thomas Frank and the Frankfurt School, Silicon Valley and Florida's own childhood skill at building wooden cars), there are only *three* moments of doubt or hesitation about the views for which he argues. These are worth citing in full:

> [The creative economy] is not a panacea for the myriad social and economic ills that confront modern society. It will not somehow magically alleviate poverty, eliminate unemployment, overcome the business cycle and lead to greater happiness and harmony for all . . . left unchecked and without appropriate forms of human intervention, this creativity-based system may well make some of our problems worse.[36]

> My statistical research identifies a troubling negative statistical correlation between concentrations of high-tech firms and the percentage of the non-white population . . . the Creative Economy does little to ameliorate the traditional divide between the white and nonwhite segments of the population. It may even make things worse.[37]

> Creativity is not an unmitigated good but a human capacity that can be applied toward many different ends . . . Massive, centralized experiments in new forms of economic and social life led to fiascos like the Soviet Union, while here in the United States, free-market creativity has turned out a great deal that is trivial, vulgar and wasteful.[38]

There is no comment offered following the first two quotations; they come at the end of sections, after which Florida's cheerleading resumes unabated. The third warning about the potential dangers of creativity comes in the book's conclusion, in which he directs his energies toward convincing the US public and their governments to recognize and support the Creative Class. There is a meek defense offered concerning the potential for creativity to be put toward totalitarian uses or result in the detritus of consumer culture. Put simply, since creativity is now at the core of the economy, and since it is only an increase in resources that will enable the potential to do good in the world, creativity remains essential, no matter that its results include everything from the atomic bomb to the superfluous commodities lining the shelves of dollar stores around the world.

What emerges in these three passages is what is almost entirely absent in the rest of the book: the *political*. Why a creativity-based system might make our problems worse is never specified; it also comes as somewhat of a surprise, given the tone and triumphalism of the book, to learn that it is *not* a panacea. One realizes in reading these passages that little or no mention has been made of a whole host of issues related to work and labor in the era of globalization: poverty, unemployment, outsourcing and offshore work, or the business cycle – or race and ethnicity, for that matter. Yet these are all crucial factors in shaping the experience of work and one's degree of economic participation, whether in the United States or elsewhere. There are other ways to make sense of Florida's list of cities, and their existing levels of Creative Class workers, which correlate *precisely* with poverty, unemployment, race, lack of access to education (required for Creative Class jobs), lack of mobility, and lack of opportunity.[39] These are deeply political issues, not mere externalities or afterthoughts to the system he describes. When ethnicity or immigration is discussed, it is framed by Florida as mere context or backdrop in an urban setting – the urban coloring that gives a place its feeling of diversity and tolerance, much the same, in other words, as a good alternative music scene: part of the necessary make-up of a city that allows white Creative Class members to feel good about themselves and the place they live. One of the reasons the political is missing – beyond, that is, that its inclusion would spoil the elegance of Florida's systems and its apparent strong correlations between job type and "tolerance" and "diversity" – is announced in his response to the problem introduced in the last passage above. When it comes right down to it, the logic of the economy trumps everything, even the possibility of the terrible new weapons that some members of the Creative Class are (without doubt) commissioned to design. Whatever its sociological reality, creativity begins to sound like another name for neoliberalism – or if not equivalent, then an important factor in the operation of the latter, especially in post-industrial economies.

At one level, it would not be going too far to see the absence of the political as the absence of the *world* in general: the contingencies and challenges that shape economic decisions and those of city councils and urban planners are nowhere to be found. This is one of the reasons, perhaps, that there seems to be a fundamental structuring confusion of cause and effect in Florida's work when imagining how urban spaces operate: *rarely* does one have the production of creative city spaces that *then* attract creative workers (away from other creative cities, one can only imagine). More commonly the reverse is true, with certain kinds of cities emerging out of historically contingent processes of industry and labor. (Can one imagine China, for instance, developing a Brasilia-like creative city from scratch? What would it take to make such a place one that would cause "thought leaders" to jump from Beijing and Shanghai to go and live in it?) But it is perhaps more productive to focus on a smaller element of the book that nonetheless captures some of its wider absences.

The limits of Florida's construction of the Creative Class and its future promise can be seen in the fact that in a book whose fundamental theme is labor, a real discussion of work is entirely absent. The Creative Class engages in the creation of meaningful new forms. It does so, however, as *work*, as an activity within corporations and institutions familiar to all of us (the ones that capture Florida's interest are high-tech giants such as Dell, Microsoft, and Apple). In championing creativity, Florida seems to have forgotten about work, whether accidentally or deliberately. Work within capitalism has a number of social and economic functions, the most important of which – the reason why a corporation or institution might hire a member of the Creative Class – is to generate a product or offer a service (transferable and useful, whether material or immaterial). This process is not carried out for the good of humanity, or because it allows members of the Creative Class to exercise their impulses, but to generate profit. As any fourth grader knows, profit can only be realized if the amount one pays the creative staff (and the rest of the workers) is less than the income that can be generated by means of the product.

This sense of capitalist work – as part of a system of profit – never appears in *The Rise of the Creative Class*. Instead, it is essential for Florida to make the point that members of the Creative Class *aren't* motivated by money, and that the Super-Creative Core make even less than their Creative peers.[40] In surveys which he cites, IT workers indicate that work challenge, flexibility, and stability all come before base pay as reasons why they choose their jobs, with many other values (vacations, opinions being valued, etc.) standing only a few percentage points behind.[41] For Florida, this interest in factors other than salary is viewed as a defining element of the Creative Class. Their desire for flexible and open forms of work, which allow them to avoid wearing a tie, to come late to work, or, better yet, to continue to work wherever and whenever (at home, on the subway, while shopping, while reading messages on their Blackberries, etc.), is seen as a sign not just of a new mode of labor freedom, but a form of social freedom more generally.

Numerous social and cultural critics have drawn attention to the ways in which this apparent new-found freedom in fact covers up an expansion of the traditional, 9 to 5 work day to every aspect of one's life.[42] For those with a more systemic understanding of the capitalist economy and the changes it has undergone over the past two decades in particular, this liberalization of the work environment appears as little more than a new mode of labor management, whose overall aim remains that of generating as much profit as possible for companies and shareholders. If workers see their jobs as sites of self-definition, challenge, and freedom instead of the opposite, so much the better for the bottom line! The training of bodies willing to work at any time of the day – and to do so not due to external compulsion, but because of some innate, self-defining drive – is an easy way of increasing productivity without having to increase pay. Florida expresses no anxieties about this redefinition of work, and even argues that such worries are overstated and beside the point.[43]

At its core, what is expressed in Florida's book is a fantasy of labor under capitalism: the possibility *within* capitalism of work without exploitation, of work as equivalent to play. What might give those of us who study the arts and culture pause here is how closely this vision approximates that of the ideal social function and purpose of culture – if in reverse. The aim of the historical avant-garde was to reject the deadened rationality of capitalist society through the creation of "a new life praxis from a basis in art."[44] Florida's characterization of the Creative Class suggests that this new life has in fact been achieved. For the historical avant-garde, the passage to the utopia of a new life praxis was supposed to occur via the transformation of life and work by *art*, such that art as a separate, autonomous sphere of life cut off from more pragmatic life activity was no longer necessary. The division of art and life that first made the autonomous activity called art what it is would be undone through the critical practice of art itself. In Florida's vision of our creative present, *work* tends toward art by means of changes in the character and nature of labor, partly as a result of technological developments and partly due to what can only be described as new-found enlightenment about the way in which the workplace should be configured. Equating the Creative Class with the activity of the avant-garde might seem far-fetched. It is, however, the fundamental way in which Florida envisions the social function of the Creative Class. For him, the Creative Class has brought different spheres of life together to allow that innate element of creativity that makes us human and distinguishes us from the beasts to finally be expressed socially. He writes, "[W]e are impatient with the strict separations that previously demarcated work, home and leisure."[45] Luckily, in the era of globalization these separations have become undone. "The rise of the Creative Economy is drawing the spheres of innovation (technological creativity), business (economic creativity) and culture (artistic and cultural creativity) into one another, in more intimate and more powerful combinations than ever."[46] And again: "Highbrow and lowbrow, alternative and mainstream, work and play, CEO and hipster are all morphing together today."[47] CEO and hipster, professor and banker: maybe. But what of the workers who make their clothes and their laptops? And those who assemble their iPhones?

Florida's vision is, of course, more wishful thinking than actually realized utopia. He imagines capitalism to have achieved what the avant-garde had wished to bring about as a means of *undoing* capitalism. How can this be? What enables and sustains the fantasy of capitalism as an avant-garde – capitalism as having gone beyond itself in the way art once imagined it could – is the concept of creativity itself. The history of the concept of creativity and the changes it has undergone over the centuries is enormously complicated.[48] Suffice it to say that in terms of its recent history, creativity is most commonly associated with the act of generation in the fine arts. The idea that the production of a painting or musical score involves generation ex nihilo – the emergence of the new out of nothingness – sprang in part from the individualization of artistic practice at the beginning of the nineteenth century and in part from the break with strictly determined formal categories within which such activities were supposed to be carried out. Artists are the model for the creative individual; they are also the model of a kind of self-motivated labor done for intrinsic purposes and outside of the formal institutions of work.

Over the course of the twentieth century, creativity has come to be associated with all manner of activities: scientific discovery, mathematics, economics, business activities, and so on – anything thought to involve the production of newness of any sort. Despite its residual Romantic humanism, one effect of this expansion of the term is to have rendered creativity into a synonym for originality or innovation. In Florida's use of the term, creativity becomes an act with even less specificity, being understood at times as little more than "problem solving" of a kind that takes place all the time in work and daily life. Yet it is also essential that in virtually every one of its invocations in his work creativity retain its link to the arts and to (the imagined) freedoms and autonomy connected with such work. This is reinforced by the equivalences Florida repeatedly draws between the work of artists and engineers, musicians and computer scientists. There would be something critical missing in Florida's account if he was to champion the work not of the Creative Class, but that of "knowledge workers," the "postindustrial class," the "professional-managerial class," "symbolic analysts," or even "cognitive laborers." "Creative" obscures the work function of this Class, transforming it into something much grander than just a label for a new category of work in late capitalism. The genius of making use of "creative" and "creativity" in the way that Florida does is to render the world into something comprised – if not today, then someday just around the corner – of *nothing but artistic activity*, if carried out through different forms of labor (not with paint, but XML; not by videos intended for the artist-run space, but for clients on the internet) and with different ends in mind. The distinctions between engineer, computer scientist, and lawyer thus become something akin to that between painters, sculptors, and filmmakers –

variants of the same fundamental creative impulse. At the same time, filling the world with art empties it of the vagaries and injustices of work under capitalism – that is, of the world that we in fact inhabit and to which we need to attend.

The group that most fascinates Florida are workers in the high-tech industry in places such as Silicon Valley and Austin, Texas. His understanding of the nature of technological innovation, the creation of wondrous new hardware and software, shapes his sense of what constitutes creativity. Though he does not say as much, if artistic work stands as the model of what constitutes creative labor in general, new technology is the mechanism by which it is imagined that creativity can form the life activity of more and more people: innovation can eliminate tedious work, leaving only challenging work behind. There is, however, another level at which artistic labor and that of technological industries in which Florida is so interested can be seen as connected. At one point in *RCC*, Florida boasts that the number of people who identify themselves as artists and cultural workers expanded dramatically over the past half-century in the United States, from 525 000 in 1950 to 2.5 million in 1999, "an increase of more than 375 percent."[49] He declines, however, to consider how such workers actually make a living, which is understandable since, for him, artists and cultural workers value the opportunity to enact their creative freedom much more than they worry about how they might eat.

Florida may be correct in identifying a connection between artists and workers in the knowledge industries of the "new economy." Where he is mistaken is the precise nature of this relationship. What is being carried over from artist to IT worker through the medium of creativity is the "cultural discount" that has long accompanied artistic labor of all kinds (not to mention issues related to ownership of intellectual property, which we will leave aside). One of the reasons why most artists aren't able to survive on the fruits of their labor is that it is assumed that they are "willing to accept non-monetary rewards – the gratification of producing art – as compensation for their work, thereby discounting the cash price of their labour."[50] Though the IT worker is typically far better compensated for his work than the artist, the adoption of an artistic relation to their work effects a similar labor discount that benefits their employer – even if the IT worker believes that the primary benefits are his own. The characteristics of the post-industrial knowledge worker that is the exemplum of Florida's Creative Class are that they are "comfortable in an ever-changing environment that demands creative shifts in communication with different kinds of clients and partners; attitudinally geared toward production that requires long, and often unsocial, hours; and accustomed, in the sundry exercises of their mental labour, to a contingent, rather than a fixed, routine of self-application."[51] We are all artists now, which doesn't mean a life of unfettered freedom and creativity. Rather, it means that, if we're lucky, the labor of crunching code for long hours can be offset by no longer having to wear a tie to work and by getting to play with your colleagues at the corner football table once in awhile.

There is much more that one could criticize about Florida's vision of our collective futures. There is the fact, for instance, that despite the link he wishes to make between art and the Creative Class, in the end artists and musicians don't really get to play with the big boys of the IT world. The Bohemian index, which measures the presence of Creative types in a city, confirms that they are simply the humus out of which the creativity of technological types grows: just like ethnic diversity, they give a place its color and maybe provide an occasional evening's entertainment. The limited vision Florida has of creativity – the almost complete crowding out, say, of any sense of the intrinsic value, or political or social function, of certain kinds of human activity – is indicated by his use of patents as a means to measure it, and the unembarrassed description of creativity as pure utility, transferability, and economic functionality. Florida imagines the gradual expansion of the Creative Class so that it would one day encompass *everyone*. Who would be left to pull the espressos and cappuccinos so beloved by professors and bankers is unclear. What is clear, however, is that even amidst all the creativity that the Creative Class and Florida himself engages in, there is one "new" thing ruled out from the beginning: an entirely new economic and social system, one in which work would have a very different social character than liberal capitalism, even at its most utopic, might be able to provide. For a start, such a system might not be organized around ever-increasing levels of profit and productivity. Despite all of the interesting new ways of thinking about work in the global era on display in Florida's work, in the end it remains startlingly timid about thinking new ways of being and living, preferring to place its hope on the idea that capitalism will turn out – by the magic of technology – to be the grounds for the best possible world we could live in.

To be clear: Florida's views on creativity are less idiosyncratic than they are *symptomatic*. One finds these ideas circulating widely in the culture at large. It is endemic today especially in the language of business and economics. As Paul Krugman writes (to take but one example), "in the 1990s the old idea that wealth is the product of virtue, or at least of creativity, made a comeback."[52] In some respects, the redefinition of business as art via the concept of creativity might not seem to be an especially worrisome development. It certainly doesn't seem to traipse on the space where one might think it does: the field of cultural study and analysis. After all, creativity was never really a feature of older conceptual vocabularies of cultural study (from Johann Joachim Winckelmann to Immanuel Kant to Gotthold Lessing) and it is certainly not important in more recent ones. At the same time, creativity has been tied to the activity of art, literature, and culture in the quotidian vocabulary of the social. Our criticisms of Florida are directed to the ongoing ideological redefinition of work and social experience and expectation under neoliberalism. But do we need to go further and consider what this contemporary redefinition of creativity means for the practice of art and culture?

Borrowing creativity from the arts to use in describing the activity of work does have repercussions that we can't pass over. In Florida's worldview, what was once dangerous or revolutionary about art appears fully domesticated. The freedom of the artist with respect to some aspects of the organization of their work becomes a model for work in general. As a result, it is thus only the social or political *content* of art or cultural practices and not their social *form* – as a kind of labor distinct from all others – that might be threatening or dangerous. Artistic labor once exemplified the possibility of modes of work other than either the factory floor or the manager's office, each of which in its own way beholden to the rhythms of capital. Once art becomes universalized through the spread of the discourse of creativity, even this potential political challenge, too, is diluted. It is in the adventurous radicality of the artists exhibited in independent galleries and contemporary art museums that Florida locates the kindred spirits of creative workers in other parts of the economy; established museums that display the classics of Western art don't interest him or (so he claims) the Creative Class in the least. If everyone is participating in the same narrative of social development through creativity − artists and IT workers, professors and bankers − what remains of art is perhaps only to furnish the capitalist economy with ideas indirectly, through the spark or flash of a new concept that might emerge when a software designer is standing in front of a canvas denouncing technological capitalism and the social dominance of computers. The reign of creativity thus poses challenges for the way in which social criticism operates today, even if creativity may not be a concept with particular theoretical salience within cultural criticism as it is currently practiced.

But the challenge or threat goes beyond this. We suggested in passing at the outset that creativity was a concept being used by both left and right. In examining Florida's popularization of work as a sight for creativity, we have focused on him as the chief theorist and champion of an idea of creativity that transforms capitalism from a machine of exploitation into something that enables people to fully employ their innate capacities. The US right has criticized Florida's political motives in his assignment of Creative City status to this or that place, even as it has absorbed the larger idea of putting creativity to work. But what about those further to the left? There, too, the principle of creativity has come to form an important part of how the present social context is conceptualized. Especially in the work of writers associated with Italian autonomist thought, from Paolo Virno to Michael Hardt and Antonio Negri, the current hegemony of post-Fordist, cognitive or affective labor is seen as making evident what was always already true about work, but which has become structurally impossible to ignore today. Social prosperity is dependent on language, communication, knowledge, and creativity − that is, on the "general intellect" that Marx describes in a passage in the *Grundrisse* that has become a key part of contemporary left political philosophy. Though it might seem surprising to say so, the difference between right and left, between Florida and Virno, is not in their analysis of the structure of contemporary capitalism and the social and political developments that have accompanied it, so much as the lessons that each draws from it. The post-Fordist labor utopia imagined by Florida is for left thinkers anything but the realization of a world without work; instead, it constitutes a new form of exploitation, and perhaps an even more dangerous one given the ideological power of accounts of contemporary work such as that of Florida. Creativity *does* flourish in contemporary capitalism, but insofar as it is put to use to generate profit, the potential political implications of this new situation are typically defused, at least temporarily. For the left, the increasing dependence of contemporary societies on forms of creative labor constitutes a political and imaginative opening – recognition (at long last) that capitalism needs labor far more than labor needs capitalism, and that the sovereignty of the state can be replaced by a new society founded on the general intellect.[53]

Yet despite the different lessons drawn from the social and political implications of post-Fordist work, there is a surprisingly common view of what constitutes creativity and its links to art, culture, and the aesthetic. In recent social and political thought, creativity seems to have become nothing short of the defining element of human Being: we are no longer *Homo faber* but *Homo genero*. As in the case of Florida, creativity on the left finds its referent in an idealized vision of artistic labor and a skewed view of the character of classical aesthetics, and is also imagined as what needs to be enabled and set free in order for there to be genuine social freedom. In a recent interview, Virno points to the troubling integration of aesthetics into production, but in so doing affirms a view of aesthetics that is reminiscent of Florida's own claims about the place of creativity in human nature.[54] While admitting at the outset of this long interview that his knowledge of modern art "is actually very limited," Virno is fearless in extending several of his key concepts to discussions of art and aesthetics, such as "virtuosity," one of many names for the innate productive capacity of human beings (which in the work of Antonio Negri goes by the name "constituent power"[55]). If left discourses are attuned to the blind spots that exist in

Florida's celebration of the conditions of work under contemporary capital, they nevertheless enact the same rhetorical and conceptual gesture of transforming human activity (or at least its potential) *as such* into art – and an idea of art taken not from sociology, but from fantasies about its ideal relationship to something called "creativity."

The effect once again is to render mute the critical capacities and (at least) potential political function of art and culture, even as it becomes coterminous with human life activity as such. It places art at the center of politics, but only by doing away with the significance of art *as* art. Contemporary art and cultural production have a social specificity that plays an essential role in their political function. They don't need to think of themselves as creative. Indeed, it would seem that the farther they stay away from the intellectual and political traffic in creativity, the more likely they are able to continue to challenge the limits of our ways of thinking, seeing, being, and believing.

The issue here is limits and how we might best address them. At times in his work, Florida is at pains to explain how the work of his house-cleaner, or his gardener, or other service economy workers that he daily comes into contact with as a professional, have – or potentially can have – creative aspects. For him to suggest otherwise would be to make their lives less *human* than his own. In a sense, he's right: who wouldn't want to be a professor or banker rather than the barista serving them? It'd be different, of course, if the barista owned the shop they worked in, if the banker David Brooks names in the epigraph to this section was a teller instead of a decision-making suit, or if the professor was a low-paid contract instructor instead of a highly paid tenured Ivy-leaguer. The genius of Florida's system is to have imagined a utopia *within* capitalism – one that requires no break, transformation, or revolutionary switch in behavior. He draws on examples from the present to suggest that we are already *there* – or at least some of us are – and that we need to push things forward in order for us all to ascend to the heaven of IT work. Can we all actualize our innate human essence through creative work? Florida seems to think so. But another part of the narrative of his work – especially his writings following the 2008 financial crisis – suggests that the Creative Class constitutes a necessarily small, if highly desirable, pool of workers over whom

99

cities, regions, and nations must fight if they want to come out on top of the economic game. He can't have it both ways; without the promise of greater individual possibilities and capacities on a global scale, the story of cities fighting to attract IT workers, film and television shoots, and the like, seems to lack the grandiose insight necessary for a guru who wants to lead us into a future – even a future that looks much like the present. Though Florida rarely uses the term himself, his is a vision that operates within the landscape of assumptions and beliefs that we have come to know as globalization.[56] Our next figure imagines himself to be offering a map of this landscape and its possibilities; the how and why of this effort shows further some of the dark borders that have drawn around our understanding of the global present.

c. The Anecdotal American: Thomas Friedman

Thomas Friedman has won three Pulitzer prizes and, since 1994, has been the foreign affairs columnist for the *New York Times*. Together with writing his twice-weekly op-ed pieces for the *Times*, Friedman has written five enormously influential and best-selling non-fiction books about the Middle-East, geopolitics, international finance, 9/11, and the contemporary environmental crisis.[57] Speaking to government and business leaders around the world (not to mention high-school students, housewives, and the audiences of numerous television talk shows), Friedman has emerged as one of the most prominent voices of our time. He understands himself as something akin to a seer, but one who speaks less in tongues or riddles than in crystal-clear sentences, packed with common sense and personal anecdote.

Globalization is Friedman's object of study and the sole organizing principle of his worldview and unremitting production of ideas, opinions, beliefs, attitudes, critiques, predictions, anxieties, and hopes. In 1999 Friedman wrote *The Lexus and the Olive Tree*, in which he unveiled with gusto what he named the new system of globalization, as against the Cold War one that dominated the post-World War II period. With the fall of the Berlin Wall in the winter of 1989, according to Friedman, a new set of ideas, demographic trends, perspectives on

100

the globe, defining technologies, measurements, and anxieties came into being that functioned not to divide the world (as the Cold War logic did), but to integrate it.[58] For Friedman, globalization is "the inexorable integration of markets, nation-states and technologies to a degree never witnessed before – in a way that is enabling individuals, corporations and nation-states to reach around the world farther, faster, deeper and cheaper than ever before, and in a way that is enabling the world to reach into individuals, corporations, and nation-states farther, faster, deeper, cheaper than ever before."[59] This is all made possible by free-market capitalism and (at least in this first book on globalization, before the financial meltdown tempered Friedman's unabashed allegiance to that other Friedman, Milton) he dutifully recites the neoliberal mantra:

> the more you let market forces rule and the more you open your economy to free trade and competition, the more efficient and flourishing your economy will be. Globalization means the spread of free-market capitalism to virtually every country in the world. Therefore, globalization also has its own set of economic rules – rules that revolve around opening, deregulating, and privatizing your economy, in order to make it more competitive and attractive to foreign investment.[60]

The Lexus in the title of the book refers to the ultra-modern, efficient, and forward-thinking Japanese car factory that knocked Friedman's socks off back when he visited it in 1992, while the Olive Tree refers to the violent appeal by Palestinians about the right of return to Israel. But as Friedman is wont to do, he turns these actual objects into metaphors, so that the Lexus represents progress, prosperity, and the quest for the new, while the Olive Tree represents identity, nationalism, and the tight-fisted squeeze on what was. Throughout all of his work, though most pronounced in his books and columns following the financial meltdown of 2008 and the mainstreaming of ecological concerns, Friedman wants to recognize the need to properly integrate both the Lexus (fast-growth capitalist development) and the Olive Tree (identity, the environment, and cultural origins) – but he simply cannot help himself: the Lexus is the supreme and only vehicle to drive us into a better future. Olive trees don't have speedometers, much less radios that would allow one to keep up to date on what's happening in the world as one zips down the highway of capitalist prosperity.

Six years after publishing *The Lexus and the Olive Tree*, Friedman updated his thoughts on globalization in *The World Is Flat: A Brief History of the Twenty-First Century*. It was on a trip to Bangalore in 2004 when Friedman realized that things had changed once again, from (and now in Friedmanese) Globalization 2.0, based on the global integration of nations and corporations driven by ever-developing communication technologies (from the telegraph to the world-wide web, from 1800 to 2000) to Globalization 3.0, which is based more on individuals who, thanks to the convergence of new communication technologies (the personal computer, fiber-optic cable, and work-flow software) are able to collaborate and compete globally in radically new ways. If Globalization 2.0 was about the transforma-tions of large institutions and nations into a global system due to the Industrial Revolution and growth of information technologies (and Globalization 1.0 – from 1492 to 1800 – was more about the origins of the nation-state system and how it was shaped by "how much brawn ... your country had and how creatively you could deploy it"), then Globalization 3.0 is about the end of the nation and the birth of the empowered individual.[61]

When looking at Friedman's two books side by side, we see very different narratives of history as well as very different theories of history. In *The Lexus and the Olive Tree*, for example, the great rupture is the fall of the Berlin Wall that radically separates the two very different international systems of the Cold War and globalization. Friedman warns that to pretend that globalization is just economic fashion or a "passing trend, that it is not qualitatively different than what came before, is to miss the most significant fact of our present world."[62] In *The World Is Flat*, globalization is now understood in a much longer duration, with different phases. In this newer narrative, the shifts build one on top of the next, in a way that reaches, in the end, the great liberation of the global individual. The first narrative is dominated by a synchronic mode of writing history, while the second is characterized by a diachronic one.

Within that field known as the philosophy of history, the synchronic mode (meaning "at the same time") organizes the events and phenomena of a historical moment into a separate structure that stands in radical contrast (if not incommensurability) to other structures. Synchronic historiography follows a spatial logic, one that emphasizes the relations among the units of any given slice of time, while a diachronic historiography follows a temporal logic, one that emphasizes the movement of phenomena from one structure to the next ("across time" as its etymology suggests). The synchronic mode emphasizes rupture, discontinuity, and the integrity of the discrete historical moment, while the diachronic emphasizes accumulation, continuity, and the integrity of phenomena that transcend historical periods.

Of course, Friedman is not concerned with the theoretical problem of organizing and narrating history. But all of his arguments are inescapably shaped by how he mismanages this problem. It is precisely the attention to theorizing history that drives the most important work on globalization. Take, for example, the geographer David Harvey. In his *The Condition of Postmodernity*, Harvey marks the shift from modernity to post-modernity by stressing the new flexible forms of accumulation enabled by developments in communication and information technologies.[63] For Harvey the important break is in the 1970s with the oil crises. Industrial capitalism (based on Henry Ford's assembly line) became too rigid – such a hierarchical, vertical, and utterly compartmentalized model could not respond quickly and effectively enough to crises – whether a crisis of resources, of overproduction or underconsumption, or a crisis of labor unrest. What emerges with post-Fordism (based on many of the same characteristics described by Friedman) is a much more flexible capability of managing crisis. If, for example, labor unions in Haiti become too powerful, then the post-Fordist corporation can easily and quietly move the factory to a country with a much more docile labor force, such as Malaysia or Vietnam.

What Friedman calls the "flat-world platform," Harvey calls the "compression of time and space," and both notions of change shape the limits and possibilities of individuals, nations, and transnational organizations. The great difference between these two thinkers,

103

however, is their account of the fundamental basis for this crucial historical transformation. Friedman sees the great shift to globalization as an outgrowth of technological development. And from where does this great technological development come? Great individuals working in free environments! And from where do these great individuals and environments come? From America and from God (an insistence of the necessity of the United States that puts one in mind of Zakaria's claims in *The Post-American World*)! When looking out at the flattened world, Friedman's greatest fear is that "America's losing its groove" and that the God-given genius of human beings will not be allowed to flourish so that they might have the opportunity to build new Lexus factories (a view of the human that can't help but put one in mind of some of Richard Florida's claims and ideas).

Harvey, by contrast, explains the sea change to post-Fordism by analyzing the transformations within capitalism. For Harvey, capitalism is the system that shapes the Cold War and globalization, not the other way around, as Friedman would have it. Capitalism has a logic that is organized on commodity production and the social relations that emerge from this specific form of production. There are some fundamental rules of capitalism (such as the imperative to produce profit, the uneven social relations represented in the production of commodities, and the continual necessity to expand) that define and structure this mode, from its transition from feudalism up to the present. The cutting-edge form of accumulation might have shifted from manufacturing to financial speculation, but the fundamental rules have not. By focusing on the identity and difference of capital over its long history (identity in terms of how its rules remain constant and difference in how its dominant form of accumulation changes), Harvey is also able to analyze the identity and difference of human beings, nations, and cultural formations over time.

We bring Harvey into the discussion in order to show how far out of his league Friedman is when thinking about globalization. It's one thing to articulate one's opinions and make arguments about the world (as he does in his *New York Times* columns), but it's quite another to pretend, as Friedman does, that he is offering a systemic and rigorous critique of a historical moment. For example, Friedman begins *The*

Lexus and the Olive Tree with the strong assertion that globalization is an international system that "has now replaced the old Cold War system, and, like that Cold War system, globalization has its own rules and logic that today directly or indirectly influence the politics, environment, geopolitics and economics of virtually every country in the world."[64] This is the category mistake we wrote of earlier. The Cold War was not a political-economic system. It was a way of describing geopolitical relationships that were governed by two competing social formations – one capitalist and the other socialist. Likewise, globalization does not influence anything, because it is not a system; it is an effect or outcome of the globalizing system of capitalism, a point (probably one of the very few) on which both neoclassical and Marxist economists agree.

Unlike Paul Krugman, his colleague at the *New York Times*, Friedman doesn't really care much about political economy. True, he references Joseph Schumpeter's idea of "creative destruction," celebrates David Ricardo's theory of comparative advantage, and is stunned to learn that Marx actually had something lucid to say about capitalism. For Friedman, however, capitalism is not an economic logic, but an older, less exotic plot-point in his schoolboy history. Friedman teams Francis Fukuyama with celebrity CEOs (Bill Gates of Microsoft, Michael Dell of Dell Inc., and Andrew Grove of Intel Corporation) in order to bury any analysis of capitalism save the share prices of the companies in which he invests. In the end, for Friedman, any critique of capitalism must come to terms with his understanding of history: "The democratizations of finance, technology and information didn't just blow away all of the walls protecting alternative systems – from Mao's little red book to *The Communist Manifesto* to the welfare states of Western Europe to the crony capitalism of Southeast Asia. These three democratizations also gave birth to a new power source in the world – what I will call the Electronic Herd."[65] The Electronic Herd is Freidman's name for the combination of stock, bond, and currency traders as well as multinational corporations who, according to him, have become the main generator of capital growth, replacing governments in the process. How and why governments may be in perfect coordination with this Electronic Herd (as has certainly been the case beginning from the Clinton administration in

effects not because of the greedy and unfair actions of individual capitalists, but because of how this unevenness is internal to the very system itself, most fundamentally in the logic of the commodity. It is for this reason that *Capital* begins with an analysis of the "simple commodity." Only from the most basic unit of capitalist production can the larger system of capitalism be understood.

The form *Capital* takes, its movement from the particular case of the commodity form to the general system of capitalism, is meant to teach its readers how to make sense of their lives, not by moralizing against their greedy bosses or by blaming themselves for their miserable situations (both of which are counterproductive), but to understand how their situation came into being in the first place and the manner in which it is reproduced daily and systematically. For Marx, it is only this more objective critique that can provide the clearest map of how the system works. Moreover, and most crucially, this objective critique (mirrored formally, like the great literary and philosophical *mise en abymes*) reveals that the inequality produced by capitalism indicates not that the system is broken or temporarily disrupted, but that it is working well. It is easy to criticize capitalism when fires burn down dilapidated factories or bosses refuse to pay workers, but the most important and most difficult challenge is to formulate a critique of the system when the contract is obeyed and the boss acts with integrity and compassion. Such a structural critique requires a more removed and abstract style than one might find in a typical op-ed piece.

The dilemma here (and the point that returns us to the work of Friedman) is that such a style is not easy to follow and not immediately attractive to a diverse set of readers. Journalism, by contrast, is exceptionally suited to drawing in readers with its compelling and immediately absorbing narratives. And now we are getting at the crucial generic limits of academic and journalistic work: the former emphasizes scholarly abstraction at the expense of accessibility and engaging flair, while the latter emphasizes the small stuff of everyday life at the expense of rigorous abstraction and original research. Of course, these are generalizations and there are many writers who try to square this circle, such as academic anthropologists theorizing by way of thick description or by the long review essays in the *New York Review of Books* or the *Times Literary Supplement*. In the end, however, academic writing and journalism have inescapably different limits and possibilities, one not being necessarily superior to the other.

Both *The Lexus and the Olive Tree* and *The World Is Flat* are very large monographs (490 and 600 pages respectively) that are written in a style identical to Friedman's columns for the *New York Times*. And it is precisely this journalistic style extended into best-selling books, one that aims to contain more than a one-off opinion piece, where we locate the most powerful instantiations of the common-sense approaches to globalization and the contemporary world.[67]

The first and most powerful formal technique that stands out when reading anything by Friedman is his use of the first-person singular to deliver a profusion of personal anecdotes. One cannot get away from this: every idea begins with an anecdote that is drawn from Friedman's constant travels around the world. As prototypical, we can take the founding anecdote of *The Lexus and the Olive Tree*. While in Japan in 1992, Friedman visited the Lexus car factory outside Toyota City and was impressed, even unnerved, by how technologically advanced the operations were. "I kept staring at this process, thinking to myself how much planning, design and technology it must have taken to get that robot arm to do its job and then swing around each time, at the precise angle, so that this little thumbnail-size wire could snip off the last drop of hot rubber for the robot to start clean on the next window."[68]

Following his visit to the Lexus factory and on the *shinkansen* ride home, Friedman explains that while reading the newspaper he paused over an article about how a US State Department spokeswoman had started a furor in the Middle East when commenting about Palestinian refugees. "So there I was," Friedman explains,

> speeding along at 180 miles an hour on the most modern train in the world, reading this story about the oldest corner of the world. And the thought occurred to me that these Japanese, whose Lexus factory I had just visited and whose train I was riding, were building the greatest luxury car in the world with robots. And over here, on the top of page 3 of the *Herald Tribune*, the people with whom I had lived for so many

years in Beirut and Jerusalem, whom I knew so well, were still fighting over who owned which olive tree. It struck me then that the Lexus and the olive tree were actually pretty good symbols of this post-Cold War era: half the world seemed to be emerging from the Cold War intent on building a better Lexus, dedicated to modernizing, streamlining and privatizing their economies in order to thrive in the system of globalization. And half of the world . . . was still caught up in the fight over who owns which olive tree.[69]

What exactly is an anecdote? How does it function? How does its formal strategies relate to its content? What would Friedman's books be like if the anecdotes were removed? How does the anecdote relate to Friedman's politics – his common sense, his understanding of the nation, of capitalism, and to his moral positions?

The anecdote is a short tale narrating a real incident (usually, but not always biographical) whose main purpose is to reveal a truth that exceeds the particularity of the incident itself. The Greek for anecdote is "unpublished," meaning that the incident cannot be confirmed or cross-referenced by anyone save the person relaying the tale. Despite the brevity of the anecdote, it usually shares the tripartite structure of longer narratives: the presentation of a situation, some tension or crisis, and a resolution. The defining quality of an anecdote is less its brevity than its lack of complexity. In "Anecdote and History," an essay tracking the history and use of the anecdote in Europe, Lionel Gossman explains that the anecdote may be invoked to illustrate "a problem or even a paradox, but will not usually lead to a rethinking of the terms of the problem or paradox."[70]

As a formal intervention, the anecdote has a double potential: both reactionary and radical. As a reactionary trope the anecdote confirms and reproduces common-sense views of the world and the human condition. It is also positivistic: it grants meaning to the incident itself by delinking it from a larger context of meaning. In other words, the anecdote fetishizes the incident; it freezes the dynamics of the larger system in which the incident functions, and invests too much meaning into the delinked fragment. As for Friedman's Lexus and olive tree anecdote, this fetishization begins with Japan.

Even if we suspend the fact of the Japanese recession (already quite severe at the time of the publication of *The Lexus and the Olive Tree*) and pretend that Japanese efficiency and corporate flexibility had not been called into question since at least the early 1990s, there is still the need to consider the context out of which the Japanese economic miracle was born. The Japanese high-growth economy, from the end of the US occupation in 1952 to the Tokyo Olympics in 1964, must be understood in terms of the larger geopolitical context – protected by the US nuclear umbrella and nourished by the reverse course (the betrayal of the immediate post-war promises of democratization and demilitarization) enacted by the one-party rule of the Liberal Democratic Party from 1955 on. For most of the high-growth period, civil liberties were seriously curtailed as any expression of dissent was usually stamped out – "How could you complain given how fast the economy has grown?" was the usual retort. But it was not very hard to distinguish (as did the huge Japanese student and peasant movements throughout the 1960s and 1970s) between economic growth and economic prosperity. Japan may have become the second largest economy in the world, but the Japanese people were not feeling very rich.

The Japanese economic miracle (double-digit GDP growth for decades) was based on a national economic policy in which there was absolutely no division between Japanese private and public institutions. The United States would have never encouraged such a command economy (the Japanese Ministry of International Trade and Industry meticulously facilitated the reciprocal relationship between commercial, banking, and financial sectors of the Japanese economy) if it weren't for the need to defend against China and the potential threat of socialism spreading throughout East and Southeast Asia.

In addition to this, Japanese nationalism has returned with a vengeance over the past few decades. The mayor of Tokyo, Ishihara Shintaro, had made one anti-immigrant comment after another and the longstanding mistrust of Japan by its ex-colonies (Korea and China, in particular) is notorious. In fact, one could argue that there are more olive tree skirmishes in Japan than Lexus cars. Instead of providing wisdom and an off-center route to deeper meaning, Friedman's anecdotes strengthen the stereotypes that block critical thinking.

110

The anecdote, however, does not always have to serve such a reactionary function. Rather, the use of an anecdote can upset dominant narratives of the world and history precisely by how they fall out of line, by how they get caught in the throat of history. For example, in "The History of the Anecdote" Joel Fineman calls the anecdote the smallest unit of the historical record (the historeme), and as such the anecdote "is the literary form that *lets history happen* by virtue of the way it introduces an opening into the teleological, and therefore timeless, narration of beginning, middle, and end."[71] As such, Fineman argues that the anecdote can liberate thinking from the "great man" theory or "great event" theory of history.

The point here is that the guerrilla historian who elevates the anecdote above the orthodox archive can only do so by listening very carefully, by hearing something almost imperceptible in the incident from which the anecdote comes. This is something akin to psychoanalytic listening – the way the analyst hears the smallest detail and pursues it (rather than the supposedly big problems) so as to get at the heart of the matter. Since the dominant narratives of the patient's life function to keep the patient stuck in his or her symptoms, the contingent detail (the slip, the joke, the banal observation) usually provides the royal road to the unconscious. To listen in such a way requires a certain engaged detachment, and more importantly it requires restraint to prevent imposing meaning onto the issue or event. Rather than putting the anecdote to instrumental use, the anecdote must be given room and allowed to exist disconnected from dominant narratives. Only then will the anecdote erupt, offering powerful new ways of thinking about the world.

But such a radical deployment of the anecdote comes not only by way of a careful, patient, and subtle reconfiguration of a detail, but also through a piercing, didactic, and methodological deployment of it. Take, for example, Bertolt Brecht. From the 1920s through the 1950s, Brecht composed an assortment of anecdotes and other short excerpts, some of which have been collected under the title "Anecdotes of Mr. Keuner."[72] Neither pedantic nor populist, academic nor intellectual amateur, Brecht's Mr. Keuner, or Mr. K, is a surrogate to comment on a variety of different subjects. For example, the following anecdote entitled "A Man of Purpose":

> Mr. K. put the following questions: "Every morning my neighbor plays music on his gramophone. Why does he play music? I hear that it is because he does exercises. Why does he do exercises? Because he needs to be strong, I've heard. Why does he need to be strong? Because he has to get the better of his enemies in the town, he says. Why must he get the better of his enemies? Because he wants to eat, I hear."
>
> Having learnt that his neighbor played music in order to do exercises, did exercises in order to be strong, wanted to be strong in order to kill his enemies, killed his enemies in order to eat, he put the question: "Why does he eat?"[73]

One answer to this last question is "to survive." To which, Mr. K. might ask, "why survive?" And so on. Indeed, the "whys" add up ad infinitum. This frustrating regression of asking "why," however, is not only a schoolboy game leading to meaninglessness, but a rhetorical strategy to provoke a productive silence, a speechlessness that interrupts the smooth and tautological function of a discourse. At some point in the process, the answer shortens to a paternalistic "because, that's why!" followed by silence. And it is precisely at this "unreasonable" inter-vention that the true political moment has been reached – when the opposing sides own up to the uneven power relations involved in the dispute and understand their actions based on different ideological interests. This is also the moment when all moralizing stops and the clear articulation of power begins. But this is the moment that Friedman, with his string of narcissistic sentences and storehouse of personal anecdotes, cannot reach.

When we ask Friedman "why" America is best suited to lead today, he answers by appealing to America's great past. Why is America at the forefront of the worldwide development called globalization? Because it has been the leader of the free world, and so must of necessity continue to lead it if the future is going to be better than the past. And that's that. In contrast to how Brecht deploys the anecdote to up-end presumptions, Friedman deploys it in order to confirm them. Every one of Friedman's anecdotes is like the one articulated about the experience on the bullet train. From apparently random events – the visit to the plant followed by the chance glance at a specific section of the paper – he builds an entire theory of the present, something he does in the same fashion whether he is working with 1000 words or 600 pages. The flash of insight that emerges from the anecdote appears to reconstitute the world in a new way. Yet it should be evident that the only way to frame these chance encounters as something meaningful is to always already know the system in advance. The settings for Friedman's anecdotes are as telling as their content: a bullet train in Japan, or the balcony of a sheik's condo in Dubai: this movement around the world seeking the truth of globalization is already figured *as* globalization. Readers permit Friedman's collection of anecdotes to mutate into world-historical claims (Globalizations 1.0, 2.0, and 3.0) in part because they show how well traveled he is: the experience of the globe allows him to know what globalization is. Indeed, it sometimes seems as if the world system is already legible in the system of these personal anecdotes, that there is thus no need for the kinds of theoretical and analytical tools that one finds in the work, for instance, of David Harvey.

Friedman, the global traveler, knows globalization because of his travels. As a traveler, Friedman seems to discover novelty wherever he goes. The "new" is a key component of his articles and his books, and suggests a laudable attentiveness to a world changing in front of his own eyes. But as the example of the Lexus shows, one can imagine finding something new and yet miss the big picture entirely. Indeed, without realizing it, Friedman is the bad American tourist – not the one who throws his money around and demeans locals, but the one who imagines that of necessity he will experience new, mind-expanding things abroad, and so can only ever attend to those things. The Lexus will make a positive impression. The world of the Olive Tree? Never. Part of the limit Friedman encounters is that he travels in a world now fully Americanized. While Zakaria can point to this as success of a system, as the bad tourist Friedman has to suppress the sameness he might find everywhere, only ever attending to those things that are new in the right way – within the circuits of that technological view of the world with which Florida is so enamored.

113

Modernizing, streamlining, and privatizing: for Friedman, there are clearly winners and losers in the system of globalization. Why some might fight over, or think about, the Olive Tree more than the Lexus (the natural, one can't help point out, versus the artificial), even today isn't something that Friedman is able to consider, just as he can't see that the global dominance of these values might well be the correct answer to the question "why" America. Despite this circular logic (or perhaps because of it), Friedman's relentless affirmation of the values of the system has been enormously influential. It affirms the United States' place in the world (e.g., the individual is pre-eminent, speed rules, etc.) even as it takes didactic pleasure in anecdotally pointing out which other parts of the world have sped ahead. The overall effect is a powerful one, simultaneously suspending a more rigorous and critical attention to the character of globalization and its multiple dimensions as well as to its politics and particular future-orientation, while at the same time affirming the solidity of the present forms of political and social organization even in the face of so many supposedly new forms of doing things.

Friedman may be a talented and influential storyteller; he tells us almost nothing, however, about one of the central dynamics of globalization that we have insisted on: the fate of national sovereignty vis-à-vis a global market. This is one of the central themes of his newspaper colleague, economist Paul Krugman, whose more public writing has turned away from economics and toward a defense of the productive conjunction between liberalism and capitalism in the twenty-first century. Krugman is the more nuanced thinker, not beholden to the conceptual limits that usually attend the common sense of the anecdote. Which is not to say that common sense of the global moment doesn't frame his own thoughts in seemingly unavoidable ways.

d. Confidence Game: Paul Krugman

Paul Krugman secured his place in the history of economics by winning the Nobel Prize in the field for his work on trade theory in relation to geography. However, unlike some Nobel winners, his but of the grand narratives of progress and reason. While economic systems might misfire and produce crises from time to time – usually, in Krugman's view, as a result of poor decision making guided by ideology instead of science – nothing that has happened over the course of the twentieth century (or indeed, even the most recent economic crisis) suggests that there is anything like a dark side to economic enlightenment. The comfort one finds in Krugman's view of the world is that, in the end, there is no need for any massive systemic change in order to address pressing social and political problems. For the most part, things are fine as they are: with the return of Keynesian ideas – of a very timid and minimal form, it has to be said – and the elimination of ideologues from government (on the right *and* left), current systems of liberal-capitalist representative democracy can do what they are designed to do: provide justice and opportunity for all.

Krugman's Nobel Prize was received for research attentive to the dynamics of production and consumption on a global scale.[75] It is surprising, then, to find so little feel in his work for the complexities – social, political, *and* economic – of the global era. In an article in *Slate* written in the days before the World Trade Organization (WTO) meeting in Seattle in 1999, Krugman berates those who would oppose globalization.[76] He imagines the protesters as having very little understanding for what is at stake in globalization, picturing them as groups and individuals who see the WTO as at "the center of a global conspiracy against all that is good and decent . . . a super-governmental body that forces nations to bow to the wishes of multinational corporations. It destroys cultures . . . it despoils the environment; and it rides roughshod over democracy, forcing governments to remove laws that conflict with its sinister purposes."[77] He challenges the idea that national economies perform best by aiming at self-sufficiency rather than producing for the world market, though it is questionable whether any of the protesters opposing the WTO were doing so because they wanted a return to import-substitution strategies of the 1950s and 1960s. He also takes on the idea that globalization results in a "global monoculture," a worry that he sees as paternalistic – a vision of the world that sees it as designed for the amusement of Western tourists hoping for diverse and novel experiences on their trips abroad, instead of "for the benefit of ordinary people in their daily lives."[78] He mentions nothing, however, about globalization's impact on the environment, its effects on democracy, or its role in shaping government decisions to reflect market rationality (the logic we now call neoliberalism). Globalization is imagined narrowly as having to do with economic trade, and, secondarily, with cultural flows; and in Krugman's view, the nation-state remains the primary site at which political decisions are made and the organizing unit of global affairs. In other words, globalization is understood in its most common guise: the flow of money and goods beyond borders. For Krugman, little else seems to be implicated, impacted, or affected by this flow, even pre-existing political and economic systems.

The nation-state plays an especially large role in Krugman's thinking. The governments of nation-states are the ones ultimately responsible for the decision making that shapes the operations of global markets, just as they are for what happens within their domestic boundaries. And so it is to these policy makers to whom his writing often seems to be directed. Can capitalism save us by slow degrees through the more proactive involvement of the nation, as Krugman and other liberals suggest? And is the "us" that Krugman imagines the United States alone or are we all in this together in some way? In a nutshell: what does Paul Krugman's liberalism look like? Should we give into the temptations of its pragmatic left-centrism or treat it with the suspicion that a fly might view the sticky sweet offering of a Venus fly trap?

* * *

We have always known that heedless self-interest was bad morals; now we know that it was bad economics.

Franklin Delano Roosevelt, 1936

The subtitle of Krugman's *The Great Unraveling* is "Losing Our Way in the New Century." The "our" is, of course, the US public that Krugman imagines as his main readership (à la Friedman and the other figures whom we've been examining). The implications contained in the rest of the title are perhaps more significant. There is a claim made

117

about a path being traveled, a direction once taken, now abandoned or lost. The clear suggestion is that the United States was heading in the "right" direction over much of the twentieth century (if indeed not over its whole history), and that only in the first decade of the new century has the thread of that narrative been lost. The collection of op-ed pieces in *The Great Unraveling* presents evidence both of the multiple ways in which the United States has lost its direction and of what steps it should take to get back on the path. As one might expect from a series of occasional essays written in the heat of specific economic or political events, the overall message that one comes away with is indirect and unfocused. So much of the criticism is directed at Bush and members of his cabinet that one might expect that all the United States would have to do to get back on track is to get rid of the bad guys who unexpectedly happened to show up in DC to run the biggest economy and military in the world for close to a decade.

A similar narrative of loss and return shapes Krugman's *The Conscience of a Liberal*. First published in 2007 (with a new introduction added in 2009), the book offers an outline of the economics and politics of the United States from the Gilded Age to present, with concluding chapters on the problems of health care and economic inequality in the United States. The intent of this historical overview is to try to stage an argument with some depth about the direction that the United States should now take. There is little new in the book, either factually *or* conceptually: on the whole, Krugman works through a fairly typical set of issues, concepts, and historical situations, organized around a standard division in US political life – the divide between conservatives and liberals. Unlike much of Krugman's other writing (both academic and popular), *Conscience* is a frankly *political* book that hopes to win readers over to his way of seeing things by re-narrating recent US history, and in so doing, making a case for a new way of doing things; the case he makes here does not rely on his economic expertise so much as the skills he has developed for assessing American social life during his time as a popular writer.

Whether the United States follows the ideas and ideals of "movement conservatives" (like the Tea Party stalwarts) or their liberal opponents, in both cases the future, for Krugman, appears to be a return

118

enfranchisement of woman and minorities, but the basis for a just society had been established and the United States was moving in a direction when these issues, too, would be resolved for the better.

There are numerous questions one could pose to this rather rose-colored view of the 1950s, 1960s, and 1970s. To begin with, given the general agreement on values and political bipartisanship and agreement, one might want to ask on what basis US citizens decided to vote for one party over the other if it was all the same in the end. (Was it just habit? Why not create one-party rule?) But let's focus first on the *second* point that Krugman makes in the opening chapter. It is a claim that frames the argument of the entire book; it is also a claim that is astonishing less for what it asserts than what it suggests about his understanding of the place of economics in society and politics. The growing economic inequality that has characterized American life during globalization – an ever-growing gap between the rich and poor, a declining middle class, and expanding poverty – is described *not* as the result of "impersonal forces such as technological change,"[82] that is, from the push of an economic invisible hand, but as the result of politics. Krugman writes: "I've become increasingly convinced that much of the causation runs the other way – that political change in the form of rising polarization has been a major cause of rising inequality."[83] To most commentators and members of the public, this would hardly come as a surprise. Krugman's faith in economics as a social master discourse is evident, however, in the need he feels to provide evidence of the priority of politics over economics. "Can the political environment really be that decisive in determining economic inequality?" he writes. "It sounds like economy heresy, but a growing body of economic research suggests that it can."[84] He offers four points to defend this position: the post-war middle-class society he values was created through institutions, norms, and the political environment of the time; the timing of economic shifts seem to suggest that they are led by political changes; an erosion of social norms and institutions over the past 30 years have created inequality in the United States (as opposed, say, to technological change being the cause); and – a highly questionable claim – the United States is the only country to experience greater inequality during globalization: if it was due to the market,

Krugman argues, one might have expected similar levels of inequality across the globe.

What is surprising then is Krugman's own surprise at the power of politics to determine economic developments and changes. What he thus understands as the nature and content of politics cannot help but come to occupy the center of the book, even if he himself spends little or no time reflecting on the character of the political as such. For Krugman, politics is ultimately not a matter of power, historical form, or the intricacies of social structure, but a question of – as the book's title suggests – *conscience*: that inner play of morality and ethics that pushes one to act in the right way. From its opening pages, *Conscience of a Liberal* is established as a drama involving villains and heroes. The villains of the book are the "movement conservatives" – a group animated by a whole chain of publications, people, thinks tanks, and news organizations – who have taken over the Republican Party with their anti-government, low-taxation ideas. Krugman writes:

> Money is the glue of movement conservatism, which is largely financed by a handful of extremely wealthy individuals and a number of major corporations, all of whom stand to gain from increased inequality, an end to progressive taxation, and a rollback of the welfare state – in short, from a reversal of the New Deal . . . because movement conservatism is ultimately about rolling back policies that hurt a narrow, wealthy elite, it's fundamentally antidemocratic.[85]

The greed of a few individuals and their lack of conscience about how best to act toward their fellow man derails what might be the otherwise smooth and sane operation of the economy. One can only assume that there was a greater degree of moral virtue in the era from FDR to the 1960s, which has now been replaced by the values of Gordon Gecko and others of his ilk. But why? And if it is a minority, why has this shift been tolerated, especially given Krugman's insistence that polls on a variety of issues suggest that the United States is in fact a predominately center-left country?

The bulk of the book consists of a detailed, often insightful history of the rise and fall of middle-class America from the New Deal to the present – as Krugman puts it, from the high time of the Great Compression to the social and economic inequalities that define the Great Divergence of our own era. It is the story of a right-wing capitalist conspiracy (named directly as such). Two points are emphasized throughout: that the story of changes in US social and economic life in the twentieth century is a matter of politics ("rather than narrowly economic phenomenon"[86]), and that conservatives have repeatedly – with astonishing insight into the shifting landscape of US politics – played on social fears (such as the fear of communism) and divisions (especially race) to place themselves into a position of power in which they could enact their policies. It is incumbent on Krugman the political theorist to try to make sense of *why* voters might be willing to elect politicians who work solely for elite business interests. There is no hint that something like ideology might play a role, that is, that voters might well imagine themselves as having much in common with the values and norms championed by movement conservatives, even if economically they end up paying the price. Instead of looking at the big picture of why anyone would vote for a Republican Party that has been "taken over by radicals,"[87] he looks to the politics of majority voting. "Why have advocates of a smaller welfare state and regressive tax policies been able to win elections, even as growing income inequality should have made the welfare state more popular?"[88] Since he only has to identify that small segment of voters that would push the conservatives over the top, it becomes easy to find the problem: a change in voting patterns by white Southerners. Krugman writes:

> The overwhelming importance of the Southern switch suggests an almost embarrassingly simple story about the political success of movement conservatism. It goes like this: Thanks to their organization, the interlocking institutions that constitute the reality of the vast right-wing conspiracy, movement conservatives were able to take over the Republican Party, and move its policies sharply to the right. In most of the country this rightward shift alienated voters, who gradually moved toward the Democrats. But Republicans were nonetheless able to win presidential elections, and eventually gain control of the Congress, because they were able to exploit the issue to win political dominance of the South. End of story.[89]

The racism of white Southerners draws them to the "Grand Old Party." As to what else they think they might be getting out of voting against their own economic interests, he is either unable or unwilling to offer an answer.

And as for a solution to the political bind in which the United States finds itself? If the economic elite wasn't already punished by the 2008 financial crisis, Krugman appears confident that demographic changes will necessarily push movement conservatism out of favor: "Over the longer term, immigration will help undermine the political strategy of movement conservatism ... movement conservatives cannot simultaneously make tacitly race-based appeals to white voters and court the growing Hispanic and Asian share of the electorate."[90] Policies passed by the Arizona state government in 2010 and the election of Scott Brown to the US Senate in Massachusetts in the 2010 special election might make one question the confidence with which Krugman asserts the coming change in the political landscape.

It might be too much to expect an establishment thinker like Krugman to question the very nature of what passes for democratic voting as an accurate representation of the electorate's opinions or longings. One might expect, however, more than the argument we are offered here. His challenge to movement conservatism *and* his appeal for a kinder, gentler capitalism are both built around a moralizing critique. In place of an ideological analysis that could describe with full complexity a whole range of developments that have taken place over the past three decades – everything from the rise of 24-hour news, the global trend of mass political disengagement, the challenges and opportunities afforded by the economics and politics of globalization, and so on – Krugman provides a narrative of good guys and unconscionably bad ones. It is impossible for him to imagine, for instance, that the drives and imperatives of the capitalist economy itself might shape norms and behavior in a fundamental way. By shifting the focus to politics and to morality, economics assumes (for him) its proper place of a science of market. As he traces the birth of movement conservatism, he notes that "the conservative economic intelligentsia emerged first, because the real truths of economics create a natural propensity in economists to go all the way to free-market fundamentalism."[91] Why don't these truths generate the same propensity in Krugman? His conscience saves him, pushing him to imagine a need not for an alternative economic system, but for a kinder, gentler version of the existing one that would still take profit and private property as its founding axioms.

In his Introduction to the paperback edition of *Conscience*, Krugman speaks confidently about the opportunity for Barack Obama to realize a progressive agenda – to return us to the conditions of Krugman's childhood, but with the addition of universal health care. With the good guys now in charge, the economy can function as it's supposed to, not just to make the rich richer, but organized and regulated in such a way that it can once again produce a predominantly middle-class society. "The claim that America is ready for a new New Deal – which some readers considered quixotic when the hardcover edition was published – is now more or less conventional wisdom."[92] After two years of the Obama presidency, one can assert with some confidence that conventional wisdom can sometimes be wrong.

* * *

Nobody thought that such a thing could happen in the modern world, but it did, and the consequences were startling.

Paul Krugman[93]

One of the key assumptions in *Conscience* is that with the right leaders in place, governments will be able to make appropriate decisions with respect to the economy, shaping its impact and its effects on populations. This is hardly an earth-shattering assumption: it's common sense. In *The Return of Depression Economics and the Crisis of 2008*, Krugman takes on a very different set of questions. In *Conscience*, the analysis of the past century of US politics takes place with a limited discussion of the broader, global circumstances that might have an impact on the economic and political directions taken by the country. On the other hand, *Return* is explicitly about the new global order and the challenges it poses for the operation of economies. Taken together, these two books give us the full scope of Krugman's liberalism: the possibilities for state intervention into the economy at both a global and national level, and its very real limits as well.

Return begins by outlining what Krugman takes to be the reality within which economic decision making has to operate today. Post-1989, we live in a world in which socialism is no longer "an idea with the power to move men's minds"[94] and in which a fully global capitalism has involved the developing world in production (and thus, in the world economy) to an unprecedented degree. To put it bluntly, "we live in a world in which property rights and free markets are viewed as fundamental principles, not grudging expedients; where the unpleasant aspects of a market system – inequality, unemployment, injustice – are accepted as facts of life."[95] It is clear from even this quote that Krugman's analysis of the global economy is not going to involve questions of morality, conscience, or even to some degree, politics. This is a book of economic analysis, which aims to make sense of the instability of the global economic system. The economics of *depression* – as distinct from *recession* – have returned at the moment of capitalism's supposed post-1989 victory. How and why, and what might be done about it, is what Krugman outlines by working through currency crises in Latin America (Mexico 1994, Argentina 2002) and Asia (1997–1999), and an assessment of Japan's Lost Decade (1990s), as well as providing analyses of stock market bubbles in the United States (the dot com bubble of the late 1990s and the more recent housing market bubble) and a brief commentary on the global crisis of 2008.

In many respects, the specifics of the argument are less important than the form and larger claims that emerge out of Krugman's analysis. For Krugman the political analyst, financial crisis provides opportunity: just as the Great Depression led to the New Deal, the current crisis threatens to undercut movement conservatism and introduces the possibility for a new New Deal that might undo the inequities of the Great Divergence. In his role as an economist, the return of depression economics introduces a potential system failure whose cause has to be identified in order for capitalism to keep operating, whether or not its operations and outcomes are morally laudable. The essential mechanism by which to prevent economic downturns and to maintain private property and private decision making is well known, having been developed to deal with the consequences of the Great Depression. Krugman describes this as the "Keynesian Compact":

> What restored faith in free markets was not just the recovery from the Depression but the assurance that macroeconomic intervention – cutting interest rates or increasing budget deficits to fight recessions – could keep a free-market economy more or less stable at more or less full employment. In effect, capitalism and its economists made a deal with the public: it will be okay to have free markets from now on, because we know enough to prevent any more Great Depressions.[96]

The question that animates the book – and has fueled much of Krugman's response to what he has seen as the too timid response by the Obama administration to the current economic crisis – is why this Compact seems to have failed or broken down, allowing depression economics to return not just to the peripheries of capitalism but to its US center. It is worth mentioning that despite its importance for his argument in the book, he offers very little elaboration of what constitutes this Compact. It seems limited to the fact that the state will intervene by cutting taxes and raising spending to avoid recessions, and does not extend to the broader dynamics of the New Deal, which included mechanisms to (for instance) reduce the yawning gap in division of wealth during the Gilded Age (to which we have returned at the present) or to try to ensure full employment and to mitigate the effects of the sometimes cruel whims of the market.

Even in this restricted fiscal mode, the Keynesian Compact is not without problems. In an era in which the bulk of government revenues comes from private individuals rather than corporations, the use of public monies to prop up private companies has generated enormous criticism across the globe, regardless of the macroeconomic rationale involved and its supposed benefits to the system in the long run (it was Keynes, after all, who famously commented that in the long run we are all dead). Perhaps the deal once made with publics about the continuation of free markets – a gesture of accommodation that, in the first place, was carried out to mitigate political challenges to the very legitimacy of liberal capitalism – is one which many would now want to reconsider. In any case, two causes for the return of depression economics emerge from Krugman's analysis. The locus of the *first* is changes in financial practices in the United States, both as a result of deregulation of the banking sector at the end of the twentieth century and the emergence of a shadow banking system "that were never regulated in the first place."[97] For anyone who has paid attention to myriad discussions of the problems in the US economy that led to the fall 2008 crisis, the culprits that Krugman raises are familiar ones: excessive levels of risk and speculation in a financial system that had become detached from the real economy; the creation of new financial instruments with promises of spectacular returns, but whose elements and risk were impossible for investors to understand; changes in lending practices to homeowners, underwritten by an excessive and irrational faith in the unending upward progression of property values; the practice of hedge funds to arbitrage away liquidity, especially given that "for many illiquid assets they *were* the market";[98] and an over-leveraging of all manner of financial institutions, both of the bricks-and-mortar (or glass and steel) and the shadow variety. Krugman advocates increased regulation, but also "temporary nationalization" of some elements of the financial system, as long as they are "reprivatized as soon as it's safe to do so."[99] When it comes to assigning blame on home turf, it comes down to illogic, neglect, and "irrational exuberance" in markets, as well as the failure of key policy makers to make tough decisions, most notably Alan Greenspan during his time as chairman of the Federal Reserve's Board of Governors (1987–2006).

The market bubbles and economic crises endured by the United States are, of course, linked to the global market as never before; this is why, one might expect, Krugman offers analyses of the currency crises in Latin America and Asia – as exploratory test cases to understand what happens next in the United States. But in the course of his analysis, the problems for the United States appear in fact to have little connection (until perhaps recently) with the return of depression economics elsewhere. The Keynesian Compact secures faith in free markets; in the United States, governments routinely intervene in markets in order to stabilize them, whether through the desperate heavy hand of big government spending when necessary, or through the more quotidian

regardless of what they do. Once there is a loss of confidence in a country's economy due to some financial problem, a process is set into motion from whose consequences it is difficult to recover. Whether or not a particular problem speaks to larger, underlying macroeconomic issues, it can set off a loss of investor confidence; this produces a fall of currency and a rise in interest rates in an attempt to attract investors back, but a *slump* in the economy because foreign currency and debt becomes more expensive, which leads to further financial problems for banks, households, and companies in the country, and thus a further loss of confidence, and so on. Krugman writes, "because speculative attacks can be self-justifying, following an economic policy that makes sense in terms of the fundamentals is not enough to assure market confidence. In fact, the need to win that confidence can actually prevent a country from following otherwise sensible policies and force it to follow policies that would normally seem perverse."[101] What is true for national governments is equally true for the IMF:

> Because crises can be self-fulfilling, sound economic policy is not sufficient to gain market confidence – one must cater to the perceptions, the prejudices, the whims of the market. Or, rather, one must cater to what one *hopes* will be the perceptions of the market ...
>
> It became an exercise in amateur psychology, in which the IMF and the Treasury Department tried to persuade countries to do things they hoped would be perceived by the market as favorable.[102]

Did foreign governments and the IMF have to play these games? In each of the situations that he analyzes, Krugman suggests that other paths could have been taken. His conclusion, however, is unambiguous: "the bottom line is that there were no good choices. The rules of the international financial system, it seemed, offered many countries no way out. And so it was really nobody's fault that things turned out so badly."[103]

The Keynesian Compact on which the fate of markets rest would appear to operate only in the case of Western developed countries; elsewhere, the science of economics becomes a game of amateur psychology dependent on a different kind of Keynesian: "animal spirits."[104] In the age of a truly global economy, however, recent events have shown that these animal spirits have infected the entire planet. The Keynesian solution to the Great Depression – always already helped along by the appearance of World War II, with its massive demand on government coffers – has continued to work to the degree that it has only because capital everywhere could come home to roost in the relative safety of the United States. The United States was a space exempt from confidence games; such an exceptionalism was necessary in order for the whole system to continue to operate. The size and strength of the US economy is one reason for the (relatively) unwavering confidence that one might have had in it; another was its permanent war economy (i.e., akin to what World War II was to Keynesianism), which underwrites the US currency (what Robert Kurz calls the "arms dollar")[105] as the unit of universal exchange. This stable center seems, too, to have been important for the epistemic self-certainty of economics.

What now, now that economics has been replaced by amateur psychology and confidence games *everywhere*? The apparent illogics and quick collapses of markets and currencies (followed by equally quick recoveries) are only in part due to the villainous hedge funds and shadow banks to which Krugman draws (sometimes admiring) attention. The scale and scope of financial markets, the speed at which decisions can be made via information technology, and the realities of a system in which there is no longer any outside – the outside of the socialist world or of developing economies not yet fully integrated into capitalist markets – has exposed the animals spirits lurking within economic decision making from the beginning. Can governmental policies or regulations by nation-states rein these in to a degree that would make a difference? Shouldn't we question the realities of the Keynesian Compact and imagine other ways to organize ourselves globally? Or couldn't we insist on a Compact that was more Keynesian than Krugman seems to want (that is, more than the state intervening at the level of interest rates, taxes, and spending)? For Krugman, this is unthinkable. Instead, the whims of the market are allowed to rule, and, in the absence of other ideas, we will have to just live with "the facts of life": inequality, unemployment, injustice, all exacerbated by depression economics.

* * *

So what *does* Paul Krugman's liberalism look like? Can we depend on it to offer us a way into the future – a future better than the present we are living in?

Liberalism requires one to live several contradictions, and to have faith in a worldview that for many has become equivalent to reality itself (and so needs no further comment). The contradictions – and elisions, and missing arguments, and holes in logic – are in evidence in these two books by Krugman. In *Return* we are shown a virtual economy that is becoming difficult if not impossible to control; the mechanism by which governments could keep capitalism operating – and thus, one assumes, the good times rolling – is in danger of becoming an anachronism. At a different scale, that of the nation-state rather than the economy of the globe, *Conscience* makes an argument for an almost equitable economy through government intervention, with a seemingly simple solution (higher taxes for the rich!) which is derailed not by epistemology but by political ill will and self-interest. To an unexpected degree, in Krugman's texts such decisions at the level of nations aren't impeded or impacted by the developments in the global economy that have generated the conditions for a return of depression economics. The failure to raise taxes is never linked to (for instance) the need of states to entice and keep businesses by minimizing taxes as a result of competition between nation-states, but is merely a local drama connected to the rise of movement conservatism. National and global don't intersect; nor do the political and the economic, each of which keeps to its own geographic sphere of influence.

What is missing or elided in this picture – besides, that is, the very fact of globalization and its implications for national policy making and financial markets – is something that is usually at the core of liberalism: the future. Liberal political visions are not usually arrested in flight. There is always work to be done to make things better – more justice and more equity (political *and* economic), opening up life opportunities for everyone. But in Krugman's liberalism, time is arrested. In *Return*, he sounds perilously close to figures such as Robert Kagan or

Francis Fukuyama in asserting the inevitability of capitalism, with all of its attendant outcomes (unemployment) and injustices (disparities in income and thus all manner of life opportunities). As an economist, capitalism is for Krugman something more than an historical system of human social organization – *not* just a system with a history, but also one *prone* to history, which is to say, potentially open to change and modification in order to generate different outcomes and to minimize social injustices. Capitalism and the economy are the self-same for this liberal. The self-justifying character of economics – its tendency to create and maintain its object of study, and to forget its roots in ideology and politics on the path to being a science – is starkly evident throughout his writing.[106] He cannot frame his thinking against the fact that capitalism's emergence on a global scale after the end of socialism is the coming-into-being of the economy – that object which economists study scientifically – proper, which had been impeded from full world-historical self-expression by amateurs who had wanted to arrest progress by messing up economics with politics.

The problem, however, is that this economy proves to be cruel. But this is a problem only if one has a conscience – or rather, if one has the conscience of a *liberal*. What is missing in *Conscience* is any outline of ethical principles or a vision of a social good. Doesn't an appeal to conscience and the description and naming of good (liberals, progressives) and bad (movement conservatives) demand an outline of principles, such that what is good (good government, good governance) can be measured and imagined? One could, for instance, assert that in principle everyone is always already equal and, as such, social systems need to be redesigned to enable this possibility. Krugman offers no such account, because it goes against what is possible within capitalism. Capitalism is treated as the governing principle of society; all politics can do is try to mitigate some of its negative outcomes and impacts. In the absence of a set of principles to assess the quality and function of these processes of mitigation, what Krugman offers is a vision of a *past* society. His conscience is built around images of American halcyon days: dad going off to work, mom in the kitchen, boys with crew cuts off to play baseball, girls in dresses playing with their dolls. Once again, time is arrested in flight: we can do no better as

132

a society – if one is in the United States – than add health care to what we already had back in the day. This is a conscience premised on a selective view even of the glory days of US society. Consider the way in which a more global view of the post-World War II era complicates this national fantasy of a once-and-future middle-class America:

> The established tale of the age of three worlds [1945–1989] is that there were three stories: the long boom of US, Japanese, and German Keynesian capital that created a global Fordist mass culture characterized by sex, drugs, and rock and roll; the long and uneven struggle between the Stalinist bureaucracy and the forces of the "thaw" and *glasnost* in the apparently separate world of centrally-planned people's democracies; and the rapid decolonization of the Third World followed by various forms of state-led development and modernization, whether through capitalist import-substitution or Soviet-style central planning.[107]

The first New Deal was constructed in order to save capitalism from itself and from the challenge of those who opposed its injustices and often violent impact on human communities. The new New Deal that Krugman advocates (and for which many of us hope) – is this not simply yet another attempt to save capitalism? Is it not a system which remains unjust and whose effects we now know are not just on human communities but on the earth itself? The future deserves better than a repetition of the fantasy of better living through capitalism, however convincing its advocates might be.

We have been offered three versions of roughly the same narrative of the present and the future, of globalization and its aftermath. Here's how the story goes. There are significant changes (e.g., in work, in society and technology, in the nature of economics) to which "we" (the referent here usually being the United States) have to pay attention to make sure that we get what we want and that we improve our societies and opportunities as individuals. The present is undergoing a transformation. The future, however, is expected to look much like the present – or even the past! – despite the fact that these didactic texts all tell us that something needs to be fixed in the present. Globalization generates new circumstances and contexts, the response to which is an indefinite present rather than a reconsideration of those social, political, and economic systems that have been shown to be lacking or problematic. The gestures made are always pragmatic and positivistic ones – this is how the world is, so we have to deal with it rationally and without stars in our eyes – and yet the imagined outcome is fantastical: a utopia of work as art and pure self-actualization (Florida), the emergence of genuine individuality with the aid of technology and the speed of globalization (Friedman), and a capitalist society that produces a just society on a global scale in which everyone is middle class if they are not rich (Krugman). Education, morality, the nation, the future, history, and certainly capitalism: these are things which these thinkers believe *will* save us.

What ideas about the present and the future might we find in a more radical critic, one who takes on the ideologies of globalization to which we have pointed, and who attends to the limits of its common sense?

e.   The Non-Shock Doctrine: Naomi Klein

Naomi Klein has impeccable timing. She began researching her first book, *No Logo* (2000), about the shift in corporate emphasis from the production of goods to their global branding, not long after the Zapatista uprising against the North America Free Trade Agreement (NAFTA) in 1994 and published it right after the emergence of the anti-globalization movement in Seattle in 1999.[108] Likewise, Klein's bestseller *The Shock Doctrine*, about the rise of what she calls disaster capitalism, was written only shortly before the great economic crisis of 2008.[109]

Articulate, perspicacious, measured, but brimming with critical fire, Klein tracks the worldwide corruption of capitalist accumulation and its political effects of war, torture, labor exploitation, and criminally greedy leaders. For every VIP hotel lounge that Thomas Friedman has visited to meet with the global elite, Klein has visited the crime scenes of sweatshops, the hospital beds of torture victims, the asbestos-infested FEMA trailers of New Orleans, and the demoralized shrimpers in the Gulf of Mexico following the BP oil explosion. But like Friedman,

Klein also relies on her own experiences and an array of personal anecdotes to tell her stories to an ever-growing number of receptive readers, from young anarchists in need of a lucid narrative to explain their discontent to incredulous older liberals in need of disabuse as they face the contradictions of capitalism.

Take, for example, the beginning of *The Shock Doctrine*. Klein describes being in New Orleans right after Hurricane Katrina. Together with victims of the disaster, she listens to politicians revel in the upside to all the destruction, explaining to their audience how Katrina had effectively produced what so many politicians and developers could not: a "fresh start" and "clean sheets" to remake the city. Klein is appalled. "This isn't an opportunity. It's a goddamned tragedy. Are they blind?" Klein overhears one victim saying.[110] Another responds, "No, they're not blind, they're evil. They see just fine."[111]

The Shock Doctrine is Klein's history of this evil: the way that a certain form of capitalist accumulation (one that grants almost total freedom to corporations and that rejects the welfare state though deregulation, privatization, cutbacks) waits for — indeed produces — catastrophic events in order to impose its market fundamentals on socially vulnerable and psychologically shocked populations. Beginning with the overthrow of Prime Minister Mohammed Mossadegh in Iran in 1953 and the CIA-sponsored coup in Guatemala one year later, to the university training of Latin American students to install neoliberal ideas throughout the Southern Cone in the 1960s and 1970s, all the way up to the Iraq wars, Katrina, and even the economic crisis of 2008, Klein's argument is clear: neoliberal capitalism feeds off disaster, and this feeding frenzy is mobilized by a small group of evil individuals, from Milton Friedman to Alan Greenspan to Donald Rumsfeld.

But the history in *The Shock Doctrine* is different than the history of evil in Klein's first book, *No Logo*. In her first book, Klein is less interested in neoliberal capitalism and its questionable political leaders than in tracking the places of corruption and individual transgression by corporate executives and factory bosses. Indeed, the new priority on corporate branding and image control addressed in *No Logo* effectively hides the actual practices of corporations. With advertisements no longer directly referencing the products themselves but the fantasy lifestyle and affect associated with such products, there is a delinking not only of what a product is (its use) and what it says it is (its brand), but – and more insidiously – also a delinking of what a corporation says it is (its whitewashed representation of itself) and what it *actually* is (how it produces, who it contracts to produce, and the actual effects of its products on consumers). *No Logo* is a detective narrative. At the scene of the crime are the Nike shoes, but to nab the guilty parties Klein must piece the clues together on her way to the real criminals – first to the local boss of the overseas sweatshop and then to the evil CEO himself.

Klein's history in *No Logo* is a history of transgression, of corrupt individuals caught red-handed. Indeed, this is precisely what was presented as the moral force of the anti-globalization movement at its beginning. If young consumers knew from where their clothes came, if they were able to map all of the networks involved in serving their Starbucks coffee, they would be disgusted, their desire for the commodities would whither, and they would resist, thus effectively changing the world. There are three key assumptions here: first, that knowing about how something works will necessarily change how one behaves; second, that changing one's behavior will necessarily lead to systemic social change; and third, that the origins of corruption are located in the transgressive act itself. To grasp what is at stake in *No Logo* and situate it vis-à-vis *The Shock Doctrine*, we must take up these assumptions one by one.

Knowing about how something works will necessarily change how one behaves. If psychoanalysis has taught us anything, it is that merely understanding our symptoms does not necessarily interrupt our compulsion to repeat them. We might know very well that we become irrationally aggressive when criticized by others, and we may know very well that this is a habit we have repeated since childhood, but knowing this history and understanding the triggers do not necessarily reconfigure our behavior. In fact, often it is precisely our knowledge and understanding of such symptoms that charge and sustain them. The greatest horror is not that there are illegal prisons and torture occurring on Guantanamo Bay, but that these prisons and practices exist with our full knowledge. "If only they knew, then they would change," is a false promise – "if only they knew about the abuses at Abu Ghraib, about

Saddam's lack of WMDs, about BP's calculated negligence, about how their tennis shoes are made, about how they lash out when confronted, if only they knew the truth of the situation, then they would change." This has revealed itself to be utterly false and ideologically deceptive, especially in today's saturated mediascape, in which politicians are unfazed by so many clever "YouTube" montages that expose their inconsistencies and hypocrisies. In fact, the exhausting ubiquity of these revelations is matched only by the exhausting ubiquity of the inconsistencies themselves. No one seems surprised and no one seems to care very much.

This leads to the second assumption that *changing one's consumer behavior will necessarily lead to systemic social change.* By calling this assumption into question, we do not mean to argue against boycotts or mass consumer actions. It is true, of course, that commodity capitalism could not continue if commodities were no longer purchased. But the most profitable commodities (the ones that drive the system) are ones that many people have no choice about whether or not to consume. Here we are referring to weapons, medicine, and food, three industries that combine for almost three trillion dollars spent annually, approximately 6 percent of worldwide GDP. This is to say that quite a bit of commodity production does not come down to individual consumer choices and, thus, consumer behavior. If consumer behavior does change (so that one votes by way of one's consumer choices) even while more and more people are not even in a position to consume (due to poverty and impoverishment), but the commodity system carries on as it is, *then* where does this leave things? Where does this leave a world in which capitalism continues even as many no longer invest in it – and this lack of investment is more on the level of ideology than money? Another way to put these questions is to stress that dominant capitalist ideology does not operate by generating some sort of false consciousness toward the problems of capitalism (so that one is duped into believing that capitalism is inviolable), but that capitalist ideology works precisely by revealing the very problems of capitalism itself – but in a way that makes these problems seem permanent and irresolvable.

Indeed, we are tempted to argue that a new ideological dominant (of an old capitalist reality) is coming into being, one in which the way the world is understood and represented is closer to the way the world actually operates. People the world over seem to know exactly how capitalism works (through the extraction of surplus value from those who toil in fields, factories, and the service industry) and what it engenders socially (class conflict, gender inequality, imperial violence, brutal dispossessions, ecological destruction, and psychological suffering). This does not mean that we have arrived at the end of ideology, but only that *today the dominant ideology is the truth of the capitalist system itself.* But, and again, knowing about a system and coordinating one's behavior in relation to this knowledge does not necessarily change the system itself. It does, however, make for a much more open and honest (if not necessarily more violent) political struggle: the line that separates winners and losers, minorities and majorities, rich and poor, capitalists and anti-capitalists is clear for everyone to see. These lines certainly existed at the time when Klein wrote *No Logo*; they were, however, mediated in a much less candid and direct way: the tortuous logic of modernization theory ("we will all rise … some a little later than others") and Cold War ideologies ("economic divisions exist as a temporary political sacrifice for freedom") still held sway. In other words, at the time of *No Logo* we were still shocked to learn that before our breakfast arrived at our table it went through a slimy network of slave labor, colonial residue, and high-tech labor exploitation. But by the time of *The Shock Doctrine*, no one (save those who had checked out long ago) was surprised anymore.

The origin of corruption is located in the transgressive act itself. Transgressions occur in capitalism not because capitalism has gone wrong, but because it has gone right — it has worked as it was designed to work. We have made reference to this before, but it is essential to recognize how this functions. Indeed, without recognizing this greater logic of capitalism (a logic that operates unseen as we obsess over the latest scandal or corruption), one effectively abandons politics as such. To criticize capitalism based on its transgressive acts (e.g., factories burning down, contracts betrayed, child labor being used) is to forego an analysis of how capitalism produces inequality even when it works well (e.g., when the factories are clean, the contract is obeyed, and when workers get to enact their creativity à la Richard Florida). Does

138

one really need to be a Marxist today to recognize that the system is structured in dominance, structured to produce great wealth for a privileged minority? Does one really need to be a so-called Red Green to recognize that commodity culture is destroying the environment? Does one really need to be trained in dialectical materialism to recognize that war and prisons are not only highly profitable industries but indispensible for the reproduction of capitalism?

The answer to all three of these questions is a resounding "No!," as Klein demonstrates in *The Shock Doctrine*. If *No Logo* resorted to a history of transgression (looking for the "gotcha" moments), then *The Shock Doctrine* presents a history of crisis (one that is less occupied by sinister acts and more focused on the active sins of neoliberal capitalism). In fact, it is Milton Friedman himself who supplies Klein with her crisis mantra: "He observed," Klein writes, "that 'only a crisis – actual or perceived – produces real change. When that crisis occurs, the actions that are taken depend on the ideas that are lying around. That, I believe, is our basic function: to develop alternatives to existing policies, to keep them alive and available until the politically impossible becomes politically inevitable.'"[112] Klein punctuates this quote with an exclamation point: "Some people stockpile canned goods and water in preparation for major disasters; Friedmanites stockpile free-market ideas."[113]

Disaster capitalism, for Klein, is precisely this "kick 'em while they're down" installation of economic fundamentals. And the neoliberals go one step further: they kick them down before kicking them while they're down. They mastermind and finance the coups, they exacerbate the natural disasters, they provoke the recessions, so that they can then work their magic with as little opposition as possible. All of this is not too difficult to confirm in the historical record, with (as Friedman has done in the quote above) the neoliberals themselves unapologetically admitting to their tactics. But the neoliberals have two simple and powerful ripostes – ones that in a debate with Alan Greenspan, Klein was unable to sufficiently make a case against. "Name me a better system, a system that has generated more wealth for more people than capitalism"; and, Greenspan continues with what he takes to be his *coup de grâce*, "corruption is human, but capitalism is the best system precisely in the way that it keeps corruption under relative control." Greenspan effectively asks, "what are you telling me . . . that the Soviets weren't corrupt?"[114]

Before being cut off, Klein responds to the first question of an alternative system with the phrase "mixed economy." In *The Shock Doctrine*, Klein elaborates on this:

> I am not arguing that all forms of market systems are inherently violent. It is eminently possible to have a market-based economy that requires no such brutality and demands no such ideological purity. A free market in consumer products can coexist with free public health care, with public schools, with a large segment of the economy – like a national oil company – held in state hands . . . Markets need not be fundamentalist.[115]

With this Klein has returned us to the debate between Keynes and Hayek, and we find ourselves backed into the same corner we identified with Krugman. Ultimately and however inadvertently, Klein and Krugman are in accord with Greenspan, holding that capitalism is the best of all systems and despite all of the brutality that has been registered on its watch, it still comes out ahead of other systems now *and* in the future. This is why, of course, Klein cannot adequately respond to Greenspan's second point about corruption.

It is precisely this problem of corruption that needs elaboration. There are two key points. The appeal to corruption, either in a more broadly accusatory way against all capitalists, or in a more selective way against neoliberals, always draws attention away from the systemic critique to the bad people in the system. Of course, there are "bad people" and they should be held accountable, but it is a strategic error to privilege them over other critical approaches. Indeed, we are arguing for a critical approach that might be called a non-moralizing critique of capitalism, one that addresses itself to the structures and strictures of its common sense and focuses on the success rather than the failure of the system. But what would the principles of such a non-moralizing critique be?[116]

First, it would not be personally motivated. Of course, every action is personally motivated insofar as it comes from an individual person and is necessarily fashioned by conscious and unconscious desire. In this case, a non-personal critique of capitalism means that one first recognizes that one is *necessarily* part of capitalism, necessarily wrapped up in its ideologies, and that one shares this complicity with others, both friends and enemies. There is no escaping capitalism since capitalism is not only the production and consumption of commodities, but is a mode with special forms of exchange, meaning making, social relations, desire, communication, and thought that necessarily imbue themselves into our very beings, so much so that attempting to avoid them is like trying to avoid our deepest habits. This inextricable relation to capitalism (which affects the very way we understand and represent it) leads to the recognition that any critique of capitalism is necessarily social, necessarily part of something that exceeds the individual producing the critique.

Second, this non-moralizing critique is not personally directed. The critique, rather, is directed toward the structure, system, and logic of capitalism, which requires less a scathing rhetoric against individuals and more of an analytic understanding of how capitalism works. As mentioned above, crisis occurs in capitalism not because capitalism has gone wrong but because it has gone right – it has worked as it is designed to work. Indeed, without recognizing this greater logic of capitalism, one that goes hiding when we obsess over the latest scandal or corruption, one effectively abandons politics as such.

This leads to the third criterion of a non-moralizing critique of capitalism: since there is always something within a system that escapes the systemic logic itself and which any critique cannot fully incorporate, *one must be open to – and try to hold – the contradictions of capitalism rather than try to immediately manage, resolve, or repress them.* This is to say that capitalism can produce magnificent things while still causing heart-breaking destruction. To recognize this is also to recognize the history of capitalism, especially the unquestionable liberating effects that its founding revolution enabled. But to recognize capitalism's historical coming-into-being is also to recognize that it can have an historical going-out-of-being. This simple fact sustains a non-moralizing critique since it denaturalizes capitalism, opening up a comparative analysis with other social formations.

This comparative analysis (which also means comparing capitalism to other formations that do not yet exist) is based not on the ideological claims and desires of different systems (democracy and freedom, for example), but on what each system delivers, such as health care, a healthy natural environment, opportunities to experience diverse pleasures, social equality, individual justice, nourishing food, and secure shelter. *A non-moralizing critique, therefore, prioritizes outcomes and remains unconvinced by non-social and ahistorical justifications and arguments, such as the complacent recourse to the scarcity of natural resources or the inherent greediness and goodness of human beings.* This comparative impulse also inspires formal experiments with alternatives, from social modeling to science fiction narratives. Indeed, such exercises should themselves not be justified based on any moralizing critique, but neither should they be discouraged by the constraints of practicality or impossibility. To make the impossible might very well be impossible, but the very act of imagining it can change the realm of possibility.

This leads to the final criterion for a non-moralizing critique of capitalism: *if one appeals to evil or righteousness, then these qualities and acts should be understood as symptoms rather than causes of the very system under question.* Evil acts do not cause capitalism's crises and then recuperate these crises by dispossessing individuals of their wealth and dignity. This process of crisis and dispossession is built right into the system itself and, like any machine, can do certain things, but not others. Instead of anthropomorphizing capitalism with histrionic claims of how evil or righteous it is, a non-moralizing critique sees it for what it is – a human-built machine that performs various functions based on certain rules and fundamental principles. Indeed, such a critique generates a certain degree of respect for capitalism based on how capable it is at performing such tasks, even if such tasks are as cruel as destroying a family-owned business or expropriating people from their land. Instead of incredulity and counterproductive anger, a non-moralizing critique generates a clear voice (however angry) and a measured response (whether clinical, rational, or poetic) that does not retreat from the most painful and beautiful aspects of everyday capitalist life.

This returns us to the distinction between journalism and academic writing, which we introduced in our discussion of Thomas Friedman.

142

Is the greatest strength of Klein's work – her clear and compelling journalistic prose – also its greatest weakness? For her work to operate as effectively as it does, that is, for Klein to maintain the popular appeal and influence of her writing, is she compelled to moralize, to lead the protestors in the inevitable chants of "shame, shame, shame" against the power elite? We don't think so. But as long as Klein concentrates her efforts on the guilty, shameful, and evil individuals, then her critique will never have the full force it deserves. This limit is not due to a self-indulgent penchant to point fingers or some oppositional tic of the young (this, in fact, is the most patronizing dismissal of Klein and some of the other impressive investigative journalists of her generation, such as Matt Taibbi and Jeremy Scahill, and one that gets repeated from Washington to Ottawa).[117] Klein's limit, rather, is due to the theory of crisis on which her work depends.

To resist a moralizing critique requires an understanding of crisis that does not get caught up in the fires and floods or the "shameful" deals brokered by Milton Friedman's disciples, let alone by Bill Clinton (probably the greatest Friedmanite of them all) or Barack Obama (who gave himself away as a relative to Friedman when, at the very beginning of his first term, he selected Lawrence Summers as his top economic advisor). A non-moralizing critique understands that crises are built right into the system itself and daily reveal themselves in between the great disasters and capital "C" crises that consume media attention as well as individual consciousnesses. In fact, the lower-case "c" crises, the ones that make up the banality of our everyday lives (the ones that don't even look or feel like crises, but keep the whole system going) consume not only our non-mediatized lives but also our unconscious. And this is doubly so for disaster.

It is at this point, however, that we need to distinguish between disaster and crisis. For although Klein is tracking an array of post-World War II disasters and attributing their causes to neoliberal capitalism, her history is organized around a theory of crisis – and these two categories (disaster and crisis) are not the same. Disaster is that moment when the sustainable configuration of relations fails, when the relation between one thing and another breaks down.[118] In a capitalist economy, disaster hits when goods cannot be related to markets, when idle capital and idle

143

labor cannot be connected, or when currency bubbles burst, replacing so much cold cash with so much hot air. In ecology, the disaster of global warming hits when the emission of carbon dioxide no longer relates to the planet's natural capacity to absorb it. For those with HIV or cancer, disaster comes when the logic of cells overproduce so that they no longer relate to the logic of the living body, or disaster hits when one is denied anti-retroviral or chemotherapeutic drugs due to the inability to pay for them. In philosophy, disaster is that moment when thinking is cut off from history, while individuals are in psychological disaster when they are no longer able to relate to the world. As for political disaster, it comes with the severed relation between those desiring representation and those authorized to grant it.

One thing we invariably learn when natural disasters strike (such as the tsunami in Southeast Asia or the earthquake in Haiti) is that such events are not natural, or at least the effects of such events are not natural. Their fallout, quite obviously, is social – products of human choices, political systems, even cultural assumptions. Extending this understanding to the limit, however, effectively evacuates the category of disaster itself. This is because although disaster is contingent (coming "from the stars," as its etymology suggests), its effects are almost always predictable and quite logical. Most people in power knew exactly what would happen if the New Orleans levées broke, just as any epidemiologist can predict how many will die of AIDS if people are left untreated. Those in power simply cross their fingers and hope that such events will not occur. When they do occur and their tragic consequences ensue, calling them disasters is like calling a dying man a hypochondriac.

However much their effects may be completely predictable, the contingency of disaster is what sets it apart from crisis. Unlike a disaster, there is something necessary about a crisis, something true to the larger systemic form. In other words, systems are structured so that crises will occur, strengthening and reproducing the systems themselves. The boom–bust cycle of capitalism is only one of the more obvious examples of this logical necessity. Both contingent disasters and necessary crises, therefore, are linked in the way that their breakdown in relations is built back up again by a different set of relations within the same system.

144

Revolution, in contrast, is that moment when a new set of relations takes hold within a different system. This crude distinction better explicates the new ubiquity with which disaster and crisis have been invoked over the past 20 years, while revolution has been driven underground, not only rendered unspeakable but, more important, unthinkable. This trend has everything to do with the political-economic situation of the post-Cold War era, a symptom of our own historical formation, which currently, for good or ill, goes by the name globalization.

Disaster and crisis have always been quick off the lips of those wishing to justify mishap and misfortune. If it were not for that earthquake, the town would not be in such disrepair; if it were not for the crooked officials, or those crony capitalists, then there would be better public transportation, better health care, and more wealth to go around; if it were not for the new terrorists, then we would be free from anxiety, sleeping comfortably on cushions bought by the peace dividend. Crisis and disaster are those props pulled out of the bottom of the bag when all other explanations lose operational force or cannot be spoken.

With the end of the Cold War, anomalous and non-systemic disaster and crisis (that is, events from the outside – like a meteor or a madman) have been even more likely to be employed to explain inequality and injustice. During the Cold War, for example, to speak the language of disaster and crisis was at once to speak the language of revolution: one discourse could easily slip into the other. Disaster and crisis were truly dangerous. With "mutually assured destruction" the watchwords of the day, one crisis could accumulate into so many crises until the quantitative curved into the qualitative and the whole system was in tatters. We only need to think about the Cuban missile crisis or the oil crises of the 1970s to remember what a cat's step away crisis and disaster were to revolution. But with the transformed geopolitical situation following the Cold War in which the United States was left as the sole superpower and the "end of ideology" became the ruling ideology, it *seemed* riskless (not to mention utterly gratuitous) to call upon crisis and disaster. At that moment, crisis and disaster were as far apart from revolution as heaven from earth. What needs to be considered in the

145

current post post-Cold War moment – that moment that comes after globalization in which no after can be thought – is whether or not this is still the case. Is something changing so that crisis and disaster are becoming dangerous again, no longer the trump cards of those in power? Is something changing so that revolutionary discourse is creeping back into everyday consciousness, into the way we understand not only radical social change, but also into the more banal ways in which we understand ourselves and think about the future?

We think something is changing, but this can only be understood when we understand crisis and disaster as non-spectacular and in terms of the everyday. Capitalism is reproduced and recuperated not by disasters and crises, but by everything that happens in between the disasters and crises. Klein's book is most brilliant, therefore, when we invert its inner form, when we understand the shock doctrine to be about the rise of non-disaster capitalism. But how does one write a book about a non-disaster? About a pervasive crisis? How to write a book entitled something like, *The Shock of the Everyday: Capitalism as Doctrine and Disaster*?

WikiLeaks wrote such a book when it released over 200 000 pages of classified military records on the everyday events of the war in Afghanistan from 2004 to January 2009.[119] The biggest leak in US military history, the archive documented in unadorned military language thousands of unreported civilian kills, dubious cooperation between the US military and the Taliban, and the way in which a black-ops Special Forces unit targets enemies for assassination or detention without trial. WikiLeaks defines itself as "a multi-jurisdictional public service designed to protect whistleblowers, journalists and activists who have sensitive material to communicate to the public."[120] The accumulated WikiLeaks text on the war in Afghanistan blows the whistle on the banality of war. In fact, this is precisely how those in power attempted to recuperate any damage the leak may have done.

The Obama administration emphasized that there was nothing new in all the documents, nothing that anyone with a mouse and a computer or enough change to buy a newspaper did not already know.[121] Additionally, Obama emphasized that it was information precisely like that released by WikiLeaks that he took into consideration in order to change the war strategy in Afghanistan. Speaking in front of the Senate Armed Services Committee at the US Central Command confirmation hearing, General James Mattis described the leak as "appallingly irresponsible."[122] At the same time, he insisted, "It didn't tell us anything, that I've seen so far, that we weren't already aware of. I've seen no big revelations. One of the newspaper headlines was that it's a – the war is a tense and dangerous thing. Well, if that is news, I don't know who it's news to that's on this planet."[123]

The General is quite right and the head of WikiLeaks, Julian Assange, agrees. When asked about what he thought was the most important revelation in the 91 000 documents, Assange responded:

> So, everyone's asking for a specific revelation that is the most important – you know, a massacre of 500 people at one point in time. But, to me, what is most important is the vast sweep of abuses that have occurred during the past six years, the vast sweep of sort of the everyday squalor and carnage of war. If we add all that up, we see that in fact most civilian casualties occur in incidences where one, two, ten or twenty people are killed. And they really numerically dominate the list of events, so it's, of course, hard for us to imagine that. It's so much material. But that is the way to really understand this war, is by seeing that there is one sort of kill after another every day going on and on and on in all sorts of different circumstances.[124]

Indeed, this is why the leak is so frustrating to political leaders and leading journalists: there is nothing to highlight except the war itself, and we already know that war is hell. Without an Abu Ghraib or Guantanamo, there is nothing for which to apologize or ask forgiveness; there is nothing to obsess over before burying such a sensational event into the footnotes of history.

The WikiLeaks archive is, in fact, an accumulation of footnotes without a main text, an accumulation that, in effect, *is* the main text – is history itself. What is revealed, therefore, is the very *logic* of the war in Afghanistan, the geopolitical *structure* of south-central Asia, and the *system* of global capitalism. Logic, structure, system: not the type of objects of investigation that sell newspapers or best-selling books of non-fiction. And on top of this tedious set of abstractions are the utterly concrete events that make up the leak, not the type of sensational, unbelievable, and singular irruptions that distract us from the cold reality of the world, but the cold reality of the world itself, much of it in the military code used for so many bundled operations. Moreover, it is the unmediatized aspect of the material (documenting approximately 20 000 civilian deaths) that contributes to the force of the revelation.[125] We have not been caught red-handed, but caught just as we are. And, most profoundly, we don't know what to do with such a revelation except to pretend that we have learned nothing new and to repress – once again – the trauma of looking at ourselves in the mirror.

This shift in register from the social to the individual (from the exposure of the theoretical abstractions of *logic*, *structure*, and *system* to the exposure of our very subjectivities) does not happen by mistake, but is a slippage that must be accounted for. And this returns us to Naomi Klein, since the organizing principle of *The Shock Doctrine* is precisely the analogy between the heartless and criminal electric shock experiments administered to mental health patients and the heartless and criminal economic shock experiments administered to whole populations. The first chapter of *The Shock Doctrine* begins with Klein visiting Gail Kastner, the woman who was the tragic victim of 63 electrocutions as part of a CIA covert operation in the 1950s. Klein writes, "Like the free-market economists who are convinced that only a large-scale disaster – a great unmaking – can prepare the ground for their 'reforms,' Cameron believed that by inflicting an array of shocks to the human brain, he could unmake and erase faulty minds, then rebuild new personalities on that ever-elusive clean slate."[126]

Ewan Cameron is the psychiatrist who administered the shocks to Kastner and who masterminded the theory of "psychic driving" (that torture incited de-patterning of the mind) that Klein applies to the neoliberal charged "economic shock therapy" of the Friedmanites. What we get with Cameron is the diabolical brainwasher and the focus on the heinous crime, the heartbreaking exception that everyone can agree is utterly despicable. By focusing on Cameron, Klein effectively de-emphasizes the de-patterning of the mind by everyday culture. The more interesting analogy to pursue would be one that draws attention to the way dominant capitalist ideology works by way of all the small stuff to produce cooperative and docile subjects (from the spatial organization of a family home to the temporal organization of schools and workplaces), and dominant capitalist accumulation strategies function to produce inequality by instantiating a similar array of seemingly neutral techniques (from the organization of labor power to the ceaseless production of commodities).

The fantasy that capitalist ideology is delivered in lethal doses with a hypodermic needle (*The Manchurian Candidate* model) is as far off the mark as the fantasy that capitalist economics is reproduced in board-rooms by disaster capitalists (*The Shock Doctrine* model). Or, we should say, it is not altogether wrong, but a tactical mistake to approach it in this way. Indeed, the capitalist system works to produce greedy and corrupt capitalists (ones who certainly deserve condemnation). Yet to begin with a criticism of them is counterproductive – not only because the dominant system of representation (media, mass culture, pedagogy) is based on a sophisticated defense of these very individuals and their practices (so that to engage in a shouting match in the contemporary mediascape is to risk neutralizing all critique), but because to go after the successful capitalists means to undermine the analytical skills required to understand the larger system. Capitalism is a tremendously complex system, which was proved once again during the 2008 financial meltdown when the derivative schemes that pushed things over the edge were so intricate that the only people who were capable of dismantling them were the very individuals who invented them in the first place. Finally, to direct a critique at the system and not at the individuals who manage and defend it is to reaffirm a belief in the system itself – in system as such. When we argue that crisis occurs in capitalism not because capitalism has gone wrong but because it has gone right, we are arguing that there is a certain cause-and-effect logic that can explain such events as war, poverty, and corruption. Of course, these effects are products of other systems as well, but the specific configuration of war, poverty, and corruption within capitalism is qualitatively different than these configurations within different systems, which is why Greenspan's point about Soviet corruption is a red herring.

Another problem with Klein's analogy between the individual and the social is that individuals are of a different order than social or economic entities. Still, we often see this analogy pursued, for instance when a nation is diagnosed as presenting symptoms such as an "identity crisis" (such as France in response to immigration issues) or repression and amnesia (such as Japan in response to crimes committed during World War II). Indeed, nations are often spoken about as if they are patients lying on a couch. As far back as J.A. Hobson's classic 1902 work on imperialism, however, we learned that nations do not rise or fall en masse, but that certain segments of national populations rise and fall quite unevenly from other segments.[127] Which is to say that to move too fast from an individual to a nation is to risk forgetting that there is a class of native disaster capitalists (many of whom supply Thomas Friedman with anecdotes!) who are instrumental in installing (and benefiting from) the economic fundamentals required by global capitalism. Individual subjects might very well be split (compartmentalizing a series of diverse and even contradictory character traits), but this split is qualitatively different than the splits within the national population.

The 2003 film *The Corporation* (for which Klein is interviewed) is one of the most compelling examples of relating psychiatric concerns to a social entity, in this case the capitalist corporation. After hitting upon Noam Chomsky, who argues that corporations are "a person without a moral conscience," the film (closely based on the book written by law professor Joel Bakan, *The Corporation: The Pathological Pursuit of Profit and Power*) reveals the way in which corporations betray the same characteristics as clinically diagnosed psychopaths, such as the inability to show remorse, callousness and lack of empathy, the failure to accept responsibility for one's own actions, and a grandiose sense of self-worth.[128] This is particularly relevant since the corporation attained "personhood" after the 1886 Supreme Court decision granting them protection under the Fourteenth Amendment. This pathologizing of the corporation might not be moralizing, but it does steer us away from the fundamental logic of the capitalist corporation. By overemphasizing the unfairly protected corporation (a protection that is reinforced by Article 11 of NAFTA which allows corporations to sue

150

Mexico, Canada, or the United States when actions taken by those governments have adversely affected their investments), *The Corporation* effectively disregards an economic analysis for a too narrowly configured political one (or perhaps we should say post-political one), one that views the problem primarily in terms of deregulation and unfair protection. The fatal assumption is that the capitalist corporation is benign when regulated and unprotected – an assumption shared on a larger scale when one imagines that a kinder, gentler capitalism can be sustained through the avuncular intervention of the state.

The weakness of this argument is particularly unfortunate given that *The Corporation* begins with a spot-on criticism of the "bad apple" defense of capitalism. From Enron to the wholesale ruin of various national economies (Russia, 1998; Argentina, 1999–2002), this defense upbraids the transgressive individuals, labeling them as "bad apples" before sacrificing them, all the while leaving intact the institutions and the very logic that created the possibility for such ruin in the first place. To their credit, the directors of *The Corporation* reject this stock and lame explanation, leading to the examination of the corporation itself. But when the film reaches "the Corporation" as a general category (and not simply as a particular case), it proceeds to invest it with the very same mental-health characteristics presented by the "bad apples": it effectively criticizes the corporation as a sick individual, returning us to the flawed strategy that the film promised to avoid in the first place. Likewise, when Klein goes after the neoliberals as disaster capitalists she effectively submits her own analysis to the tired Hollywood script that blames Mr Potter for the whole town's demise, while celebrating Jimmy Stewart's George Bailey as the sentimental savior and successful manager of a crisis that is, in reality, a logical effect of capitalism.[129]

Instead of treating the corporation as an individual, we propose treating individuals as a corporation, not a capitalist corporation that cannot suspend its fundamental rule of expansion and profit creation, but a non-capitalist corporation: one that comes closer to the term's Latin root of "corpus," the "body of the people." This collection of many individuals united into one body surviving longer than any of its particular members, and organized by logics, values, and beliefs other than the rule of profit and expansion, is not only a way to rethink

151

collectivity today but also a way to resist narratives of Potters and Baileys. The fact that capitalism cannot continue if such non-capitalist corporations become dominant is a hard fact worthy of serious consideration. Rather than allowing such a limiting fact to submit our hopes and desires to only what is possible, we believe that to contemplate the impossible (that is, to think non-capitalist corporations and non-capitalist individuals within the context of capitalism) is the very crucible of the political. Instead of returning to a mixed economy of properly regulated capitalist corporations (ones run by fair and moral executives as celebrated by Klein, and overseen by those fair and moral politicians with a conscience to whom Krugman appeals), we prefer to hold out room for an alternative social formation that would not be dependent upon a capitalist logic. Perhaps all of this turns on how the impossible (radical otherness) becomes possible; or, how the impossible (as impossible) shapes the possibilities of the present. Still, the moment we organize our critical commitments around the corruption of the puppet masters is the very moment we give up the radical project of pursuing the impossible – of moving beyond common sense (of, say, believing that liberalism is the best we can hope for) to a new common. A strong and clear voice like Naomi Klein's is indispensible to such a project, even though her own work often tends to compromise it. The idea that Klein stands at a distance from writers such as Florida, Friedman, and even Krugman in the radical force of her criticisms of globalization and the limits of current political and economic systems has the unfortunate tendency to allow the system as a whole to march on. There's no "after" to globalization to follow its end for her, too. The way to deal with bad systems isn't to fill them with good people, but to create new systems. Unfortunately, she would be no more likely to agree with our theses than the others whose ideas we have examined here.

f. The Limits of Hollywood: *Michael Clayton*

It has become sport to bash Hollywood celebrities for their political naivety. When someone as well heeled as a famous Hollywood actor speaks on behalf of justice and the underprivileged today, it cannot but come off as sanctimonious, if not a little slimy. The apparent hypocrisy compromises the millions of dollars raised and social awareness generated. Even seemingly heroic acts, like Sean Penn rescuing children from Katrina's floodwaters or John Travolta flying relief supplies into Port-au-Prince with his own Boeing 707, are easy to poke fun at and dismiss. But why? Is it because these stars are ignorant of the complex contexts and disputed histories of the issues for which they are campaigning? Is it because such charitable behavior turns into just another public relations spot? Not necessarily. What really cranks up the resentment of both left and right is that such celebrity acts appear to be utterly hypocritical. This pushes those offended into one of the most profound ideological traps of contemporary society: the trap of purity, or the belief that the only clean acts (charitable or critical) are those performed by individuals who are themselves clean. If one is dirty, so the logic goes, then one's act is simply compensation for, if not disavowal of, so much bad faith. And yet, in a culture in which one cannot help but be dirty – to be saturated with the logic of capitalist inequality – this purity argument is a reactionary gold mine, not to mention utterly debilitating for any type of democratic struggle, which will necessarily have to confront its own contradictions. And even if one is relatively successful at dodging the defiling logic of capitalist economics (by either obsessive-compulsive avoidance or Luddite retreat), then there is the psychological power of capitalism to contend with, in which one might feel dirty despite being clean (as when an innocent person becomes unreasonably nervous when questioned by a police officer). Indeed, this ideology of purity is the pivot on which our seven theses turn. Such an insistence on purity operates either to affirm common sense or to disable critique – which is one and the same thing in the end. The left melancholia of which Jacques Rancière and others have spoken is occasioned by a test of purity: the admission that "all our desires for subversion still obey the law of the market and that we are simply indulging in the new game on the global market – that of unbounded experimentation with our own lives."[130]

This is also to argue that the easy critique of the Hollywood elite is more insidious than even the most disingenuous acts of these elite

Clayton is a lawyer for a large New York law firm that has been defending a global agrochemical corporation (U-North, based on Monsanto) against a multi-billion dollar class action lawsuit. U-North is accused of contaminating ground water in a Wisconsin town, leading to serious illness for hundreds of its inhabitants. U-North's legal department is led by Karen Crowder, played to obsessive perfection by Tilda Swinton in a notable performance of a woman going to great lengths to succeed in a male-dominated corporate culture. U-North's legal department has outsourced the class action suit to Clooney's law firm, where Arthur Edens (Tom Wilkinson) is the brilliant litigator who has been working tirelessly on the case for the past six years. But Arthur is melting down – not only because he's gone off his meds, but also because he's finding it impossible to continue fighting for such a repulsive client. In fact, Arthur has been secretly making the case for the plaintiffs and has incriminating documents in his possession that will surely blow everything up. Clayton, played by Clooney, is not a litigator, but a fixer – someone who has the unique skill set to clean up all types of messes, from drunk driving offenses, to rough divorces, to the most recent mess with Arthur and U-North.

The fixer is a rich cinematic theme. From Harvey Keitel in *Pulp Fiction* to Jean Reno in *La Femme Nikita*, this is the type of person you want by your side in the middle of a crisis, someone to whom you gladly give yourself over when the wrong move can cost you your life or, at least, a few years in prison. Michael is particularly suited for this role: he is calm and reassuring, and knows how to look you in the eyes and keep it together while you're losing it. And he knows whom to call to get things done. It takes someone who's been through a few crises himself and who now leads a solitary life to dedicate himself to such janitorial work (which usually requires working nights and weekends). Indeed, it is the competence of the fixer that is so attractive. They deal with the political, social, legal, emotional, and psychological aspects of a crisis with precision, even as the clock keeps ticking. Michael is like one of those hard-boiled detectives in a Raymond Chandler novel who move effortlessly from snobbish dinner party to seedy bar to the dame's bedroom. This free movement from the top to the bottom of the class ladder is precisely why the detective served as a utopian figure

155

in modern fiction: the detective functioned to provoke the reader's desire to transcend the fixed structure of social class while, at the same time, flashing the false promise of such mobility.

But Michael is not the only competent character in the film. Sydney Pollack plays Marty Bach, the senior partner of the law firm, who oversees both a huge merger just about to go down and the U-North debacle through the reassuring bass tones of his authoritative voice. The assassins who kill Arthur work with surgical care as they inject him with poison between his toes so that it will look like a suicide. The underground poker game, to which Michael returns after a year off from gambling, is run with meticulous, ballet-like precision and via effortless silences among the Chinese dealers, elevator operators, and lookouts. Even Karen, who makes some wrong moves, is a highly competent lawyer who practices her speeches with the same painstaking attention to detail as she does when laying out her pantyhose before a crucial appeal to U-North's main shareholders. When she is forced to "fix" Arthur's destructive turn of commitment, she meets one of the assassins on the street. Not knowing how to give the order to kill Arthur, she listens to the assassin (Mr Verne) explain that he has some "good ideas" on how to handle the situation. Karen responds, "Okay." And Mr. Verne asks, "Is that 'okay' you understand or 'okay' proceed?" Again, the supreme attention to detail is striking and powerfully appealing.

Michael Clayton, the film, is also phenomenally competent. From the acting (too much affect in Arthur and not enough in Michael) to the cinematography (almost all shot with a color pallet of steely blues and grays) to the editing (which cross-cuts between the characters so that each supplements the others in a way that gets to the thing that exceeds the characters themselves, namely the system), the film rises to the top of the genre – and by genre we mean less the corporate crime film than the genre of Hollywood itself. And it is right at this pinnacle that we can best pinpoint the limits of Hollywood and, by extension, the limits of global capitalism. This is to say: *Michael Clayton* succeeds precisely by how it fails to overcome its own structural limits.

The first limit is the limit of competence. The fixer is attractive because it provokes the fantasy that capitalism can be managed – that with the right skill set, preparation, and connections every crisis can be averted. From genetically modified seeds that can outsmart a drought in advance to targeted drug therapy that turns formerly terminal illnesses (such as cancer and HIV) into chronic ones, there is a tremendous amount of desire invested in the possibilities of management, if not full-blown pre-emption. But the Real of capitalism cannot be managed and it is precisely this radical necessity of its eruptive logic that is most terrifying and beautiful. Cinematically, *Michael Clayton* cannot suspend its own reliance on formal competence. If it did, if its narrative went off the rails or its actors were less proficient, then it would no longer be a Hollywood film. Likewise, capitalism cannot suspend its own reliance on the formal categories that define its logic, such as commodity expansion and the logic of profit – itself a sort of political-economic competence. If it did, if its corporations didn't conduct elaborate cost–benefit analyses when deciding on whether to recall a faulty product and simply "did the right thing," then it would no longer be capitalism.

The second structural limit of *Michael Clayton* and capitalism is that of subjectivity. The film alludes to mental health at various moments, most directly in terms of Arthur's "episodes." When Michael is sent to Wisconsin to bring in Arthur, he loses him after Arthur escapes from the hotel room where they both spend the night. On the bathroom wall, Arthur scribbles a note for Michael: "make believe it's not just madness." When Michael catches up with Arthur back in New York, he tries to lure him back with the following monologue:

> If you're willing to start with that [that there's something chemical going on with you], then I'm willing to meet you halfway and say that "yes this situation sucks, U-North sucks." We can start with that. I'm telling you that you're crazy, that your behavior is out of control, but I'm telling you that you're right. You called it, we're janitors. I get it. But we came to this, Arthur, we made decisions, this didn't happen over night. You can't just give up. Say game over, I'm into miracles. Arthur, come on.

Is Arthur "right" about U-North and the whole interlinked system of corporate power because of his mental illness or in spite of it? Is there something about a late capitalist subjectivity that requires certain blind spots in order to be functional? And if one were to see clearly then would the truth be too brutal to handle – making one actually sick? Again, there is an analogy to Hollywood. If *Michael Clayton* were to expose itself so completely so that all of its formal components became the center of attention, then we would no longer be in Hollywood. For the Hollywood film to work, the viewer must not see its working parts too vividly or else it would be impossible to invest in the film enough to be moved by it. Of course, there are many Hollywood films that push this limit to the limit, but in the end these films, by their very cleverness and technical aplomb, invariably recuperate the Hollywood system itself. Likewise, capitalism requires a similar necessity of repression: the necessity to reproduce ideological symptoms that cannot be "cured," for if they were, the subject would be so radically different that he or she could not survive. Or to switch to a more political register: the revolutionary cannot completely overcome the existing ideological system or else they would lose the required connection to the majority of others, the very connection (and thus collectivity) upon which any revolution relies. And this returns us to purity, the seven theses, and globalization.

Krugman, Friedman, Florida, and Klein all call into question the flaws of contemporary global capitalism. Something needs to change in order for it to work more effectively. More or less regulation, more or less of a hegemonic role played by the United States, more or less trade – regardless of the argument, there is an assumption that with more common sense and education we can clean up capitalism in such a way that history will continue, the future will be saved, the nation will prevail, and the good people will win by doing the right thing. This assumption, which forms the positive core of the seven theses, forces political desire into a corner that effectively limits the imagination. To move in another direction, however, submits one to the trap of purity, to the charge that one is hypocritical and not true to the agreed-upon solutions that we're told present the only escape from the stark reality of the world. We argue otherwise and are in search of another path altogether. It is only by acting in light of these seven theses, not submitting to the current hopes placed in education, in the nation, and so on, that it is possible for us to move closer to this reality. And this eccentric path starts by imagining what comes after globalization. In the following section, the students we interview care very little for the seven theses. But they also seem uninterested in imagining what comes after globalization. How to get to the latter without embracing the former is the tightrope we are compelled to walk.

Notes

1. Wendy Brown, "Neo-liberalism and the End of Liberal Democracy," *Theory & Event* 7, no. 1 (2003): para. 9.
2. Slavoj Žižek, *First as Tragedy, Then as Farce* (New York: Verso, 2009), 5.
3. Robert Kagan, *The Return of History and the End of Dreams* (New York: Knopf, 2008), 3.
4. Kagan, *Return of History*, 97.
5. Fareed Zakaria, *The Post-American World* (New York: W.W. Norton, 2008), xx.
6. Zakaria, *Post-American World*, 36.
7. Ibid., 70.
8. Ibid., 78.
9. Ibid.
10. Ibid., 218.
11. Kagan, *Return of History*, 81–82.
12. Sarika Chandra, *Dislocalism: The Crisis of Globalization and the Remobilizing of Americanism*, unpublished manuscript.
13. We take the phrase in the title from Jamie Peck's excellent, "The Creativity Fix," *Eurozine*, June 28, 2007: www.eurozine.com/articles/2007-06-28-peck-en.html (accessed October 29, 2010). Originally published in *Fronesis* 24 (2007).
14. Karl Marx, "The German Ideology: Part 1," *The Marx–Engels Reader*, ed. Robert C. Tucker (New York: W.W. Norton, 1978), 160.
15. David Brooks, *Bobos in Paradise: The New Upper Class and How They Got There* (New York: Simon and Schuster, 2001), 10.
16. See *The Flight of the Creative Class* (New York: Harper Business 2005), in which he examines the global competition of states and cities to attract members of this class; *Cities and the Creative Class* (New York: Routledge 2004), which constitutes an elaboration of his description of the communities creative workers are attracted to and in which they

flourish; and *Who's Your City?: How the Creative Economy Is Making Where to Live the Most Important Decision of Your Life* (New York: Basic Books, 2008), which puts his analysis to use in the form of a city guide for members of the creative class.

17. Though the CCNC predates Florida's books, its growth and expansion since becoming a not-for-profit organization in 2002 has been enabled by the spread of the idea that city spending on culture supports economic development. The CCNC acts as advocate of and clearinghouse for ideas linking culture and economic development. For example, the January 2010 Creative City News reports on the investment of $5 million by the City of Woodstock in the creation of a new art gallery; the December 2009 newsletter includes stories on urban investments in culture in places such as Barrie and Collingwood, ON, Halifax, NS, and Barrie, ON.

18. Governments across the world have in recent years produced planning strategies for their cultural sector in relation to its economic impact, or have developed new departments of government to manage the economics of culture. To give a few examples: Winnipeg is concluding its year as Cultural Capital of Canada with the production of an arts and culture strategy document, "*Ticket to the Future*: The Economic Impact of the Arts and Creative Industries in Winnipeg." In the UK, the Creative & Cultural Skills unit of the national government announced £1.3 million to create 200 culture jobs for young people claiming unemployment benefits, including positions "such as theatre technician, costume and wardrobe assistant, community arts officer and business administrator." See www.thestage.co.uk/news/newsstory.php/26804/government-announces-13-million-fund (accessed October 29, 2010).

The action is just as great on the international level. Numerous international conferences focus on culture and economics, such as the annual Culturelink Conference (the third meeting of which was held in Zagreb, Croatia, in 2009) and the World Summit on the Arts (the fourth meeting held in Johannesburg in 2009). The recently released report of the Commonwealth Group on Culture and Development, a body established in 2009, links the achievement of development goals with the support of culture. And UNESCO's November 2009 World Report, "Investing in Cultural Diversity and Intercultural Dialogue," warns governments against cutting funding to culture during the current financial crisis, not just because it will impact on the issues contained in the report's title, but because such fiscal cost saving will have a deep impact on any possible financial recovery.

19. See Florida's review of Thomas Friedman's *The World is Flat,* "The World is Spiky," *Atlantic Monthly* (October 2005): 48–51.

20. Richard Florida, *The Rise of the Creative Class* (New York: Basic Books, 2002), 260.

21. Florida, *Rise of the Creative Class,* 250.

22. Ibid., 4.

23. Ibid., 31.

24. Ibid., 32.

25. Ibid., 190–211.

26. Ibid., 14.

27. Ibid., 320.

28. Ibid., 317.

29. Ibid., 37. The quotation Florida includes here is unattributed.

30. Ibid., 69.

31. Ibid., xiii. The number of times this claim is asserted is too frequent to cite, but take for instance statements such as these at opposite ends of the book: "Today's economy is fundamentally a Creative Economy" (44) and "creativity is the fundamental source of economic growth" (317).

32. Florida, *Rise of the Creative Class,* 21.

33. The critical importance of tolerance to managing the perpetuation of hegemony appears in numerous works in the genre of popular books on current affairs. See, for example, Amy Chua, *Day of Empire: How Hyperpowers Rise to Global Dominance – and Why They Fall* (New York: Doubleday 2007).

34. Florida, *Rise of the Creative Class,* xiii.

35. Ibid., xiii.

36. Ibid., 23.

37. Ibid., 262–263.

38. Ibid., 325.

39. Mobility is presumed to be a central characteristic of the Creative Class. They can go wherever they want, which is why cities have to make certain that they have the appropriate environs to attract them. Yet even in the case of certain members of the Super-Creative Core, this mobility is close to a fiction. For example, academics find it extremely difficult to move; the nature of their work means that they have to participate in

specific kinds of institutions (universities and colleges) that aren't found in the same proportion as institutions of private industry and many of which are located in smaller cities and towns. There's a reason why Durham, NC and State College, PA rank highly on his rankings of creative cities: it's not because they have a huge number of amenities (art, coffee houses, alternative music, etc.) that exist outside of work, but because the nature of the institutions that exist there render large numbers of PhDs (especially relative to population) immobile.

40. Florida, *Rise of the Creative Class*, 77.
41. Ibid., 88–101.
42. See, for instance, Jill Andresky Fraser, *White Collar Sweatshop* (New York: W.W. Norton, 2002); Christian Marazzi, *The Violence of Financial Capitalism* (Los Angeles: Semiotext(e), 2010); Andrew Ross, *Nice Work If You Can Get It: Life and Labor in Precarious Times* (New York: New York University Press, 2009); Juliet Schor, *The Overworked American: The Unexpected Decline of Leisure* (New York: Basic Books, 1993); and Tiziana Terranova, "Free Labor: Producing Culture for the Digital Economy," *Social Text* 18, no. 2 (2000): 33–58.
43. "The no-collar workplace is not being imposed on us from above; we are bringing it on ourselves . . . We do it because as creative people, it is a central part of who we are or want to be" (134).
44. Peter Bürger, *Theory of the Avant-garde*, trans. Michael Shaw (Minneapolis: University of Minnesota Press, 1985), 49.
45. Florida, *Rise of the Creative Class*, 13.
46. Ibid., 201.
47. Ibid., 191.
48. For an overview of the uses and abuses of creativity, see Rob Pope's enormously helpful *Creativity: Theory, History, Practice* (New York: Routledge, 2005).
49. Florida, *Rise of the Creative Class*, 46.
50. Andrew Ross, "The Mental Labour Problem," *Social Text* 63 (2000): 6.
51. Ibid., 11.
52. Paul Krugman, *The Return of Depression Economics and the Crisis of 2008* (New York: W.W. Norton & Co 2009), 24.
53. Section 2 of Hardt and Negri's *Multitude* (New York: Penguin, 2004) remains the most useful and compelling description of the long emergence of the common in and under capitalism.

54. "There is an aesthetic base component in human nature." Paolo Virno, "The Dismeasure of Art. An Interview with Paolo Virno," *Open* 17 (2009). Available at: www.skor.nl/article-4178-nl.html?lang=en (accessed October 29, 2010).

55. See Antonio Negri, *Insurgencies: Constituent Power and the Modern State*, trans. Maurizia Boscagli (Minneapolis: University of Minnesota Press, 2005).

56. The single reference to globalization in *The Great Reset* confirms that his ideas about creativity and innovation are situated within its general parameters: "As globalization has increased the financial return on innovation (by widening the consumer market), the pull of innovative places, which are already dense with highly talented workers, has only grown stronger." Florida, *The Great Reset* (Toronto: Random House Canada, 2010), 152.

57. Friedman's books to date are *From Beirut to Jerusalem* (New York: Anchor, 1989); *The Lexus and the Olive Tree: Understanding Globalization* (New York: Anchor, 2000); *Longitudes and Attitudes* (New York: Anchor, 2002); *The World Is Flat: A Brief History of the Twenty-First Century* (New York: Farrar, Straus and Giroux, 2005); and *Hot, Flat, and Crowded: Why We Need a Green Revolution – and How It Can Renew America* (New York: Farrar, Straus and Giroux, 2008).

58. Friedman, *The Lexus and the Olive Tree*, 7.

59. Ibid., 9.

60. Ibid., 9.

61. Friedman, *The World Is Flat*, 9.

62. Friedman, *The Lexus and the Olive Tree*, 7.

63. David Harvey, *The Condition of Postmodernity: An Enquiry into the Origins of Cultural Change* (Oxford: Blackwell, 1991).

64. Friedman, *The Lexus and the Olive Tree*, ix.

65. Ibid., 109.

66. Karl Marx, "The German Ideology: Part 1," *The Marx-Engels Reader*, ed. Robert C. Tucker (New York: W.W. Norton, 1978), 172.

67. See David Bell's "Does This Man Deserve Tenure?" *The New Republic*, September 6, 2010. Bell criticizes the holes and gaps that exist in Mark C. Taylor's *Crisis of Campus: A Bold Plan for Reforming Our Colleges and Universities*. The problem? The deformations and mutations of ideas as they grow from an 800-word op-ed piece into a 50 000-word book. He

writes, "far from reinforcing the original logic and evidence, the new accretions of text only strain them further, while smothering the original provocations under thick layers of padded anecdote, pop sociology and oracular pronouncement. Call the syndrome Friedmanitis, after a prominent early victim, the *New York Times* columnist Tom Friedman." Friedmanitis is possible only through rapid and unending appeals to common sense. Available at: www.tnr.com/book/review/mark-taylor-crisis-campus-colleges-universities (accessed November 1, 2010).

68. Friedman, *The Lexus and the Olive Tree*, 30.
69. Ibid., 31.
70. Lionel Gossman. "Anecdote and History," *History and Theory* 42 (2003): 167–168.
71. Joel Fineman, "The History of the Anecdote," in *The New Historicism*, ed. H. Aram Veeser (New York and London: Routledge, 1989), 49–76. Fineman goes onto write, "The anecdote produces the effect of the real, the occurrence of contingency, by establishing an event within and yet without the framing context of historical successivity." Gossman also quotes this on pp. 163–164 of his essay.
72. Bertolt Brecht, "Anecdotes of Mr. Keuner," *Tales from the Calendar*, trans. Yvonne Kapp and Michael Hamburger (London: Methuen & Co., 1961), 110–124.
73. Brecht, "Anecdotes of Mr. Keuner," 121–122.
74. Paul Krugman and Maurice Obstfeld, *International Economics: Theory and Policy*, 8th edn (Boston: Addison Wesley, 2008).
75. The two papers usually cited as the first elaborations of Krugman's "new trade theory" and "new economic geography" are, respectively, "Increasing Returns, Monopolistic Competition, and International Trade," *Journal of International Economics* 9.4 (1979): 469–479, and "Increasing Returns and Economic Geography," *Journal of Political Economy* 99.2 (1991): 483–499.
76. "Enemies of the WTO: Bogus Arguments Against the World Trade Organization," *The Great Unraveling* (New York: W.W. Norton & Company, 2004), 367–372.
77. Paul Krugman, "Global Schmobal," *The Great Unraveling: Losing Our Way in the New Century* (New York: W.W. Norton, 2004), 367–368.
78. Ibid., 370.
79. Paul Krugman, *The Conscience of a Liberal* (New York: W.W. Norton, 2009), 265.

80. Krugman, *Conscience of a Liberal*, 4.
81. Ibid., 4.
82. Ibid., 6.
83. Ibid., 7.
84. Ibid., 7.
85. Ibid., 10–11.
86. Ibid., 145.
87. Ibid., 163.
88. Ibid., 172.
89. Ibid., 182.
90. Ibid., 193.
91. Ibid., 115.
92. Ibid., x.
93. Paul Krugman, *The Return of Depression Economics and the Crisis of 2008* (New York: W.W. Norton & Company, 2009), 133.
94. Krugman, *Return of Depression Economics*, 10.
95. Ibid., 14.
96. Ibid., 102.
97. Ibid., 163.
98. Ibid., 136.
99. Ibid., 186.
100. Ibid., 103.
101. Ibid., 113.
102. Ibid., 114.
103. Ibid., 118.
104. "Most, probably, of our decisions to do something positive, the full consequences of which will be drawn out over many days to come, can only be taken as the result of animal spirits – a spontaneous urge to action rather than inaction, and not as the outcome of a weighted average of quantitative benefits multiplied by quantitative probabilities." John Maynard Keynes, *General Theory of Employment Interest and Money* (London: Macmillan, 1936), 161. See also Christian Marazzi, *The Violence of Finance Capitalism* (New York: Semiotext(e), 2010), especially chapter 4.
105. Robert Kurz, "World Power and World-Money: The Economic Function of the US Military-Machine within Global Capitalism and the Background of the New Financial Crisis," trans. Imre Szeman and Matt MacLellan, *Mediations* 25 no. 1 (2009–2010), forthcoming.

106. How might Krugman react to the historicization of economics? Take, for instance, Immanuel Wallerstein's description of the roots of the contemporary organization of academic social science: "From the dominant liberal ideology of the nineteenth century which argued that state and market, politics and economics, were analytically separate ... Society was adjured to keep them separate, and scholars studies them separately. Since there seemed to be many realities that apparently were neither in the domain of the market [economics] nor in that of the state [political science], these realities were placed in a residual grab-bag which took as compensation the grand name of sociology ... Finally, since there were people beyond the realm of the civilized world, ... the study of such people encompasses special rules and special training, which took on the somewhat polemical name of anthropology." Immanuel Wallerstein, *The Essential Wallerstein* (New York: New Press, 2000), 133.

107. Michael Denning, *Culture in the Age of Three Worlds* (New York: Verso, 2004), 27.

108. Naomi Klein, *No Logo: Taking Aim at the Brand Bullies* (Toronto: Vintage Canada, 2000).

109. Naomi Klein, *The Shock Doctrine: The Rise of Disaster Capitalism* (Toronto: Vintage Canada, 2008).

110. Klein, *Shock Doctrine*, 4.

111. Ibid., 4.

112. Ibid., 7.

113. Ibid., 7.

114. *Democracy Now*, September 24, 2007, *Alan Greenspan vs. Naomi Klein on the Iraq War, Bush's Tax Cuts, Economic Populism, Crony Capitalism, and More*. Available at: www.democracynow.org/2007/9/24/alan_greenspan_vs_naomi_klein_on (accessed November 3, 2010).

115. Klein, *Shock Doctrine*, 24.

116. An earlier version of these paragraphs on a "non-moralizing critique of capitalism" can be found in Cazdyn's *The Already Dead: The New Time of Politics, Culture and Illness* (Durham: Duke University Press, forthcoming).

117. Matt Taibbi, "The Great American Bubble Machine," *Rolling Stone*, April 5, 2010; Jeremy Scahill, *Blackwater: The Rise of the World's Most Powerful Mercenary Army* (New York: Nation Books, 2008).

118. This delineation of crisis and disaster is taken from Cazdyn's "Disaster, Crisis, Revolution," in *Disastrous Consequences*, ed. Eric Cazdyn, *South Atlantic Quarterly* 106, no. 4 (2007): 647–662.

119. WikiLeaks published this "Afghan War Diary" or, as the archive is also called, "The War Logs," on July 25, 2010. Prior to releasing these documents on its web site, WikiLeaks made the records available to the *Guardian*, the *New York Times*, and *Der Spiegel*, which published many of the records on that same day.

120. WikiLeaks. Available at: http://wikileaks.org/wiki/WikiLeaks: About.

121. The White House, Office of the Press Secretary, "Press Briefing by Press Secretary Robert Gibbs," July 26, 2010. "And, again, I think it's – let's be clear, and I want to make sure that I'm clear on this – based on the fact that there's nothing – there's no broad new revelations in this, our concern isn't that people might know that we're concerned about safe havens in Pakistan, or that we're concerned, as we are, about civilian casualties. Lord, all you need is a laptop and a mouse to figure that out, or 50 cents or $1.50, depending on which newspaper you buy. I don't think that is, in a sense, top secret. But what generally governs the classification of these documents are names, operations, personnel, people that are cooperating – all of which if it's compromised has a compromising effect on our security." Available at: www.whitehouse.gov/the-press-office/press-briefing-press-secretary-robert-gibbs-7262010 (accessed November 3, 2010).

122. *Democracy Now*, transcripts from July 28, 2010.

123. *Democracy Now*, transcripts from July 28, 2010.

124. *Democracy Now*, "WikiLeaks Founder Julian Assange: 'Transparent Government Tends to Produce Just Government,'" July 28, 2010. www.democracynow.org/2010/7/28/wikileaks_founder_julian_assange_transparent_government (accessed November 3, 2010).

125. Estimated by WikiLeak researchers. See *Democracy Now*, "Julian Assange Responds to Increasing US Government Attacks on WikiLeaks," August 3, 2010.

126. Klein, *Shock Doctrine*, 31–32.

127. J.A. Hobson, *Imperialism: A Study* (London: George Allen & Unwin, 1902).

128. Joel Bakan, *The Corporation: The Pathological Pursuit of Profit and Power* (New York: Free Press, 2005).

129. *It's a Wonderful Life*, dir. Frank Capra, Liberty Films, 1946.
130. Jacques Rancière, *The Emancipated Spectator*, trans. Gregory Elliot (New York: Verso, 2009), 33.
131. See Fredric Jameson's Introduction to *Archaeologies of the Future* ("Introduction: Utopia Now"). Jameson writes, "For even if we can no longer adhere with an unmixed conscience to this unreliable form, we may now have recourse to that ingenious political slogan Sartre invented to find his way between a flawed communism and an even more unacceptable anti-communism." *Archaeologies of the Future* (New York: Verso, 2005), xvi.

Part III
The Global Generation

a. Next Generation

We probably don't need to state the obvious: there's been an enormous amount written about globalization over the past two decades. Much of this has consisted of debates between academics over what constitutes it; much of the rest has been an attempt by politicians, policy makers, and political and economic elites to put the concept of globalization to use for their own ends. It is important to view globalization as an ideological project and as a system of belief that, as we have argued, makes a claim about the inevitability of the present and, as such, the future as well. A simple question one needs to ask is whether this belief system has its intended effect, shaping the ways in which we think about today and tomorrow – that is, whether it manages to convince us that the problems of the present can be solved by the solutions of the past; or, that after globalization comes ... more globalization, whether imagined as system, fate, or ideology.

In order to better understand how and to what degree the ideas and ideals associated with globalization have found their way into con-temporary discourse, we conducted a series of interviews with

After Globalization, First Edition. Eric Cazdyn and Imre Szeman.
© 2011 Eric Cazdyn and Imre Szeman. Published 2011 by Blackwell Publishing Ltd.

university students around the word. We carried out 60 interviews in six countries: Colombia, Croatia, Germany, Hungary, Russia, and Taiwan. Our aim was to see what globalization meant for those who came of age in the era of globalization: those for whom there has only ever been a period *after* the Cold War, dominated politically by the United States and defined economically by a capitalism left unchallenged.

Why students? And why these countries? University students are the most likely people to come into contact with the discourse of globalization. They are also a segment of the national population who have one of the largest stakes in it, as they describe the coordinates of the world that they inhabit and outline their potential to move within it. In the nations in which we conducted our interviews – and indeed, in most countries in the world – university education continues to be an imagined means of class advancement. Whether they swallow whole the ideology of globalization or challenge its economic and political mystifications, students of the global generation have to think about the implications of globalization discourses. This is true of students studying across a wide range of disciplines in the human sciences, from languages to sociology, from political science to business. Though we found varying degrees of interest in some of the questions that we asked, every student had an opinion on globalization – what it meant and what its significance was for them and their countries.

As for the countries: as soon as one proposes not only to conduct a survey on globalization, but to do it in a global comparative perspective, the question of which countries – why some and not others – cannot help but arise. If our aim was to capture ideas about globalization around the world, why not make use of a tool like the Pew Global Attitudes Survey, a survey that was cited frequently by media in the years following 9/11 to gauge shifts in opinion about the United States and its actions in the world? Why not undertake a study of more than six nations, or conduct interviews in countries thought to be more directly affected by globalization, such as Brazil, India, and China, nations in the Middle East and Africa, or even the United States itself? These are legitimate questions. We wanted to avoid starting from assumptions about which countries have been most directly affected by globalization as a guide to where to find our interview subjects. After all, one of the presumptions of the discourse of globalization is that once the global era begins, *everyone everywhere* belongs to it: older ideas of developed and underdeveloped, advanced and belated are suspended. The countries we chose to study include "friends" of the United States (Colombia), a former and once again emerging superpower (Russia), a respected middle power at the center of the Cold War (Germany), and a number of smaller countries struggling to define their national identities and build their economies as the geopolitical valences of the globe shift around them (Hungary, Croatia, and Taiwan). There is no claim to comprehensiveness or to some complete view of the planet; at the same time, conducting in-depth interviews in these places opens up much-needed vantage points on globalization as ideology and reality that is missing from most of the literature on the subject.

b.   From Anti-Americanism to Globalization

The interviews were carried out in 2006–2009; each interview averaged one hour in length. We used a set series of questions for each interview, though we also followed up on issues that arose over the course of our discussions and deviated from the established order of questions, as necessary. Our interviews *were not* focused directly on globalization as a topic. Rather, we framed our work as a study on contemporary anti-Americanism, as well as a number of issues related to the contemporary moment: globalization, capitalism, contemporary culture, the problems and prospects of the countries in which we were doing our interviews, as well as the outlook of each individual student on their own future possibilities.

Although these interviews have been instrumental in shaping this project, we do not privilege them as sacred source material. And although we set out with a rigorous set of methodological concerns (around confidentiality, student selection, documentation), we still treat the interviews less as ethnographic texts than as *literary* ones. This is

173

to say that the students' comments (like the works of the figures in the previous section and like our own prose) are symptoms of globalization, expressing in conscious and unconscious ways (in form as well as content) diverse ways of coming to terms with the world. By "literary" we do not mean to call the interviews fiction, or to smooth over each subject's idiosyncrasies in the service of a structural analysis of so many types and characters. We mean, rather, that the forms of narrativization, the use of language, and the attention to temporal tense (durational and non-durational aspects of representing past, present, and future, for example) are as significant to their representations of the globe as their more concrete arguments about the world.

We started our interviews at a time when anti-Americanism was rampant; by the time of our last interviews, in February 2009, this anti-American feeling seemed to have disappeared entirely. The reason is obvious: the election of Barack Obama in November 2008, which students anticipated in 2008 and mentioned directly in the interviews in Colombia in 2009. This reversal is troubling, if only for the rapidity with which a set of affective and cognitive dispositions can change their valence from negative to positive without evidence of any substantive institutional change other than the shifting around of seats (i.e., change of elected officials) within an existing political structure. In President George Bush's second term in office (2005–2008), it seemed that the United States was becoming associated with the practices and policies of globalization – the extension of political, economic, and cultural power under the guise of an historical force – to such a degree that anti-globalization sentiments were becoming mixed up with anti-American ones. So we wanted to enter into discussion of globalization by proposing to talk first about anti-Americanism, in order to see if the connection between the two was as strong as we intuited it was.

There are a huge number of works that have been written about anti-Americanism, primarily by authors in the disciplines of history, sociology, and political science.[1] The tendency has been for studies that address anti-Americanism (or more broadly, attitudes toward the United States) from the vantage point of a single nation; French and

Canadian studies of anti-Americanism and the vicissitudes of the idea of America both within the United States and at home are especially common, with a number of new volumes appearing in the wake of the shifting attitudes toward the United States after 9/11.[2] Against the backdrop of globalization, new volumes appeared that focused on anti-Americanism in comparative perspective, usually in the form of a collection of essays dealing with different regions or nations.[3] This focus on anti-Americanism across nations introduces some new depth to the phenomenon. However, the actual insights provided about these sentiments seem to have remained much the same. There are studies that try to explain and justify anti-Americanism and those that acknowledge its existence – even if they might think it is misplaced or misguided ("*this* is why people are anti-American") sentiment – and offer ways to manage it for geopolitical reasons. Others provide accounts of shifts in its character and development over time – an accounting that reveals interesting changes in the nature of US power in the world – or a taxonomy of the levels at which anti-Americanism operates (attitudes toward the US government, US mass culture, etc.). The feelings of opposition to the global hegemon, whatever their character, don't seem to be especially surprising; what's missing in all of these studies is another aspect of anti-Americanism that we wanted to explore and understand – the way anti-Americanism (and the lack of anti-Americanism) could be understood as an engagement (however unconscious) with the ideological limits of globalization. In other words, given the "time limit" of globalization, we've come to understand anti-Americanism as a placeholder, as a symptom of thinking an "after" to globalization when this very thought is forbidden, if not unthinkable.

Since at least the time of the Vietnam War, and certainly in the wake of the post-9/11 wars in Afghanistan and Iraq, anti-Americanism has constituted a form of *negative* belonging – a weak form, but, nevertheless, a way of affirming one's place in the world by identifying what one is *not*. We know what it is like to affirm an identity, and what the negative (exclusions and paternalisms) and positive (feelings of connectedness and group belonging) consequences of such affirmations are. But what does it mean to *deny* such an identity? What is the form

175

and content of such denial? Can, for instance, one be anti-American and not affirm one's own nationalist belonging? (Or, for that matter, can one be an American who is anti-American but not self-hating?) By asking our interview subjects to talk about anti-Americanism, we were in part probing the kinds of group identifications and connections that they felt at the time. If we had just asked directly about globalization – a concept that already implies to many the end of just such identifications in favor of some abstract internationalism, whether desired or unwanted – these ideas and ideals would have been missed.

Anti-Americanism also constitutes a *map* of larger political circumstances. In most cases, the content of anti-Americanism is much less important than its form. Caught in a sound bite on a network television news broadcast, an expression of anti-Americanism on the streets of some foreign (read: non-US) city can sound irrational, full of hatred toward an entity that only exists as an abstraction: America – something other than and yet inclusive of the US government, its leaders, its citizens, its foreign policy, its institutions, its culture, even the (post) modernity with which it has come to be allegorically associated. But one can read too much significance into a sound bite and certainly one can read it incorrectly. As the responses of the students in our study show, such indiscriminate or unjustified anti-Americanism (an opposition to anything and everything American) is rarely felt. Rather, it is clear that anti-Americanism constitutes a ready-to-hand map of the power in the contemporary world, a first-order explanation of networks of political force and influence. It is a map that connects physical and economic power to cultural forces. Globalization now offers the same kind of map: it has become a shorthand term for the way the world is now and how it is likely to be for at least the near future. Globalization processes, however, also have a tendency to transform political forces into a force of history, or even of nature. There are no dominant actors in globalization; it is not led or shaped by any group or state; it simply *is*. This is part of its ideological power. Anti-Americanism might seem very much out of step with the breathless analyses of the political present and future that have poured forth in recent years, a politics shaped by concepts and theories that insist on the *new*. It seems archaic in comparison to everything associated with the global, a term and a sentiment connected to an earlier moment of cultural and economic nationalism, fiscal dramas about development through import substitution, and so on. However, if one wants to comprehend how power is understood, investigating anti-Americanism helps to expose the organization of the world during the era of globalization in a way that taking the topic of globalization head on simply doesn't. At a minimum, anti-Americanism throws globalization into new relief, not just bringing to light the latter's ideological function but also causing one to consider more closely just what (if anything) changed at the moment of 1989.

Let us be clear. By approaching globalization through the topos of anti-Americanism, our intention was not to prejudge the ways in which our interviewees understood globalization – to name it in advance, in other words, as a ruse of political power. We wanted, rather, to get students to tell us about the way that they feel the world works, how ideas of globalization fit into the operation of the planet, and what this means for both planetary futures and their own future to come. As we discussed in Part I, in the final years of the Bush administration, anti-Americanism became part of discussion of globalization in ways we felt we could not avoid. We were not expecting from the students – and did not get – an echo of playwright Harold Pinter's harsh comments about the United States in his Nobel Prize acceptance speech in 2005, in which he described it as (amongst other things) "brutal, indifferent, scornful and ruthless ... [and] also very clever."[4] We were much more interested in an interrogation of the views – of what we have described as a kind of hegemonic "common sense" – informing New York columnist James Traub's article *anticipating* Pinter's comments.[5] Titled "Their Highbrow Hatred of Us," the article describes the Nobel laureate's politics as being "so extreme that they're almost impossible to parody."[6] Pinter imagines the Iraq War as being about control over resources – the latest in a long list of foreign (mis)adventures arising from the United States' hegemonic impulses – and described the US bombing campaign in Kosovo as "a criminal act." Traub points out:

These views are hardly unfamiliar in the United States; you can hear them on any major university campus. Among public intellectuals or

177

literary figures, however, it is hard to think of anyone save Noam Chomsky and Gore Vidal who would not choke on Pinter's bile. But the situation is very different throughout Europe, where the anti-American left is far more intellectually respectable.

He continues:

All this talk about "resistance" and "antifascism" betrays the origins of this virulent strain of anti-Americanism: support for the "liberation" struggles in China, Cuba, Vietnam, Zimbabwe and elsewhere. Iraq, in other words, is being superimposed on the old "anti-imperialist" grid, with disgruntled Baathists playing the role of the Vietcong. You might have thought that the end of the cold war would have knocked the starch out of this Manichaean struggle, but the far left has been unwilling to surrender the exhilarating moral clarity of that era.

Traub understands that "no nation as dominant as America now is will be accepted as a benevolent actor; indeed, no nation so easily available to advance its own interests will act benevolently most of the time." Indeed, he admits that the United States could help its case by accepting international rules and institutions, such as the International Criminal Court, which most countries in the world have ratified and take as binding. At one and the same time, Traub suggests that there is some merit to anti-American sentiments, but is also at pains to treat the views of Pinter, Noam Chomsky, Gore Vidal, and others as not just mistaken, but irrational, a joke: the unrealistic, misguided leftist views one might expect to find on university campuses, but which students plunged into the realpolitik of the world manage to overcome, even if their professors seem unable to do so.

The best way for the United States to address such sentiments, according to this cartoon, is to act better in the world. Who could disagree? The real issue is, of course, *why* the United States does not do so; there is a reason why hegemons don't take courses in ethics, which Traub seems to miss entirely. Moralism is no substitute for structural analysis. But this is almost always obscured in the common-sense rendering of the world as a place made up of good and bad actors, whose motivations, successes, and unfortunate missteps can easily be comprehended. Anti-Americanism is illegitimate, Traub suggests, and then argues that it is perfectly legitimate, which is why one needs to take action to address it. At the heart of such contradictions is a map of the world that we see repeated within the official discourses of the policy elite: the world needs desperately to change, but only by becoming more like it already is – or *could* become, if only it could approach a state of its own perfection (think here: Zakaria's post-American American capitalism, Krugman's liberal capitalism, Friedman's green capitalism, Florida's people capitalism, or Klein's mixed capitalism).

Is this how the next generation sees the world as well? As a world held captive by these contradictions – contradictions that render logic and critical analysis as bad form or a kind of left extremism and that can be dismissed for not abiding by the rules of common sense?

c. A Map of the World

Any study that looks at countries separated by history, geography, and economic circumstance (just to begin with) will generate differences that cannot be overlooked. The attention of the students whom we interviewed in Taiwan is to China in the north – not as a site of geopolitical tension, but as a place in which they might be able to find employment after completing their studies. Germans view Europe from the vantage point of cosmopolitans who have the entire space of the continent within which to move; for them, national affiliations have diminished everywhere such that Europe comes before home and country. For Hungarian and Croatian students, the idea of Europe does offer new possibilities, though for them it is the chance at financial security and stability, should they be fortunate enough to leave their countries for more economically fertile ground. Unsurprisingly, Colombian and Russian students view the world from yet other perspectives. Such differences are to be expected.

What is perhaps more surprising are the *similarities* found across the six countries. Across different types of universities (public and private), distinct fields of study (business, philosophy, anthropology, sociology,

179

etc.), age groups (from 18 to 30), and socioeconomic status (from lower classes to upper-middle classes), what struck us repeatedly were the shared concerns and outlook of the students on the world into which they are about to emerge as participants and decision makers. The similarities are not more significant than the differences, but we have chosen to emphasize the similarities and organize our speculations around them. This strategy requires a certain resistance to what might be called an area studies or even cultural approach, in which scholarly attention to historical detail reveals how views coming from one place relate more to that place's unique past than to any shared and more general forces. In other words, the emphasis on difference usually leads to a vertical study that ultimately reveals why it is erroneous to draw such seemingly obvious connections among contemporaneous phenomena. On the other hand, the emphasis on similarity usually leads to a horizontal study that ultimately reveals why it is equally erroneous to draw such seemingly obvious distinctions. It's not too difficult to imagine where this leads: for every argument made about global similarities, the orthodox historian is right there to dismiss it, to show why the lack of any attention to deep history compromises such horizontal speculation. Likewise, for every argument made about differences, the orthodox sociologist is right there to dismiss it, to show why the specificity of the present compromises such vertical speculation.

We are not arguing that one way is necessarily better than the other. And we acknowledge that both approaches have their possibilities and limits, not to mention that each approach is already shot through with the other and that the very binary of vertical and horizontal analyses itself is unstable. Still, at this moment of globalization discourse, we find it much more intellectually and politically productive to stress the horizontal approach. This is to say that the emphasis on similarity or difference is itself dialectical and contingent on specific historical imperatives during which the emphasis is made. There were powerful political reasons to emphasize difference at earlier moments. To take just one example, in the 1970s and 1980s certain literary scholars began to emphasize difference as a strategic political act.[7] By arguing that the non-Western prose narrative should not be so quickly identified with the Western novel (as it was so often in Asian and African studies and as revealed by the obligatory blurbs on the back of so many translated non-Western works – "just like Dostoyevsky," "the next Faulkner"), appeals to universality were exposed as nothing more than thinly veiled rationales for domination. Within area and literary studies at the time, to delink and emphasize difference, therefore, was one way to expose the violence implicit in modernization theory. By the 1990s, however, the emphasis on difference had lost its progressive edge and turned into a reactionary form of humanities-based criticism, one that argues for uniqueness and radical difference in a way that meets up not only with neoliberal versions of multiculturalism but with the most insidious neo-nativist discourses. The problem now becomes how to think similarity without forgetting the sordid history of so much universalist desire.

Indeed, the most profound similarity among the students we interviewed was in the lack of affect they presented when articulating their individual and national paralysis. They were, quite simply, "cool" about the state of the world and how broken it seemed. But this coolness was not fueled by irony or sarcasm. This is not to suggest that they were content or satisfied, but only that they seemed to be lacking in the very histrionics that we located in the critics analyzed in Part II. Instead of dismissing this weak affect due to so much apathy and the depoliticizing effects of global capitalism, we cannot help but wonder if there is not something radical in it – something that not only alerts us to our own limitations, but that also contains the seeds of a much more radical subjectivity.

The questions that we posed to the students resulted in a wide range of answers – too rich and wide to summarize in any easy way, and certainly deserving of the broader comparative analysis we offer here. Before passing onto a discussion of some of the key points raised in the interviews, it is worth noting three main themes that arose from these 60 discussions that speak directly to the issues that we have been discussing in this book:

1. *The Way Things Are:* The students seem to have little *explicit* interest in the discourses of liberal capitalism that we discuss and

analyze in Part II of the book. When they do have some interest or express some knowledge of these discourses, they see it as a discourse of elites that has little to do with them. The students whom we interviewed almost all had excellent English-language skills and were studying at the university level (some at universities from which the national political class is typically drawn, such as National Taiwan University and Universidad de los Andes in Colombia). In fact, we were prepared to speak to the students in languages other than English (with a translator or with our own respective language skills), but this was, sometimes to our disappointment, not required – no doubt, another unmistakable symptom of globalization. Yet they seemed to have little idea of the work of Thomas Friedman or Paul Krugman, with whom one might have expected them to come into contact during their studies at some point, whether in the original or in translation.

This is not to say, however, that the students do not embody the ideology expressed in these works. The *common sense* view of the world that shapes these students' viewpoints, understandings, and expectations of the world are in fact to a large degree those we see expressed in and exemplified by US liberal discourse. As citizens of a post-communist world, they live in a post-ideological era. They do not have to be convinced about the dominant way of doing things, since there is nothing but the present: socialism is as quaint an idea to them as the era of kings and queens. It is not the case that they need to be persuaded that capitalism is the best form of economic organization: it is simply what is. The students are aware that, unfortunately, capitalism of necessity produces injustice. Their view is that states should address these injustices through social programs – an *ethical* injunction more than a political one, and one named more as a hope than an expectation that their own governments will act in the appropriate way, whether due to the corruption and incompetence of leaders, or because of the constraints and restrictions – mainly financial ones – that being in a global system has placed on national decision making. With the exception of the students interviewed in Germany, these students know that there is something amiss with this common sense. Since they live in countries without strong welfare systems, or with social systems that are under threat as a result of economic and competitive pressures (read: lower taxes for the rich), the world seems an uncertain and threatening place. The students both believe the fantasy of a liberal capitalist system that can if configured correctly benefit all, and don't believe it at all; with a lack of alternative narratives, the current geopolitical configuration appears to them as the given order of things.

2. *The Way Things Work:* When asked to provide an outline of the way in which the world is organized – that is, who has the power and influence to direct and shape developments not just in their own country, but on a global scale – students generally provided an astute rendering of the world. In virtually every case, students refused an easy acceptance of anti-Americanism or globalization as names for the present order of things. Anti-Americanism was divided into opinions concerning US foreign policy, US values and society, the products of American culture, and so on. Disappointment or displeasure about US foreign policy – a universally held position, it seems – had little relation or connection to other ways it is imagined that the United States shapes or influences the globe. Anxieties about cultural imperialism via the spread of American cinema, television, or music – a strong feeling amongst earlier generations of students – is relatively muted, if not entirely absent. The idea that culture can be a politics by other means is understood, but not really taken very seriously.

As for globalization? We were surprised by the degree to which it was associated narrowly with economics, that is, with the sense that it signifies that the globe is now integrated into a single economic system. This was expressed by all and accepted without question as the given state of affairs. The answers given with respect to globalization were of a kind with those given in response to our questions about other concepts naming large systems, such as capitalism, democracy, and anti-Americanism. Students were careful to show themselves to be reasonable, offering no strong statements, but falling back on an enumeration of positives and negatives. Globalization brings the world together, which means

183

less control by their own nations over policy making; on the other hand, the fact that the world is smaller means that they can potentially exploit overseas opportunities. Globalization means that there is more competition than ever before; on the other hand, it also means that they can see more, read more, experience more from other parts of the world than ever before. There were no ideologues in the group of 60 students whom we interviewed. But this careful balancing of pros and cons meant that there were no strongly held opinions either. Again and again, we had the sense of speaking with smart, insightful students, who were cautious about taking a position other than one that affirms the present and its operations, if in a slightly critical way.

3. *What Might Be Done:* Despite being able to offer an overview or sketch of global power, and despite their own subject positions as nascent elites, the students seemed to look at the world as if from the outside – as observers more than active participants. The general view expressed by most, if not all, was that the systems through which life activity is produced on the planet are too large for them to have any effect on it. Political opinions were surprisingly muted; the political class was seen as being comprised of a distant group of actors who were mainly in it for themselves. This is seen as regrettable, but also what one can expect for official politics, which is part of the reason the students avoid it. As for the future? Since the students didn't believe that there was much that anyone could do to amend or ameliorate the state of things, they mainly felt that it would be much like the present, perhaps somewhat worse. Under the circumstances, what might be done is for each of them individually to try to improve their own conditions (and perhaps the situation of their families) to whatever degree possible. Education was seen as a means to this end, though hardly a guarantee of a positive outcome in a world imagined as having once offered more stable and certain pathways through social life.

We are aware that the context of the interview and the direction of our questions may have generated some of the responses we received.

And we are cautious about making grand statements about generational differences, especially ones that might frame a younger generation as lacking in some essential quality (supposedly) possessed by those generations which preceded it. It is analytically suspect to indict a generation of students on the basis of some identified absence, especially an ethical or political one. At a minimum, one could demand to have the grounds on which one determines this lack or absence explained and identified, which would show soon enough the claim to be normative more than analytic.

Having said all this, what did the global generation look like to us? Astute and lacking in cynicism; aware of the world's problems, but without any sense of how they might be ameliorated; uncertain about the future, and so reliant on the common-sense ideology of liberalism that underpins globalization to paint it for them. And so committed to the present that they cannot even begin to imagine any future defined by an "after" to the present.

In order to give some more tangible feeling to the shape and structure of their views – so unlike the youthful subjects imagined by Friedman, Florida, Krugman, or Klein – we provide here two points of entry into the interviews we conducted. First, we provide some examples of the responses we received from students on some of the main areas in which we were interested: nationalism, anti-Americanism and geopolitics, globalization, contemporary cultural politics, capitalism, and the future. Through these examples, we hope to capture both the general sentiments expressed by the students as a group *and* allow for some of the differences that we heard to come through. Second, we offer narrative case study "biogeographies" of individual student interviews – three distinct positions on the world that give further shape and substance to the claims that we make and findings that we describe above.

1 National sentiments

Globalization is famously said to be about the end of the nation. Perhaps this is the case if one once imagined the nation as the sole register within which political and economic decisions were

185

considered and made. In terms of individual, subjective identification with a community, for the students in our interviews the nation remains *the* space to which one belongs and within which one's life and life expectations operate. The global generation is also a national one. The history of the nation is an especially powerful political form of identification; after the family, it remains the primary manner in which we imagine collectivity. If the nation is an "imagined community" (in Benedict Anderson's memorable phrase[8]), it is one which has over time assumed an undeniable solidity through the institutions and structures that give it form: citizenship, schooling (from daily recitals of the national anthem to the national histories one consumes in textbooks), import/export schemas, communications systems (Anderson's novels and newspapers, but television and the internet, too), political and legal frameworks, and all manner of quotidian practices. (That this list bears a resemblance to Althusser's ideological state apparatuses should come as no surprise.[9]) Students read their lives within the nation; and it is the fate of their nation that concerns them more than the state of the globe or the actions of the United States. At the same time, the distinction between the national and the global is not so rigid for the students. Indeed, it is precisely the strength of the national *together with* the solidifying power of the global in terms of identity formation that we find particularly distinct about the current moment. This is only a contradiction if one expects the power of the national to fall relative to the rise of the global. But it is the change of *the relation itself* between the national and the global (not the relative power of the one or the other) that is most significant. And it is at the exact point of this changed relation where the students find themselves, and that is most meaningfully expressed in their various responses.

This being said, what do they feel about their nations? Though each has different ideas about what ails their nation, they fall within a cluster of related points. Social inequality, the gap between rich and poor, a specific lack of opportunity for students, and abuses of power by politicians. Official systems of all kinds are seen as wanting and in need of fixing. Some of these problems are caused by relations to the outside, but, in general, students see their national situations as in need of national (not global, or international) amelioration. One new collectivity seems to have real force and meaning: Europe, especially when understood as a new mode of social organization in competition with the model promulgated globally by the United States.[10]

They are first Hungarians, everybody. First they are Hungarians, then Europeans. Media does not help in that respect because very often, especially in tabloid newspapers, you see headlines that separate Hungary from Europe. I think that's really bad; it does not educate the population at all. You see sentences like, "Europe is doing well, but not Hungary." (Hungarian student)

Nowadays it is customary to pretend there are no pressing social and political problems facing our country; rather, it is customary to say that we have reached a certain level of stability. It is therefore very difficult to extract any information about the actual problems from what we are officially told; although on a practical, day-to-day personal level one cannot fail to notice that such problems do indeed exist. One is also surprised by the fact that these problems are not being addressed.

To give some examples, I can cite issues that I have experience with: issues related to social aid and security programs. First of all, the mere existence of socially unprotected groups of people is a problem in itself. Second of all, the structure of the social aid services is flawed: very often one finds that, in practice, these services do not help people, but rather only aggravate their situation. And that's without going into too much detail. (Russian student)

In Taiwanese society, some places are still very traditional. If you become a social activist, then people around you will blame you because they think you create a mess or chaotic condition. They don't want to protest. Sometimes they think it's not what they should do. It's other people's business. (Taiwanese student)

I think that the biggest one is unemployment and the lifestyle has been plummeting very fast in the last 10 years. I think that is the biggest problem. There are a few people that are really rich, and there is the middle class that is just slowly disappearing, and I think that the unemployment thing is the biggest issue. And then you also have

187

things like corruption everywhere in the judicial system, hospitals, everything. So I think those two are the biggest problems. (Croatian student)

In my opinion I think it's hard or difficult to fix the problem because actually we are living in an extreme society. The rich are really rich so you can see there are many Mercedes Benz on the street, but actually the poor are very poor. Under these circumstances it is really difficult to fix the problem, especially in Taiwanese society. I think most people long for stability, because the history of Taiwan is very complicated. Taiwan was occupied by Japan and after World War II the KMT government was in China and Taiwan, and we underwent colonization. So I think that's one of the reasons why everyone longs for stability, and they don't want to change or fix the problem. (Taiwanese student)

First of all, I do think this is a nonsense war. Guerrillas, nowadays, they do not have an ideology. They are not going after social distribution or peace, they're just after money. I do think guerrillas are just a way of living right now: it's a business. About the war: I think it is less real than it actually may appear. By that I mean the media, president, political parties, political environment is making something bigger, everyone is relating to the war so they can get something out of it. The president and the media are just putting people into camps of good, bad, evil, heaven . . . What I think the president is doing is giving us a security dilemma. He's telling us we're under attack, when we are not in a big, big way. We can still go to the coast, driving our cars, and it's not as if the guerrillas are all over the country. The media agrees with the president: we have to support him, we do have to hate the guerrillas. There is no other way to end the war but fighting it. I think both sides, they are actually doing business with each other. I don't think they're calling each other up saying, "hey, do we call it peace, or do we call it war?" No, I think they're just taking advantage of what we're facing right now. (Colombian student)

I think there is a very big gap between the upper level of society and the middle class, I think, is disappearing in Hungary. So there are no people who have an average salary, which could be really average between the top salary and the low salary. So I think this is a big problem. (Hungarian student)

188

I guess it's still the unemployment problem and, well this is what people are concerned with most in the last years, even though it's getting better. Right now we are quite positive. The market is quite good right now, I guess. Secondly, well for us it's the whole thing how you're gonna find a job even with a degree from the university. It won't be easy, especially the high mobility that is expected from you to go abroad or to a totally different part of Germany. At least this is for me a concern. I'm not quite sure how it's going to be after. (German student)

2 Anti-Americanism and geopolitics

How did students understand the role of the United States in the world? How do they view the nature of geopolitics? On the one hand, the global generation is shaped by a realpolitik about the nature of global power. Powerful countries pursue their own interests (especially when it comes to access to energy resources), as is to be expected and despite whatever rhetoric they might spout to the contrary. The United States is the most powerful country in the world, ergo it acts in its own best interest; the bluntness of this fact requires a set of ideological shields or screens in order to make US foreign policy less objectionable, that is, a set of actions guided by morality and not by acquisitiveness, greed, and a view of the world as a zero sum game.

The students challenge the actions of the United States in the world and the influence these actions have on the countries in which the students live. But as for Americans *themselves* – the people, not the politicos – they are fundamentally good. The students we interviewed can decipher the problems, limits, and causes of anti-American sentiments in their own countries, which arise in the main out of a confusion of US foreign policy with everything else that might be tagged with the adjective "American." The United States is therefore a nation defined by a split personality – state bad, people good – much in the same way that most of the students view their own governments. "Government of the people, by the people, for the people": something must happen to the people as a result of its passage through this formula. The better instincts on which the United States is founded (justice, freedom, liberty for all) similarly go astray whenever the United States

189

moves outside its own magical boundaries. The students don't seem to worry about such mysteries, seeing them as too obvious to bear mentioning: there are always good people and bad governments, good behavior at home and bad behavior elsewhere.

But all American people that I've met are really great people, so I've heard about that prejudice that all Americans are stupid and uneducated, but I've never had such experience with them ... What does it [America] signify? Power, and sort of dictatorship towards the rest of the world and being the world policemen – not even policemen because there are supposed to be just and good and so on, but just sort of world dictator. That's how I would sum it up. (Croatian student)

First, I have to say, I've lived in the States for a couple of years and I fell in love because I lived in South. It's not like Colombia. I did see the dialectic between the South and the North which I see reflected in the relationship between South America and the US. I do have sympathy for Americans, but not for what they do in the international system. I have to say, Americans when it comes to politics are respectable. If I was in their position, I would act the same way. What's the point of power if you don't exercise it? How do you exercise it except by pulling people under your command? I think when it comes to other things, Americans are nice, they have open minds to understand that other countries are not American and do have their way to do stuff. But there's a constant feeling that Americans do it better. (Colombian student)

I mean there are two major points I believe. The one thing is a positive idea of cosmopolitanism and individualism and individual achievement. Of course on the other hand, there is the idea that the US is at least the paragon of capitalism and they are the new imperial force and all of this. Well I think the second sentiment is stronger at the moment, which of course has to do with the Bush government. But it's always been there, I think. It probably goes back to the beginning of the twentieth century at least. (German student)

It's complex. In Taiwan we think America is friendly to us. Actually before I entered graduate school, I always thought America is a good nation and American people would like to help Taiwan to develop, or anything else. But recently, I changed my mind because it's wrong. America does everything to Taiwan for profit. We can't blame America for this reason. It's just our misunderstanding. But I think if we can cooperate with America, it's not bad because America's economic condition is better than Taiwan. Taiwan is a small island. We can't develop by ourselves. We have to cooperate with other big nations. (Taiwanese student)

They want political control as a means of obtaining economic control; they want resources. The issue of resources will become ever more acute. And they are trying to cover up their struggle for control of resources by means of some foolish nonsense – which, by the way, apparently goes down well within the US itself; the people are, apparently, unable to analyze what's going on. (Russian student)

Big brother. Or I could tell it in Hungarian; I don't know what is the equivalent in English – [says a phrase in Hungarian] – so I think America is the state who wants to influence everything, not directly but mainly with its economic power and it can do it. But I'm not sure that the US does it in a good manner. I think the main reasons for US influence in the world is its own economic growth and wealth, why it wants to influence other states. (Hungarian student)

As for the world situation, I think that the gap between the rich and poor also exists. The poor countries and the rich countries, and the strong countries become stronger and stronger like the US or the emerging men in China. They are actually to me a little threatening or intimidating. I don't believe in the so-called world peace. (Taiwanese student)

I've never been to the US, but I would like to. As a media student I had to deal with several media events that had happened in the US, and it was really fascinating for me as a student, how democratic, how free they are, how freedom of speech is working there. I thought at first that it's marvelous, I would like to work there and I think that's a cliché, an old cliché that the US is the home of everyone's possibilities. I think that's not true nowadays. (Hungarian student)

191

When I was young, I had fantasies about America. This is part of the reason I chose to study English. English is a symbol for social class. When I entered the English Department, I realized I'm alienating myself from America. For the moment, I think I'm opposing it. I'm ambivalent. Before that, it was an important projection of my desire. Now, I find myself distanced from it. For instance, when going abroad, I feel racial discrimination, racially categorized as Asian. In English departments, English major students would have some distance from other students, especially those who don't speak English, or those from working-class backgrounds. They feel they are superior. I don't like it, this social inequality.

When I read about Taiwanese history and the situation between America, Taiwan, China and Japan, I realized it's not as simple as you think. I have certain objections, especially when it comes to issues of military recruitment raised in Taiwan. Why should we always spend lots of money buying something we don't need? We are told that this is needed to protect ourselves from China. But you find it's not true, it's not as they say. It's a very tricky situation between these two countries. When Americans broke off relations with Taiwan, and now they have good interactions with China, you think it's not that simple, and have distance from them. I think our society is still, except for some anti-imperialist organization, most people buy whatever America says. Culturally and politically, most people still have strong relations to America and believe that America will protect us from China. Culturally, you see that more and more people in Taiwan are learning English. They take for granted the cultures of America – they dominate our culture industry. (Taiwanese student)

I don't think it's bad or good. It has its own logic. They pursue their interests. Sometimes they try to put democracy in the world, but always for their interests. They can do [what they want]: they confirm pacts with Mexico, Iraq, I don't know who else, but everything is pursuing their own interests, the interests for the American people. We all are American. I don't like to judge them. I prefer to judge their position with Latin American, Saudi Arabia. We have the problem, they don't have the problem. (Colombian student)

Do these ideas about the US have different valences depending on what position one occupies in society? Most students thought so, believing that the lower classes and those living outside cities expressed the greatest degree of anti-Americanism, while the interests of elites coincided with American ideas and values:

> One could, of course, hypothesize that in the hinterland anti-Americanism is stronger, while in large cities it is weaker, but this is hard to check. And as far as the stratification of anti-Americanism goes . . . If we take the low-income stratum of the population, their anti-Americanism is strong, as is their dislike of everything foreign. As regards the middle class, if we have any, which is debatable, it seems to me that a more rational attitude is prevalent: critical, yes, but without the stereotypical, wholesale accusations. As for the elite, it is hard to me to judge the attitudes of a group I have never belonged to and do not even entertain a hope of ever belonging to [laughs]. I guess their attitude is tolerant, partner-like. (Russian student)

> Everybody's Americanized! I think people who especially belong to the middle classes and upper classes are more Americanized. You actually know to classify people subconsciously – the more American-ized, the higher the class. Especially with younger people. (Colombian student)

Is there any possibility of changes in the United States that might suture the gap between good people and their bad foreign policy? On this point, there was some disagreement. A few (see "The Future" below) seemed to believe that the victory of a Democrat in the 2008 election and/or the election of Barack Obama more specifically would lead to changes. Others were not so sure. In any case, the winds of history and the changes that the twentieth-first century has already brought with it seemed to suggest new challenges ahead for the United States and a shift in the character of geopolitical power:

> I've come to expect the same, even if the person in government changes. Also, it's not a one man government, but it's something bigger. Even if there are new ideas coming from Obama, the structure will try to make those new things not happen. Those new things that he could maybe make in other contexts, the government administration won't allow

him to do. I don't think this will change the relations between US and Colombia. I think, if change comes, it will be more in economic matters. (Colombian student)

I think they have felt they own economic vulnerability; moreover, like any other country, they are vulnerable to resource depletion. So they have felt a certain uncertainty, instability – something they are not used to. There was the instability of the first half of the twentieth century, but they have dealt with it and seem to have decided that they have dealt with it for good. But life has shown there is nothing permanent. And while they used to be able to siphon resources out of Russia and other countries virtually uncontrollably, nowadays these countries are starting to set forth their own conditions, to limit those exports. Americans don't like it, because they have calculated how much they need and they are currently not getting enough. So what they are not given voluntarily, they start taking away by force. (Russian student)

What does it represent in the world today? I think politically it's the only superpower left, but it's not the only power left. So it will, I think it's again in a phase of transition. After the Cold War it was clearly victorious as a system and as a narrative, but immediately it got under pressure by different narratives and different powers and it has to sort of juggle. What will come in the next one hundred years? I think new powers will arise like China, new narratives will arise like Europe, and the US will have to find – I mean the American people, American culture and American politics will have to find – a way between new isolation and new compromise, how much [they] will engage in other narratives and other powers and how much [they] will withdraw from the political sphere because not all involvement is good involvement. (German student)

3   Globalization

Globalization is a term at the forefront of our minds (as much as we'd like to shake it), and it is a term that is omnipresent in the academy, and even, if to a lesser degree, in print media. We found less interest in globalization in our student interviewees, whether as process, system, or ideology. As an emergent part of the elite, and as participants in university communities which structure and participate in the ideological agenda in each region and country – especially with respect to foreign relations and the local understandings of the shape of the international – we would have expected globalization to ring bells of some kind or another. The reaction when we asked about it? Suddenly, we were no longer conducting an interview, but initiating a quiz in which precise definitions were demanded.

The chain of associations found in these definitional exercises pointed to globalization as a single, inevitable, era-defining process. Erasing, unifying, making simpler, eliminating borders, generating loss: it creates something single from what was once multiple. How? Technology, consumption, markets. Globalization is something that demands a normative assessment: is it good? Is it bad? In the end, though, this is a pointless exercise: it is taking place whether or not one wants to do something about it. A murky background phenomenon, the ground against which everything else stands as a figure, globalization is not the same as geopolitics, but the terrain on which it takes place. As a concept, these students greet globalization as a faintly suspect academic exercise. If one wants to understand the world, one turns to the game of great-power politics, which for the global generation means that the United States is in charge until others manage to catch up (China looms in the shadows). What they don't always notice, or at least what they seem to accept, is that the game is now played by the same rules, everywhere and by everyone.

> It is a worldwide process of erasing cultural boundaries. It is the formation of a common, unified society – like, for example, in the European Union. As far as I understand, they have common economic and legal norms; there are slight differences, but on the whole they try to have these norms unified, especially the economic ones, so that life becomes simpler: visa and customs and other similar regulations are unified in order to scour, as it were, the borders that hamper activity, exchange. (Russian student)

> Globalization is a process of unification that leads to a loss of cultural diversity. Globalization is often talked about in a positive key, and I think it is more of a negative phenomenon, because it erases the uniqueness of cultures, countries, mentalities. It forms a sort of

195

averaged-out, depersonalized, gray culture and society. (Russian student)

That is the problem. I think the US here in Colombia. With globalization, everyone wants more and more technology and consumption. I think people are not very conscious of that. I lived in London, and I saw people don't have anything very organic, they don't have lots of things with the ecosystem. Here, we have everything, but no one cares about that. In other countries, they don't have it, so they care a lot about it. These organizations, are people from the outside trying to protect this. (Colombian student)

We learn definitions [of globalization] in marketing courses, because this is important ... global products, global companies. For example McDonalds sells fish in Finland, and they don't offer beef in India. (Hungarian student)

It is the process of unification and mutual penetration of cultures and states, creation of one single cultural, economic, political field – you name it. (Russian student)

I think it's a part of this new system, which is this – I don't know – a world connection. I don't know how to call it. It has good parts and bad parts. I think that people are afraid that they will lose themselves in this big river of people and I think that's the fear in globalization. Now we are all connected actually and you can be connected to anyone in one second. (Croatian student)

I think that this concept is intrinsically vague and unspecific. Sociologists and economists use it in their descriptions of current events. Certain processes – of merging or of differentiating – are going on, which have been there before; but in order to be able to talk about these processes, to trace and study them, they have agreed to use the term "globalization."

Almost anything can be included here: the merging of different ethnicities, the merging of different ethnical groups within multi-ethnic states (i.e., states with dozens of different ethnical groups); a process which is currently going on both in culture in general and in artistic culture in particular – the mixing of Russian, European, American cultures, the mixing of traditions. It seems to me that these processes have actually been poorly explored and studied. If this situation persists, the concept of globalization will simply discredit itself. (Russian student)

We expect that this student is probably right.

4   Cultural politics of the present

One of the students above suggested that globalization leads to an "averaged-out, depersonalized, gray culture and society." The implication is direct: culture is made less interesting by globalization. Does globalization offer a new vocabulary for older worries about cultural imperialism – the reshaping of a culture by another, more powerful one with which it comes into contact? Is culture a place in which America's presence is most strongly felt?

When it comes to naming mass culture, its products, and the practices that it begets as specifically "American," this analytic confusion can start to creep in. It might well be the case that films produced in the United States are a major cultural export product; it is probably a mistake to describe consumerism in toto as distinctly and definitively American. Only a few students seemed to worry about having US products in their cinemas or on their radio stations, at least when it came to any broad-scale social impact that such products might have. All admitted high levels of consumption of US cultural products; most wanted to divorce such consumption from politics, just as most wanted to make a value judgment about these products, and about mass cultural products more generally. We *did* hear worries about the continued US hegemony over culture; just as often, however, we heard that there were plenty of local cultural narratives to learn about and consume, even if this possibility was sometimes impeded by (for example) lack of screen time for national films or media attention to local bands.

America is simply seen as the main source for cultural narratives – that's what they pick up on, that's what they live, they watch MTV and reality shows, but there is no connection to politics, because they don't see this as a political thing. (German student)

Everything is connected with the massive TV media and communications. Consume, consume, consume. The pop music is just so poor. You can hear Pacific music and it has real meaning. Now everyone makes music to make money. I hate US TV shows, so stupid. You don't have to do this. For example, with the artistic films, you just have to think, reflect on the movie. You see that, you don't have to think you just laugh at stupid things. That's the culture they want, keep people stupid to keep them under control. (Colombian student)

I think it's different. We can laugh and cry at American films, but there is something about Hungarian films that is ours, and we understand it. There's a film about two old guys and the guy goes crazy because he can't pay the bills and he goes bankrupt. Two old people, and they're just going to rob banks. Typical Hungarian reality, that's us. Pension just cannot pay. (Hungarian student)

We don't believe any politicians in Taiwan, so actually we watch TV, especially talk-shows. There are many political talk-shows in Taiwan, so we don't care about that now so much. (Taiwanese student)

If you read the daily newspapers here in Croatia, you will find more about Paris Hilton than Croatian artists who are famous in the world and that's what really makes me angry, but as I said you don't have a choice and I think it's pretty much the same in the rest of the world, or in Europe at least. (Croatian student)

They play a rather tangible role. American culture actively penetrates Russian culture, its impact is obvious. American notions and models of trade, food, fashion, entertainment (most movies we are shown in movie theaters are American). We are invited to go work in America, go for a vacation to America, go learn in America. (Russian student)

I don't think so. It's absolutely not a concern. It's just you know, pop culture. Again you have certain elements here, maybe more tradition-alists who will try to make these kinds of connections and maybe speak against it. But again, in the anti-consumerist view there is this connection and sometimes maybe someone will point it out, but I don't think that on a larger social scale that it's an issue – it's not an issue. (Croatian student)

Everybody wants to buy new things, fashion things. Like in the US, credit cards are becoming more popular. We also have American Express here, so you can spend easily your money and then think next month about how to pay it. That's influence of globalization. But I wouldn't say it's influence from the US. That's everywhere from Japan to the US. Everybody wants to buy more and more because more options we have year by year, we develop so many new things year by year like computers. Next year it's not worth anything, so we have problems with consumerism. (Hungarian student)

5   Capitalism

Over the course of the almost three years of this project, across countries with communist pasts (Croatia, Hungary, and Russia), and those that have experienced explosive capitalist growth (Germany during the years of the 1950s *Wirtschaftswunder*, Taiwan, the original Asian Tiger), we never heard a single unqualified commitment to capitalism as an economic system. Students expressed feelings of uneasiness with capitalism and a desire for a different economic (and social) system, or they expressed a satisfaction with the individualism and competition engendered by capitalism, but only with appropriate policy mechanisms in place to offset its sometimes cruel impact on individuals and communities. Capitalism was seen as a world system, but one whose particular characteristics differed from country to country, a specificity measured by a sliding scale from "pure capitalism" to Scandinavian capitalism. Socialism or communism was off this particular scale: a source of political ideas, past systems from which one might borrow component parts, but nothing one would choose to reinstitute in its entirety. The United States was imagined as closer to pure capitalism; where all the students we interviewed wanted to be was with the Swedes and the Finns.

199

The reality of global capitalism was in doubt for no one. The question then was whether it was a reality to struggle against or to which one had to accommodate oneself. Some students were game for the fight, if pessimistic about its likely outcome; most saw their task as one in which they and their nations needed to deal with the realities at hand and figure out how to make the best out of the only economic system available to them. "Like it or not, we have to consent to it for lack of choice."[11] Not the words of one of our students, but Alain Badiou's recent assessment of how we come to understand capitalism in the wake of the "failure" of socialism – a phrase which captures in outline the view of capitalism we saw expressed at different sites across the globe:

> What I don't like about capitalism coming here is that I see young people living under a huge amount of pressure, having to work very long hours in order to earn money. There are people who are really well paid, such as managers in big firms and they don't get time to spend their money. I think more and more it's becoming a rat race here as well. Even young people are not prepared for that and it seems a very unfair system for me. It's just work, work, work and no pleasure, whereas you are being shown pictures and images from the West – go on holiday to Cuba or wherever. The thing is that you don't have time to do that, no matter how much you earn, so it's pretty negative. Whenever I talk to my friends, we always think of some society where it would be more socialist like. Some things in communism were really good. I think that we should either bring them back and shouldn't have thrown them away as easily as we did. (Croatian student)

> I don't want to have that communism – never, ever – so I think capitalism is the normal system that we have and it seems to get along quite well with democracy, so we should go for it. (German student)

> It'll be a long process, but somehow, someday, the structures have to change. Right now, the economical crisis, the very core of capitalism is being questioned. I think the structure is so well-established to prevent any change, at least in the near future. (Colombian student)

> Capitalism might not be the ideal thing, but it's the best we've got – one might say using Churchill's words, I think. Capitalism is based on

people's desire to achieve their own goals, to compete with other people. Pure capitalism, of course, is not very attractive: there is no care for the elderly, no investment into the development of sport, etc., no social programs. So pure capitalism is a dangerous thing: a poor person will always remain poor and a rich person will remain rich, this gap will persist, and the number of rich people will always remain low. There is a Pareto law, I think, of 5 versus 95 percent. So, for example, in Russia 5% of the population own 95% of the capital, and the rest scrape by. And this is very dangerous. You look at Brazil for an example of what this can lead to: whole areas where the moment you leave your car, it is stolen. Looks like we are headed in this direction, and this would be very dangerous. (Russian student)

Of course we are a capitalist country as well, but that capitalism should always go hand in hand with certain social structures and social benefits for the people that probably fall short in a capitalist system. There are always winners and losers but you have to kind of provide for the losers, that's what I think. (German student)

So I think capitalism and corporations and brands are a necessity – symptoms of our age – I'm really keen on looking at how it works. Now I'm applying for a job and I try to learn as much as I can about how, for example a corporate media firm in Hungary works and it's really interesting for me. So we have to sell as much advertisement as we can and therefore we have to find the best methods. That's how it works. Our world is based on illusions and therefore it wouldn't be a good way to live in the twentieth century if you would have such a visions that not the media and the money is in everything. (Hungarian student)

You know every negative aspect of capitalism is projected onto the US and what comes out of it is that American capitalists are bad and German capitalists work for the common good and that's in an abstract way . . . I think it's kind of dangerous to go down that way. (German student)

I think Hungary is not trying to become capitalist, but the politicians are trying to build a proper social market economy. But because of lack of legislation but effective control on illegal and semi-illegal dealings, our market turns out to be more violent than general social market economies. Many who think, at least 50% of voters, we don't have to be capitalist to be successful. Sweden, Finland, and Ireland, are good examples to follow. They are capitalist, but not as much as the US. That is what objective people think is the right way to solve social problems as well as economic problems here. (Hungarian student)

6   The future

A hint of new possibilities? An opportunity for change? What does the future bring our interviewees? As we mentioned above, the general reaction: pessimism. If students hope for a social democratic, Scandinavian-style "solution" to global capitalism, they don't seem to feel as if this is likely in the near future. And so they are fated to have to endure the problems that they identified in their own countries (growing income disparities, lack of effective governments, a dearth of social programs) *and* the blunt realities of geopolitics – the rich get richer, the powerful make sure that they get their way. Such activist spirit as might exist is a quality of youth, they assert, which is likely to disappear with maturity and the need to address the realities of life (taking care of a family, facing the demands of a work life). The word "pessimism" appears again and again in our transcripts.

The future is not so bright that these students have to wear shades. What they need is a critical-political flashlight to illuminate the darkness they are confronting. It's not that a terrible future awaits them; it's just that it isn't exactly inspiring to imagine the future as like the present, only a little bit worse:

I think that it produces consciousness of those things, but I don't think that it drives them to act because you just cannot. You have to make your living. I think that they are aware and are willing to watch documentaries about it and read about it, but actually do something no, because you see everyone around you, people that have tried to do something but they fail, so you think okay why bother. It's also this one faculty that I was talking about, students from the faculty of philosophy that is kind of known for being very open minded. So it's a very small group of people who try to become educated in that area. (Croatian student)

Many people think Taiwan's future is not as good. It can't develop as good as 1970s or 1980s conditions. Many people my age, when we were little children, we think if you just study hard and enter the university, after you graduate you will find a good job and earn much money. But after we graduate everything seems hopeless. Many young people think maybe one day we have to work in China and not in Taiwan because Taiwan has no chance to develop. But we think we can't compete with China's young men. There are many reasons. Young people in China are more diligent than young people in Taiwan. In Taiwan we think our condition will be more serious after 10 years. . . . For me, I don't know what I can do in the future. I have to imagine about my life condition after ten years, because everything is going to change. But some people say that from 2008 to 2012, Taiwan's economic condition will better, but after 2012, the economic condition will face a big change. I'm not sure why the journals or newspapers say about this, but many people believe it. (Taiwanese student)

Well I see that there is a small group of people in Hungary that have big money and it's very hard to get between them or to get in that group. I don't really find it threatening because I know that in all countries there is such a group that has the biggest monies. But I think that it's not good that this group doesn't open up. I'm personally not fearing about the future of myself because what I find good in Hungary is that skilled people and the people who can find out themselves can make their own business. I think it's possible to build up a normal life in Hungary. Of course one has to work a lot and I think that in the short-term people have no possibility to raise but in the long-term with a lot of work they can. What I find unjust is that for example, somebody who works for 2 or 3 years is not able to buy even a very little flat, so I am optimistic only in the very long-term, so after 10 or 15 years. (Hungarian student)

Actually I'm a little pessimistic both in Taiwan and around the world because it seems that the prices are soaring nowadays in Taiwan. I know the soaring prices are also a problem throughout the world because of the soaring price of oil, because we depend a lot on it. We cannot live without oil. So maybe in the future ten or twenty years, I'm a little pessimistic. (Taiwanese student)

I don't know. I hope, but I'm not really optimistic. I really don't know. Actually I'm trying not to think about that. I like to live here actually, but I think I like to live here because I never lived anywhere else so. But, I don't know. Maybe someday when really this whole thing ... but I don't know, the political situation we have now we had a hundred years ago, they are very similar things, so it's our mentality. Croatian people are not very good at seeing the bigger picture, we are just seeing what's in front of us, so that's a problem with Croatian politicians. They mean well, but some of them are just fighting about small stupid things but can't see really the big picture. I don't know what's coming next. I don't know. I think that everyone is trying to make their small world better and I'm trying to do that. To do something for me which I can enjoy or something like that but the general picture I don't see coming in ten years, so we'll see it together, I don't know. (Croatian student)

Some people predict that two biggest power regimes in the next decade will be China and America. There are some anti-American movements and some anti-China movements. However, Taiwan is very dependent on these two powerful regimes. Since 1950 until now, the Taiwan economics has had some outcomes. It's time for Taiwanese people to think of some sustainable or alternative way to keep going. However, because China opened now, Taiwan doesn't think of how to upgrade to sustain our economics or our environment, they just look to China because they have cheap labor, so they don't have to think about this problem. (Taiwanese student)

My generation is not going to be able to change anything really. Our social conditions are not going to be the same for me in twenty years. If I have a friend who is rich, he's going to be even richer in twenty years, and if I'm poor, I'll be poorer in twenty years. Inhibit a lot of things I want to do in twenty years, whether it be for good or bad. Not only is it not going to be better, I think it's going to be under the command of fewer. Not very optimistic, but I think it's better to think this way, so when we face it, we're not going to think, I thought it would be better! (Colombian student)

I am not that positive about the future, especially when we face the rise of China and the situation of America, relation of Taiwan and America. The most important thing is the political divide, the dramatic difference between the two parties. People are going to extremes – independence or towards China. ... For the general public, they don't have much chance or experience to understand much. (Taiwanese student)

In Colombia, I think things will stay the same. I don't think they'll get worse, I hope they don't get worse. But I don't necessarily think there's an involvement because I think we've reached a point where people just focus their attention on that one issue, and so for most people's eyes, there's a development in that, in eradicating those [guerrilla] groups. But as I said, social issues aren't being touched. In that sense, I feel like we're staying the same. Maybe this president won't get re-elected, but someone just like him will be, because people really like what they're doing. I feel like we're going to stay somewhere in the same area. People focus their attention on one issue, and they forget society isn't just that one issue. Problems in the country are because of social structures – it's not working because there's so much discrimination. People working really hard and not getting anywhere. You have to change the social structure in a really big way for there to be even a little change. (Colombian student)

Well just from the people that I'm surrounded with, I guess we're quite positive. Not everybody knows yet what they are gonna do afterwards but somehow we are quite positive that we are gonna figure out something. (German student)

Well I don't know the wider generation, only the people who I'm in contact with, and it's typical that they don't have an optimistic vision about the future. But in spite of this they don't really care about problems in ten years or something. Well a lot of my friends say that how will I buy a flat? Or how will I keep or feed a family? But in the day to day life I don't see this pessimism, only when we are talking about some things I see that we are not so optimistic. But the day to day life it doesn't come out so. (Hungarian student)

On the one hand there's certainly this pessimistic notion that there's nothing much to be done. The whole idea that the whole social peg that defined the '50s and '60s and until the '80s in a way that this just couldn't hold for a long time and it's actually based on economic exploitation of other countries and that this all at some point couldn't work anymore. (German student)

205

There are people [activists] who write little booklets. There is a very small group of people and people who actually read the publication of theirs. It's the same group of people. I don't think there are people that they reach out to, so it's just a closed sort of group of people. Maybe yearly the number increases, because there are people at the university, for example the department of sociology who are more aware of things like that and they get such literature or publications, newspapers or magazines, but I think the number of people who sort of quit is the same because they see okay, there is no point and we have to earn our bread. And they just have to conform I think. (Croatian student)

I'm not really optimistic. Disappointment, what I was talking about, this is really a bit frightening for me. How it will lead, where it will lead because several possibilities can occur. I'm not optimistic. When I look around, people are really devastated. They don't have enough money to live and don't have enough future plans that are satisfying for them, and therefore I think in five years it will lead to something radical ...

There are forces which are basically inherited from the socialism so this disappointment is not only the disappointment of the capitalism, what was invented in Hungary, but even the disappointment of how they see themselves – how the new regime or new system would be working, and it's not. So I think in Hungary there are several steps that have to be made to be a so-called western country. But I can't be optimistic, so there are wounds deep inside and it's not easy to get through them, so maybe another generation, maybe mine or the following. So I think we could make a new country, but I think everybody as a young person says that they would like to. But I'm convinced that our generation is something else, therefore I'm optimistic. But as the regime of today, this regime, I'm not. (Hungarian student)

In my less pessimistic forecast I still say that the totalitarian-like state and totalitarianism remain. As well as authoritarianism, and even if the influence of the American kind of democracy will prevail, we cannot know what kind of result it will have in our country. It might be like a fly in the ointment and no one knows what effects it will have. (Russian student)

> *How do you see the future of Russia?*
> Again, no idea. I prefer not to think about it.
> *Why?*

* Because this kind of thoughts can be unpleasant, and basically I don't see the point. We can't predict the future. What will come, will come. You may think me typical Russian fatalist in this respect! [laughs]. (Russian student)

d. Biogeographies

The ideas, opinions, and claims about the world that we've assembled above might appear to some as arbitrary and unmotivated. What of the claims of those whom we didn't cite? More importantly, does a view expressed on any one of those points by any one of the 60 students capture the vantage point from which the global generation as a whole views the world?

The value of long-form qualitative interviews is that they introduce narrative into the issues under discussion. It is from individual interviews, taken as whole, that we learned the most about the views of these students and the sociopolitical situation of the nations in which they live. These individual narratives allowed us to see the ways in which discourse and ideology combine to shape perceptions of larger social shifts and changes. We spoke above of treating these interviews as literary texts – as forms of an experience of the globe that draw attention to representation in addition to the content of students' responses. To offer a further elaboration of the generation we encountered, we want to end by presenting three *biogeographies*, narratives of self and of place, which will help to contextualize and situate the comments we find above. As a counterpoint to the chain of pessimism above, we offer three less negative views that we encountered and a narrative of their responses to the issues raised by our questions. (The names we have given these students are invented.)

1   The social democrat: Croatia/Petra

Petra is a 25-year-old student who graduated with a degree in sociology. An aspiring academic, she offered nuanced and careful responses to the questions we posed. She is a committed social democrat. When asked to describe some of the problems facing Croatia, she identified the economy, specifically lack of employment opportunities and the financial insecurity felt by the populace as a result. However, she also identified a more abstract concern: "developing a civic culture, [so] that people can really feel part of democratic community, not only part of the state." She can speak in the language of GDP, IMF, financial investments, and share price, but she returned again and again in our discussion to the necessity of social security and social rights, including greater access to education, health care, and other public services. "Politics for me," she said, "means that all stake holders participate in creating the best possible policies for citizens of the country. Still it's political parties that are running most of the things, and the non-governmental sector and education and science sector is still not participating in creating policies and politics for the whole country."

As was the case with many of our interviewees in post-communist countries (Croatia, Hungary, and Russia), this frustration at the political limits of the post-1989 world extended to their economic system as well. Petra viewed the advent of capitalism in Croatia as little more than "an excuse to steal." The reapportioning of state assets during the shift from communism to capitalism was an occasion for political elites to make sure that their friends and colleagues came out of the transition on the plus side of the ledger. For her, the absence of a functioning civil society in Croatia at the present time and the lack of an economic system that worked for the public at large were not grounds for an indictment of democratic capitalism per se. Her hope for Croatia: that it develop a "better capitalism," as in Scandinavia.

The typical approach to America that we saw students take – a description of US behavior at multiple levels, a stocktaking of its effects, and an assessment of the reactions of people around the world – was exemplified in Petra's responses. Petra said that most Croatians think "Americans are stupid" (a phrase and a sentiment we heard repeatedly in our Croatia interviews). She says that she hears this from her professors as well: "basically they would say that Americans are stupid, they are primitive, aggressive, they have imperial ambitions."

She sees this as a mistake: "People see the US all wrong. People see the US mainly through the prism of American foreign policy, unfortunately, and quite often, American popular culture – you know Britney Spears and stuff – which is rather superficial. I wouldn't say that it's representative of America."

She wanted to add as much color as she could to this first, black and white picture of the United States. "It's really difficult to talk about American as one entity." Petra expressed a dislike of what she thought was an overriding US "moralism," a view of itself as the best possible place on the planet, and thus charged with a global didactic mission to spread its life systems around the world, through whatever means necessary: offering scholarships to study in the United States, sending religious missionaries to add converts to their flock, using its military power and political influence, and so on. At the same time, she expressed appreciation for what the United States has done for Croatia in the wake of the Balkan War (for instance, providing development aid and assistance with infrastructure reconstruction). She is impressed with the depth and strength in the United States of the civil society that she finds lacking in Croatia: "There is so much grassroots organizing in the US, so many conferences, so many demonstrations, so much activism going on." And she has academic ambitions that she believed could be best fulfilled in the United States. Over and over, she returned to discussion of the qualities of the US academy – rigor, high standards, a meritocratic ethos – in contrast to the university system in her home country, which she described as overly formal, closed, and afraid of the outside world.

Petra was worried about US involvement in the world economically, politically, and militarily. But the cultural influence of the United States didn't strike her as being all that significant, whether in Croatia or in Europe. The cultural preferences of "regular people" are shaped by US movies and television. Nevertheless, she pointed to numerous other cultural options for Croatians, drawn both from their own evolving archive of books, films, and television programs, and also from cultural input from Europe. She felt that cultural expression in the United States was overly sincere, whereas European culture is marked by a distance that generates distinct ways of being and behaving:

209

American popular culture doesn't have an ironic distance from itself, which European pop-culture has I think. There's no irony in the US. They're so pure and naive in what they're doing, in what they're filming, in what they're singing and it's very, in a way, scary to see that kind of ... people are not ... you know it's incredible. I think that's something that young people dislike. One major type of humor in Croatia is, particularly among younger people, is to be sarcastic about yourself, about your life and about your society, and they don't see that. When you see American students in a party, you don't see any ... it looks funny, it looks funny because they're so serious about getting drunk.

Petra thought that it was more interesting to talk about anti-Americanism than globalization. Part of the reason was that the focus of her energies and attention were toward her own country and its future possibilities. While many of her peers suggested that there was a dearth of political expression amongst young people – and she herself indicated as much in opening comments about the lack of an energetic civil culture – she also argued that the period since 9/11 had re-energized politics. There's much about anti-Americanism that gets things wrong and can lead to mistakes in how one thinks about not just the United States, but the world. But Petra also thought that

> this anti-American energy can have a very positive influence on making people conscience [*sic*] about politics. People more and more realize that they could find themselves in such a situation – if their country was doing things like that, what would they do? I think people are being more involved in politics and more conscious about it. If we were going to send our troops in Iraq and people would say no.

One of the many positive outcomes of anti-American sentiment: the possibility of the election of Barack Obama, which would reverse the shock much of Europe experienced at the re-election of George W. Bush. If Obama was elected, "you know it's going to be incredible ... His arms are chained because he has a lot of interests to take care of, but still I think the main foreign policies will alter, they will be more respectful to other cultures, countries, policies, politics and people."

The immediate future for Croatia looks difficult, but what about the longer term? For Petra, the path is clear. It is not just that Scandinavian countries offer the best possible form of government, but that there is no other possibility to consider. A functioning government and a strong civil society (NGOs, lobbyists, stakeholders of various kinds) help to sand off the sharp edges of capitalism. These component elements (government, civil society, capitalism) are treated by Petra as independent of one another, as if one could imagine one of the two working even if the third were broken. If one had a leader like Barack Obama in one's own country, things would go more smoothly; if the United States had such a leader, he'd be able to ensure that America would be on its best behavior – at least to the degree possible given all those interests that might impede his progressive aims and chain his arms together.

2 The unresentful: Taiwan/Che-Hsien

The students from Taiwan expressed similar affective attitudes toward their country, the United States, globalization, and the future as the students we interviewed from the other five countries. But, quite obviously, their points of reference were different. Most important was how Taiwan is positioned in relation to China and the United States, with Japan playing a crucial role as well. We conducted our interviews in Taiwan on the heels of the March 2008 election of President Ma Ying-jeou, the Kuomintang's (KMT) candidate who registered an impressive victory over his incumbent rival from the Democratic Progressive Party (DPP). The DPP tried to convince voters that a KMT victory would return Taiwan to its authoritarian past and undercut Taiwan's independence from China; but with unemployment and inflation on everyone's mind, this Cold War narrative carried little force. On top of this, the more China integrates into the global capitalist system the less such throwback political concerns seem to matter. Likewise, the roles played by Japan (as the "good" colonizer) and the United States (as the "good" superpower) also seemed to change with the new script.

Che-Hsien could not help but refract all of his answers through the lens of the frail Taiwanese economy. After remarking about how many of his friends are unemployed (even after graduating from university with advanced degrees), he recognized that mainland China represented both the potential solution and cause of Taiwan's current economic woes.

> Some of my relatives have just gone to mainland China for jobs because the opportunities there are bigger than they are here in Taiwan. Some people are saying that mainland China will take control of Taiwan because of the economy and the jobs it provides ... The current president promised us that we will have cooperation with mainland China without losing our independence. I think that's what people are hoping we will achieve.

Che-Hsien also remarked that for him a successful capitalist economy in Taiwan would be less about GDP or even military power than about what he called "cultural capital."

> I have students and friends here that are trying to figure out a way to produce more Taiwanese movies – I think that this sort of cultural capital will be one of the most important elements for us to define Taiwan. It's a very important question because you can see the conflict between different cultural groups here that is due to the fact that we don't have a clear picture of what Taiwan actually is.

Che-Hsien saw little contradiction in combining the three major external influences on Taiwanese society: economic cooperation with China (promoting more jobs), political cooperation with the United States (promoting more individual freedoms), and cultural cooperation with Japan (promoting a globally recognized popular culture, such as Japanese accomplishments in animation and pop music).

This combination of seemingly opposed forces should come as no surprise if we remember, for example, that suspicion about cultural imperialism expressed in many decolonizing and postcolonial parts of the world was less evident in Taiwan, Japan, and South Korea. With less powerful ideologies of individualism and originality, Western

212

brands could be immediately appropriated by local entrepreneurs so that something like Disneyland or McDonalds was viewed as just as much Taiwanese as American. On this theme, Che-Hsien explains how a convenience store like 7/11 in Taiwan is closer to the Japanese model in which all types of ancillary services (from a post office to a bank) are provided. This nonchalance toward what usually goes by the name "Americanization" led Che-Hsien to explain that he knew of no critical movements against US culture or any anti-Americanisms in the country.

As for the anti-globalization activities that have emerged around the world since the Seattle events in 1999, Che-Hsien expressed little interest. "To us, it's just news or a story that was reported by the media." As for globalization more generally: "in our daily life we can't resist it; we just have to accept the currency of globalization." When we arrived at the issue of the future (Che-Hsien's personal future, the future of Taiwan, and the future of the world), his tone seemed to change:

> I'm not sure now. To me, I am not that positive about the future, especially when we face the rise of China and the situation of America, as well as the relations between Taiwan and America. The most important thing is the political divide, the dramatic difference between the two parties [KMT and DPP]. People are going to extremes: independence from or closer relations with China. It's a defining position. This is done by political manipulations. For the general public, they don't have much chance or experience to understand. I am worried. As a student, I'm not that optimistic; but as a teacher, I can still do something. I still am very happy to see ongoing movements, like people who are calling for the rise of labor or for the protection of sex workers. Lots of people are doing things to help our society, to do something for social harmony in Taiwan. The other important thing is freedom and democracy. Freedom is often associated with America, but still in Taiwan, we have freedom for discussion. It's important for us to create community, where we could have more rational dialogue between different people. For that part I am positive. Taiwan is still free and democratic.

What's striking here is the recognition of, if not resignation to, the dominant structures – but a recognition that is neither apathetic nor

213

uninterested. At the same time, Che-Hsien presents very little political intensity or strong feelings toward any of the topics we discussed. His awareness of the world turns on an acceptance of how things are that is rarely troubled by a recurring sense of hope or despair. What we find particularly interesting in his case is the ongoing desire to know and participate in the world (politically and culturally), while not investing this desire with too much pleasure or despair. Che-Hsien's drive comes without expectation – and this drive to know and be involved without expectation potentially offers an excellent model for radical politics, that is, a politics free of resentment.

3   The optimist: Germany/Klaus

The students whom we interviewed in Germany were the ones who expressed the most faith in the future. Each saw their own future as having multiple possibilities and openings: it was less of a challenge or obstacle to overcome than an opportunity to be embraced. As for the future of Germany as a whole? All of the students expressed discomfort embracing a national narrative and saw the future as one in which Europe would come in short order to displace Germany as the center of collective identifications. In their view, this was not felt as a loss, but was understood as a development that would produce *further* opportunities for them (e.g., ease of travel and work in cities outside of Germany).

Klaus was one of the more confident and forward-looking students whom we interviewed. Identifying himself as coming from an upper-middle-class family, he was majoring in English/American Studies and Modern History. Asked to identify some key social and political issues in Germany at the present moment, Klaus pointed to the challenges that immigration was posing for German society and the economic impact of globalization, which included possible threats to the continued existence of the German welfare state. Klaus was aware of the necessity (due to the country's declining birth rate[12]) and inevitability of increasing levels of immigration to Germany. For him, one of the tensions produced by immigration was that newcomers tended to draw

214

more from the social welfare system than they contributed to it. He was also clear that perceived problems with immigration are explicitly connected to race: "we don't have problems with French or Swiss people coming in, but mainly Turkish people ... unfortunately we don't have much open debate about whether this is racist or not because in Germany racism is probably even more controversial than in the US, given our history."

Though Klaus identified himself as German and valued the activities of the German state, he was troubled by new nationalist sentiments that had been emerging in the country since the 2006 World Cup.[13] In discussing cheers for the national team, flag waving, and displays of flags outside of shops, it was important for him to suggest that this was still not an instance of nationalist sentiment, but support for a group of players: "I think the World Cup showed that Germans want to identify with their country, though I'm not sure whether they identified with the flag and the country, but the team, so the team symbolized the country and it was really the team they were rooting for and not Germany." During the 2006 World Cup, it was telling for Klaus that "mostly foreigners who come in, who don't have this connection to German history, whose ancestors haven't been here during that time, so they have no historic connection – they have no problems flashing their flag and showing it."

Nationalism plays an interesting role in Germany, with immigrants apparently able to be *more* nationalist than those already in the country; the discomfort that many Germans feel with increasing numbers of immigrants is intensified by the difficulty of employing the usual narrative of defense of home against foreigners that nationalism provides. In any case, Klaus sees this as only a temporary problem:

Nationalism in a traditional sense I don't think exists with the new generation ... I think Germans, how can I phrase this, there is a divide in how we see these national symbols and how we connect them to the nation state, because ... my generation has grown up already with this idea of Europe being this larger entity and being something ideal that you should strive for and work for.

Globalization has a role in making Europe come into being: "My greatest wish is that through the European process of unification, the nation-state will disappear and maybe one day we'll talk about maybe cultural regions . . . Given globalization you have another incentive so to say, to say okay since the world is shrinking into a village, why not just come together and say let's forget about borders because it's nonsensical."

For Klaus, globalization signifies the compression of space, the disappearance of borders, and worldwide competition in markets. These are positive developments, and not only because it might bring about a borderless Europe. He suggests that "it's threatening if you look at the downside of it, but . . . I have a lot more possibilities and opportunities than, for example, my father or my mom had, that's just the fact."

Klaus had a balanced view of the US role in the world. At times, he has viewed it as akin to the Roman Empire – "one enormous political power that sort of holds everything together, but at the same time is constantly under pressure from the fringes of that empire." But if the United States once had this role, he sees it as now coming to an end. Klaus expects the twenty-first century to be a period in which new powers arise, with the result that "the American people, American culture and American politics will have to find a way between new isolation and new compromise." There is anti-Americanism in Germany, which stems from the fact that because the United States seems to be involved in almost everything in the world, it also comes to bear much of the responsibility for what goes wrong. But while there may be anti-American sentiments toward the policies enacted by the United States, especially with respect to foreign policy, such feelings do not extend to US culture or society at large. Klaus describes a generation that is very astute and balanced in how it views the United States. While he and his peers are critical of (for example) the US war in Iraq or the establishment of the detention center in Guantanamo Bay, they make use of the work of US journalists and bloggers to keep informed about what is happening in the War on Terror, and find US voices critical of the US government to be invaluable. As with the majority of our interviewees, Klaus and his peers make no blanket condemnation of the United States. Indeed, he makes the point that in many ways the United States is likely to always play the role of global scapegoat by virtue of its position in the world at the present time. While there is "is a lot of criticism of European institutions, Europe simply does not play the same role, it's not as important, it's not what it seems to be, not as omnipresent. The fact that it's a lot harder for the European Union as a whole for example to get involved in something like Iraq makes it easier to just look at the US."

As for the future? Klaus is optimistic. He doesn't believe that there will be geopolitical problems on the scale of the twentieth century: the global spread of capitalism has meant that even countries such as Russia – with its "dictatorship-like democracy" – and China will inevitably have to play by international rules. Whatever problems might arise, he doesn't believe that there will be any military confrontation between major powers. He believes that such confrontations as will occur will be over values, with the main site of tension being between the European Union and the United States. In his view,

> the greatest challenge for America will be to cope with the fact that Europe is going to rise to a position where the European narrative can challenge the American narrative – prosperity, liberty, freedom – there's going to be a strong European narrative of basically the same values but put into a different social network or social ideal, that is welfare state and all that. I think US society will have to quickly come up with new, convincing symbols if they want to maintain that symbol as the beacon of liberty, freedom and all that, not to be overrun or just overtaken by the Europeans who will be a lot more rational and a lot more pragmatic about their ideals. That may be their greatest cultural challenge.

At the beginning of our interview, Klaus told us about having spent a year studying in Atlanta as a high school student. While he was prepared by his teachers to expect culture shock from the experience of moving from Berlin to Atlanta, he found the transition easy. Just as in his own personal experience of moving from one city to another, the movement of the world into the future does not pose many threats or problems for him. He believes that actually existing democracies represent the best possible political system – a system that has erected an ideal for itself (that is, in fact, democracy), which it tries to achieve despite challenges it encounters along the way (the example he offered was the influence of money in the US elections and in the policy-making process). The future is always better than the present, and so it will be in the case of his future, too.

e.   Can't Get There from Here

What we find particularly fascinating about these interviews is how directly, candidly, and cooly the students engage the problems of globalization. We view this type of engagement as symptomatic of a key shift. When globalization discourse first emerged in the early 1990s (when the word "globalization" emerged as the dominant way by which to describe the power shifts stemming from the late Cold War moment), the debate immediately split into two main camps. On one side were those touting the newness of everything and ridiculing the non-believers. On the other side were the "business as usual" deniers, deriding the celebrators for missing the obvious fact that the contemporary world operated in pretty much the same fashion as it had for the past 200 years. What these opposing camps shared in common was the assumption that the different levels of the world system shifted – or did not shift – together. There was a totalizing view, in other words, that interlocked the cultural, economic, and political levels so that each was understood to be moving at the same speed as the others. For example, the argument that the power of national economies paled in comparison to that wielded by transnational corporations would invariably be conjoined to the argument that national identities were weakening with the rise of transnational ones. Or the argument that national cultural production was indeed strengthening after the Cold War would necessarily be accompanied by the argument about the growing importance of national political representatives. What was sorely missing from the early debates about globalization, therefore, was sensitivity to the possibility that the economic, political, and cultural levels might be moving at different speeds.

In fact, it was precisely this unevenness that gets closest to how globalization processes actually work. It does not take too much imagination, for example, to recognize that national cultural activities might become more robust at the same time that national economies are challenged by the expanding power of global economic decision makers. Or that a nationalist movement might experience a resurgence precisely because of the rise in global immigration flows (as has happened repeatedly, if with varying success, from Jean-Marie Le Pen in France to John Major in Australia to the establishment of the Swedish Democrats Party [*Sverigedemokraterna*]). Once this semi-autonomy of the different realms was acknowledged and then integrated into mainstream discourse (celebrated as so much heterogeneity and diversity), another blind spot came into being: that of the nation-state. The category of the nation functioned to limit thought, as almost every conversation about globalization turned on a discussion about the nation (as either overcome or resurgent, either politically progressive or retrogressive). The debate over whether the nation-state was "more" or "less" of what it once was distracted attention away from the ideological function of globalization discourse, first, to crowd out the debate over capitalism and, second, to conceal the debate over what might come "after" globalization. To argue about the nation-state within this second stage of globalization discourse, therefore, was to effectively participate in the project to historicize the present as a linear extension of the past, as well as to colonize the future by the limits of the present.

With the economic crisis of 2008, we have entered something like a third stage of globalization discourse. This third stage is marked not only by the return of capitalism as a speakable discourse, but also by a shift in emphasis from studying capitalism as a primarily political logic (as was dominant during the Cold War) to studying it in its more economic dispensation. This is not to say that the economic wasn't always a part of discussions of globalization, but rather that it has come to predominate, and to be spoken about in new terms: less as a component part of the political – that rising tide which will "lift all boats" (a favored proverb of former US Treasury Secretary Robert Rubin) and so help spread democracy – but more directly and explicitly. When one speaks about globalization today, it is less in terms of freedom, democracy, individualism, liberty, and other political categories, and more in terms of blunt economic terms, such as distribution, production, consumption, profit, crisis, market expansion, and efficiency; a whole range of economic concepts have over the past two decades become part of quotidian discourse and are the primary measure through which we assess the success or failure of collectives. The mantra that links capitalism with democracy is as unconvincing today as linking socialism with autocracy (which is not to say that both links are not still trotted out). Rather, capitalism is judged more by what it produces, that is, its *actual* outcome: the degree to which equality, peace, justice, environmental health, and quality of life is attained via *economic* practices and transactions. It is precisely this shift – from the more romantic political ideologies of capitalism to the more practical economic ones – that we recognize in the general affective attitudes of the students we interviewed. And it is a recognition or reaction to this shift that is far less apparent in the established writers we examined in Part II. Even Paul Krugman, the economist, invariably punctuates his analysis of capitalism in terms of his political liberalism, just as Naomi Klein, the most radical analyst of capitalism in the group of thinkers we examine, cannot help but engage capitalism based on political corruption.

It would be easy to lament that the students are on the whole disengaged from and uninterested in the world, and consigned to their fate given the scale of the systems that constitute global social reality, as well as the size of the problems that these systems have thrown up. But this is not quite right. The lack of strong and easily asserted ideologies, or affirmation of political narratives touted by experts, suggests to us a political opening. The students express no surprise at all of the corruption and inequality that capitalism – a global capitalism – produces. This wariness of established ideas might not make for a comfortable era in which to live, but it does turn the students away from affirming any blind faith in the seven theses that we negate at the end of Part I. We do not mean to argue that a new radical attitude must concentrate on the economic component of capitalism at the expense of everything else, and we certainly appreciate how the economic realm is inextricably linked not only to the political, but also to the cultural and psychological ones (and that capitalism itself is a historical formation that includes all of human activity). Indeed, the students seemed to understand this while at the same time (and unlike many globalization theorists) not assuming that the various levels of this formation moved at the same speed, or were linked in any determinate way (though they, too, had a tendency to voice some of the mantras of the age about what globalization was and how it worked).

We want to argue that a provisional privileging of the economic today is one way to break through the "time limit" of globalization, the one that snuffs out any speculation on what comes after it. We also want to argue that to privilege the economic does not mean that everyone returns to school to major in economics, especially since the curricula of many academic economic departments remains dominated by neo-classical fundamentals in a way that rarely touches on politics (in North America, for example, most Political Economy departments were split in two decades ago) and never theorizes the relation between economics and the humanities or hard sciences. How to rigorously learn about the discipline of economics from outside of the university is one of the great challenges today, and one to which the students, with their attention to economics (or, at the very least, recognition of the importance of economics) in spite of not formally studying it, seem quite attuned. (Incidentally, this is also the place to stress our admiration for Naomi Klein, for despite our criticisms of her work we think that she represents an exemplary model of how to engage in such self-study.)

In addition to this growing interest in economics, we also notice a significant change in attitude toward the nation – not the particular nation from where each student comes, but toward the nation as a more general entity. Instead of modifying most responses with how things are in their respective countries, the trend in most interviews was to speak in broader terms about the future, capitalism, anti-Americanism, and other topics. Even in the section of the interviews that focused on students' specific concerns about their nation, they would usually invoke more supranational causes such as environmental destruction or geopolitical structures.

These two tendencies – first, an attentiveness to the everyday operations of capitalist economics over the more spectacular political claims of capitalism, and second, the relatively removed relation to the nation in which each student lives – strike us as quite promising. Indeed, we view these two tendencies as enabling a crucial ideological critique of globalization's dominant temporality. As was confirmed in every one of the 60 interviews, the students still could not imagine (and were not interested in imagining) what comes after globalization. Instead of viewing this as a problem, we want to argue that this penchant suggests new possibilities: a reluctance to sign on to existing narratives of how to improve the present for the future, a refusal to see in the current direction of the world some shining hope on the horizon, an unabashed critique of the political systems in which they live, and a recognition of the cold, hard, economic facts of the world. Even if most of them would settle for social democracy – the one available example of some "better" system than the one they inhabit – they are also deeply suspicious of the economic system that accompanies it: capitalism. The students are tempted to look for things that might save them – how could they not be? But on these points they agree with us: education offers no safeguards; morality has no purchase on the blunt reality of geopolitics; the nation is suspect; capitalism cannot be trusted; history has largely disappeared; and the future brings only ill tidings.

Here is inadequate, dangerous, full of uncertainty; *there* – some potential other to the systems in which we are now confined – seems hard to even imagine. So how might we get there from here?

Notes

1. See note 6 in Part I for a representative list of works that have been published on America and anti-Americanism in the wake of 9/11.
2. In Canada, Ronald Wright's *What Is America? A Short History of the New World Order* (Toronto: Knopf Canada, 2008), an examination of the social and political psyche of the United States that locates its roots in discovery of the New World, proved to be an extremely popular text. Philippe Roger, *L'Ennemi américain: généalogie de l'antiaméricaine français* (Paris: Seuil, 2002) and Jean-François Revel, *L'obsession anti-américaine*

(Paris: Plon, 2002) are examples of post-9/11 work on anti-Americanism in France.

3. See for example Andrew Ross and Kristin Ross, eds, *Anti-Americanism* (New York: New York University Press, 2004), and Ivan Krastev and Alan McPherson, eds, *The Anti-American Century* (Budapest: CEU Press, 2007).

4. Harold Pinter, "Nobel Lecture – Literature 2005." Nobelprize.org. August 13, 2010: http://nobelprize.org/nobel_prizes/literature/laureates/2005/pinter-lecture-e.html (accessed November 8, 2010).

5. Pinter had described to the press what the general tenor of his comments at the Nobel ceremonies would be in advance of his acceptance speech.

6. James Traub, "Their Highbrow Hatred of Us," *New York Times Magazine*, October 30, 2005.

7. Cazdyn develops this point by referring to the work of Masao Miyoshi and Edward Said in his Introduction to *Trespasses: Selected Writings of Masao Miyoshi* (Durham: Duke University Press, 2010), pp. xv–xxxiii.

8. Benedict Anderson, *Imagined Communities: Reflections on the Origin and Spread of Nationalism* (New York: Verso, 1983).

9. Louis Althusser, "Ideology and Ideological State Apparatuses," *Lenin and Philosophy, and Other Essays* (London: New Left Books, 1971), 127–186.

10. To preserve the anonymity of interview subjects, we identify these quotations merely by country.

11. Alain Badiou, *The Communist Hypothesis* (New York: Verso, 2010), 5.

12. For a recent discussion of demographic tensions in Germany, see "Graying Germany Contemplates Demographic Time Bomb," *Der Spiegel*, June 27, 2010, at: www.spiegel.de/international/germany/0,1518,697085,00.html (accessed November 8, 2010).

13. For a discussion of the social tensions raised by the flying of the German flag during the 2010 World Cup, see Kevin Hagen, "Immigrants Defend the Flag While Left-Wing Germans Tear It Down," *Der Spiegel*, June 29, 2010, at: www.spiegel.de/international/germany/0,1518,703533,00.html (accessed November 8, 2010). Similar anxieties appeared as a result of the flag waving that accompanied the success of the German national team during the 2006 World Cup in Germany. See Michael Sontheimer, "How Germans Learned to Stop Worrying and Love the Flag," *Der Spiegel*, June 29, 2006, at: www.spiegel.de/international/0,1518,424373,00.html (accessed November 8, 2010).

Conclusion: "Oh, Don't Ask Why!"

When I get up in the morning, my daily prayer is, grant me today my illusion, my daily illusion. Due to the fact that illusions are necessary, have become necessary for life in a world completely devoid of a utopian conscience and utopian presentiment.

Ernst Bloch in "Something's Missing"[1]

This is a book about intelligibility – about what can and cannot be comprehended and understood. During the Cold War, the future was open. Whether or not it was actually the case, the future felt uncertain, with the potential of moving in not just one of two directions (communism, capitalism), but several: the continuation of a protracted stalemate, the sorting out of differences through some social democratic compromise (the world becomes Sweden), the rise of other countries to convert the power dyad into a triad, or multiple constituencies, and so on. This uncertainty was at times a dangerous one, not just because of the real threat of mutually assured destruction, but also because knowledge about the present was as uncertain as the future: the present we were living would come to look different from the perspective of what came next.

After the end of the Cold War, globalization was a discourse that offered to make the present (time) and the planet (space) intelligible.

After Globalization, First Edition. Eric Cazdyn and Imre Szeman.
© 2011 Eric Cazdyn and Imre Szeman. Published 2011 by Blackwell Publishing Ltd.

Intelligible does not mean clear or simple. Globalization as both discourse and reality were certainly confusing enough. The resolution of the protracted political, economic, and military struggles that followed World War II occurred at the same time as the birth of new technologies and a vibrant technophilia, the emergence of pronounced anxieties about environmental limits, demographic worries (population decline in most Western countries mirrored by their near-logarithmic explosion elsewhere), and the full-blown emergence of global mass culture – an intensified and extensified society of the spectacle, redoubled in force and social significance since first described by Guy Debord in the 1960s.[2] Globalization was imagined and conceptualized by vectors of force and sites of impact running across the range of flora and fauna into which we continue to map our social existence: economics, politics, culture, and society. Still, despite its complexity, globalization *was* intelligible – a process (or set of processes), or period, or even an ideological narrative, that could be understood and graphed in detail. There was a vast academic apparatus devoted to doing just this, bolstered by new technological tools that allowed for quicker communication of results and new modes of analysis.

Globalization was a name for the moment; it was also, as we have insisted, an ideological project, one whose function was to make a claim on the character of the present. Globalization marked, at long last, the conclusion of the project of human social development, the arrival of the world's various constituencies into an accord over the governing principles of political economy. There were some malcontents and disappointed parties (no system can be perfect). But there was also broad agreement over the paths to pursue for social (read: economic) improvement and success, now and forever more.

In the process of naming and claiming the present, globalization has had an effect perhaps no one might have imagined when the "new world order" was being evoked into existence. Globalization has become a perpetual present, a project and a period without an end. The oft-referred-to crisis of the left can be summarized as an inability to mount any resistance against this restructuring of time – a redefinition of time that evacuates the future in favor of the present, translating the ontic into the ontological. The 2008 economic crisis confirms this time shift. Where once one might have expected a global reaction on the scale of the European revolutions of 1848, or the worldwide struggles between police and protestors in 1968, today we have outrage without much action. The recently announced decision by US billionaires to donate half of their wealth to good causes has been greeted in the press not with the analysis proper to it – the criticism mounted, for instance, by Slavoj Žižek of figures like financier George Soros, who plunders the public during the day only to give half back in the evening[3] – but with praise and comradely backslapping. The heroes of the digital age have done good – again![4] Today, capitalism is plainly understood as an unjust system, but instead of hopes of bringing it to an end, there is a meek accommodation, and a hope (given that there are no alternatives), that it can be made to work well for most – which is to admit that it of necessity can't work for everyone.

What is it that makes this state of affairs intelligible? In his blog "The Conscience of a Liberal," Paul Krugman writes: "Open immigration can't coexist with a strong social safety net; if you're going to assure health care and a decent income to everyone, you can't make the offer global."[5] A strong safety net can help to offset the problems generated by our social and economic systems. Immediately, however, it is admitted that only a few can be so lucky as to enjoy this safety: it is impossible on a global scale. Here is a paradigmatic case of the limits of liberalism: the necessity, as Nicholas Brown puts it, to "believe two contradictory things at once: an imperative to protect the unlucky, and an imperative not to protect the unlucky."[6] Krugman expresses unhappiness at this state of affairs – his liberal conscience at work again, allowing him to square the circle of the contradictions of the system by recourse to the arbitrariness of nationalism and a moralism marked by its immorality. This combination of moralism and nationalism which permits an evasion of the problems and limits of global capitalism is a logic we have seen at work in the other figures whose ideas about globalization we have looked at: it is an insight produced through blindness, though advocated as if the world was viewed through an X-ray rendering of hidden forces made clear only to the author's eye.

The books we examine in Part II always a US audience even as they speak about the globe. This is not just a formal or rhetorical gesture – something required for the purposes of market share and to garner reviews in the appropriate news organs of the liberal center. Rather, it constitutes an admission of the divide between the United States and everyone: an awareness of the fiction of the political rhetoric that globalization benefits everyone, and the need to maximize opportunities and limited resources for one's own nation. It is in this sense that Zakaria's post-American world is American through and through, that Florida's fascination with a capitalist utopia of creativity is framed as a competition between nations (and indeed between cities within them), and that Friedman scours the world for anecdotes that might help him to grasp the secret of the new world confronted by America so that America might benefit from it. Even the Canadian globalist Klein is ready to allow for a world of nationalist competition, not to mention one in which capitalism itself persists, if in the form of mixed markets. This is a view that doesn't resolve the problem of social and economic injustice, but repeats Krugman's contradictory logic even if it seems that her politics are to the left.

Technique, expertise, competency – the fantasy of epistemic control we see on display in *Michael Clayton* is a component part of the practice of rendering the complexities of the globe intelligible for the purposes of nationalism. It is essential for the coherence of this fantasy, however, that this technical expertise be conjoined with a morality that governs the correct use of knowledge about the globe and smoothes over contradictions that might arise from the application of technical insight to get ahead at the expense of others. As significant as this persistence of the nation is, the retreat from structural or systemic accounts back to an appeal to the logic of the bad man is equally significant. At one extreme, this takes the form of global conspiracy theories, from the idea that the planet is managed by the Bilderberg Group or The Family, to the belief that plans are exchanged amongst elites at Davos. Moralism need not take such extremes, however; the measurement of good and bad corporations, good and bad products, owners, politicians, athletes, and so on, has become ubiquitous. It is symptomatic that one of the largest companies on the planet – the corporation that embodies the tendencies of the global moment more than any other – bears a slogan that invokes the ethical. As with Krugman's conscience, Google's "Do no evil" does not in fact prevent the company from making questionable decisions about privacy or the undemocratic control and management of information, so much as it helps it to continue to imagine itself as not truly a corporation (its motives are different!) even as its market value grows ($185 billion in January 2010).[7] In the present moment, politics has become less about policies or changes to systems than the individual behavior and beliefs of those in charge. At a moment when one cannot help but attend to interconnected global systems – from the economic to the ecological – the Great Man theory of history returns, with a focus on the moral disposition of the leader. The growing disappointment over the first years of the Obama administration stems less from its policy outcomes than from shock at the fact that the world hasn't changed as a result of a "good" leader taking over from a "bad" one.

This is a book about intelligibility. What we find ourselves concluding is that what passes for intelligibility today does not in fact produce insight into our present or future, but actively works to solidify our sense of the limits we face and the possibilities available to us. It's no mystery that capitalism is the operating system of the planet. But this knowledge of capitalism is not the same as an understanding of it and of its influence on our habits, understanding, expectations, views of past and present, and what might yet be. What we are calling intelligibility here – a bureaucratic-sounding word, one lacking the gravitas of many concepts or figures – has in other contexts been called utopia. Utopianism has come to mean a certain kind of fantastical or wishful thinking about impossibilities. But this is to misunderstand the significance of utopia for both politics and the generation of concepts. If utopia engages the impossible, then it does so with the ultimate desire to shift the realm of possibility. Utopia, therefore, is ultimately about *possibility*. In particular, it is about the possibility that things might be other than they are – for instance, that we might develop a world in which everyone has access to adequate amounts of food, clean water, or even simply the opportunity to work.[8] It is the desire for this possibility, uncompromised and genuine, that we feel is missing. The students whom we interview in Part III understand the absence of this future possibility from their present, but are unwilling or unable to address it. As for the liberals? They expend energy on the development of an exit strategy situated squarely within existing relations, and then express satisfaction and even surprise at having found what they always already knew was there. As Nietzsche reminds us, "If someone hides an object behind a bush, then seeks and finds it there, that seeking and finding is not very laudable."[9]

Something's missing when instead of the possibility of radical difference, we find always and everywhere the same ideas of how we might proceed. Of course, something's been missing for a long time, even if globalization offers a different context (and thus, distinct challenges for critique) in which this is the case. This phrase comes from a discussion about political possibility which took place almost a half-century ago. "Something's Missing" (1964)[10] is the title of a discussion between Ernst Bloch and Theodor Adorno about utopia and its fate. Both thinkers find utopia to have become banalized in the modern world through the coming into being of all kinds of techno-logical inventions that are utopian in their character (television, air travel) and made ubiquitous by having become associated with even the act of purchasing an object (a fantasy that can come to fruition, a wish that can be fulfilled, even though Adorno suggests that in so doing "one sees oneself almost always deceived"[11]). The substance of Adorno and Bloch's discussion focuses on the importance of seeing utopia *negatively* – not as this or that kind of society, as mapped out by figures like Thomas More or Tommaso Campanella, but as the "capability to imagine the totality as something that could be completely different."[12] Treating utopia negatively acts as a defense against "the cheap utopia, the false utopia, *the* utopia that can be bought."[13] As a negation of what merely *is*, utopia acts as a critique of the present, pointing to what *should be*. The content of utopias is less important than the expression of a *will* for the present to be different. When it is said that some utopian goal or aim "cannot be realized," what is really being said is "we do not *want* it to be realized."[14] Bloch suggests that this utopian impulse is captured in the sentence "Something's missing" (*Etwas fehlt*) – "one of the most profound sentences that Brecht ever wrote"[15] – which Bloch takes from Bertolt Brecht and Kurt Weil's 1930 opera *The Rise and Fall of the*

City of Mahagonny. The diminishment or complete absence of this impulse by the 1960s is not an accident. Bloch suggests that "There is a very clear interest that has prevented the world from being changed into the possible."[16]

It is worth tracing this sentence back to its origins. At once an opera that criticizes bourgeois opera in form and content and a savage allegory of life under capitalism, Brecht's libretto for *Mahagonny* has been viewed as deliberately crude and didactic. Set in the American Wild West, a space of unfettered capitalism where money rules and rules are few and far between, *Mahagonny* shows what the world looks like underneath the veneer of European bourgeois culture. Jimmy and his crew of lumberjacks arrive in Mahagonny ready to spend the cash they've accumulated after seven years of working in the wilderness. After their long labor, they expect to translate this money into the fulfillment of all their desires – the happiness and freedom of consumption that one imagines is the reward for engaging in production. But things go wrong almost immediately. Grown bored of cheap gin and whiskey, fishing and smoking, and tired of the rules that Lokadja Begbick starts to institute in the once anarchic town, Jimmy decides to leave Mahagonny and runs to the pier to catch a boat out of town. His friends try to keep him from leaving, describing all that he can still do in the city: sleeping, swimming, enjoying himself in myriad ways. To all their entreaties, he repeats: "Something's missing."[17] Jimmy is in existential despair: "And why does nothing make sense at all?/You tell me, please, why nothing makes sense at all ... You tell me! What is it a man was born for?"[18]

What follows confirms the play's reputation as a blunt critique of the injustices of capitalism. After a series of misfortunes – starting with the typhoon which narrowly avoids the city and which allows Jimmy to take control away from Begbick – the play ends with Jimmy being brought in front of a tribunal to account for the city's problems. He famously receives the death sentence not for his crimes of gluttony, drunkenness, fighting, or prostitution, but for not having money to pay his debts (two rounds of whiskey and a broken bar rail). At one level, the lesson is a straightforward one. As Adorno writes in his review of *Mahagonny*, "the present system, with its order, rights, and more, is exposed as anarchy; we ourselves live in Mahagonny, where everything is permitted save one thing: having no money."[19]

But the opera is more complex than this. If it were only a critique of capitalism and its inability to produce human happiness, it would fail to explore the full significance of Jimmy's feeling that "something's missing." *Mahagonny* is, first, an exploration of the limits of bad utopianism – that is, of a utopia that imagines that it can be actualized in the form of a set of rules and procedures, or even in the supposed freedom that comes when they are suspended. Jimmy's response to his feeling that something's missing (after threatening to eat his hat – "Jimmy! Hat-eating/'S not what mankind was born for"[20]) is, in the confusion of the typhoon scare, to take control of Mahagonny, eliminating Begbick's edicts and prohibitions and reintroducing the anarchy that once ruled. The crisis allows the city to swing from recession to boom times, but it doesn't manage to fill up the absence that Jimmy experiences. Instead, the result is the tragic opposite of the pure freedom for which he hoped. Though it might have appeared that Jimmy's version of Mahagonny undid the limits of Begbick's, the larger system within which both were configured remained in place. It is a point Brecht cannot resist driving home in the opera's conclusion, in the inscriptions placed on the signs of the demonstrators:

First group. Begbick, Fatty the Bookie, Trinity Moses and supporters. The inscriptions on the first group's signs read:
 "FOR THE INFLATION"
 "FOR THE BATTLE OF ALL AGAINST ALL"
 "FOR THE CHAOTIC STATE OF OUR CITIES"
 "FOR THE PROLONGATION OF THE GOLDEN AGE"
First group:
 For this splendid Mahagonny
 Has it all, if you have the money.
 Then all is available
 Because all is for sale
 And there is nothing that one cannot buy.

The inscriptions on the second group's signs read:
   "FOR PROPERTY"
   "FOR THE EXPLOITATION OF OTHERS"
   "FOR THE JUST DIVISION OF SPIRITUAL GOODS"
   "FOR THE UNJUST DIVISION OF TEMPORAL GOODS"
   "FOR LOVE"
   "FOR THE BUYING AND SELLING OF LOVE"
   "FOR THE NATURAL DISORDER OF THINGS"
   "FOR THE PROLONGATION OF THE GOLDEN AGE"[21]

It is not surprising that Jimmy would imagine utopia to be found in the simple and direct negation of prohibition and the unleashing of individual desires – desires which are of necessity the product of those selfsame limits and thus still bound to them. As Lydia Goehr reminds us, "*Mahagonny* projects a closed world in which there is no 'noncapitalist space.'"[22] Despite all the injustices, exploitation, and chaos listed on the signs of the protestors, each ends with a hope "for the prolongation of the golden age." What is on display in *Mahagonny* is "the closed world of bourgeois consciousness which considers bourgeois social reality to be immutable."[23] What's missing is not simply an outside that would make it possible to see the laws of human happiness shaping life in Mahagonny as socially produced and not in any sense natural, but a sense of mutability or change that would open up the possibility of seeing that the golden age is anything but. The opera offers a direct critique of capitalism, but does so in a way that draws our attention to the political or conceptual blockages that need to be addressed if one is to do more than affirm it even by denying it, as Jimmy has the misfortune to do.

But *how* to do so without reaching for or appealing to an outside that doesn't exist in the world of Mahagonny? This is our problem more than it was Brecht's; there was for him not just the proximate lesson of the Soviet revolution, but also all kinds of political agitation within Germany – and even within the United States – that preceded and followed that first great system failure: the Great Depression of 1929. In the wake of *our* crash, we have few examples of counter-systems ready to hand to which we can reach for ideas, and certainly no non-capitalist space to map and explore: globalization has made this a certainty, even if there might be some small zones in which experiments with other modes of life are taking place. In the intervening years, Brecht's theatrical projection of Mahagonny into the non-space of the American West has been rendered actual. The Los Angeles Opera's 2007 staging of *Mahagonny* perceptively renders the city as Las Vegas – a place to which one goes after a stretch of work for pure leisure and secret indulgence in one's fantasies ("What happens in Vegas stays in Vegas"). In an era of deregulation and faux freedoms as a result of the retreat of the state, Mahagonny is no longer allegory of a possibility still on the horizon as much as it is the reality with which we have to contend.

Brecht provides us with an insight into how we might render visible the character of our own Gilded Age – that is, render it intelligible, which is to say, into a system with a history, which is mutable and does not confine us like fate. In his review of the opera, Adorno draws attention to a key inversion which it can be possible to miss or to mistake. In the first scene, Begbick's associates, Fatty and Moses, say that "this entire city of Mahagonny exists only because everything is so bad, because there is no peace and no harmony, and because there is nothing anyone can believe in."[24] Jimmy's response comes as a negation of this "fun of peace and concord"[25]: "Ah, no one will ever be happy throughout your Mahagonny because there is too much peace and too much harmony, and because there is too much in which one can believe."[26] It is this surplus of belief that critical thinking has to address, a surplus of the actual and pragmatic, of the prescriptions of common sense, that stands in the way of the possible. What Jimmy misunderstands is that his negation of Begbick's system has to be more *radical*, an order of thought satisfied not just with raising questions about the practices of the Golden Age, but of its very existence. And the only way to do this is to set thinking free at the same time that we break ourselves from a commitment to the reigning rule of the social, such that we can get past the limit placed on possibility.

Our seven theses on globalization are written in the negative not to shut down possibilities, but to ensure that they are enabled in the most powerful sense possible. Otherwise, as we have argued and shown, any affirmation of "solutions" to our present problems and impasses is to think within a framework that accepts as impractical the idea that everyone could – or even *should* – be included as fully as possible in the social. Negation produces an awareness of system, and of its limits, in a manner in which little else is liable to do. In his discussion with Bloch, Adorno says at one point:

> Yesterday you quoted Spinoza in our discussion with the passage, "Verum index sui et falsi" [The true is the sign of itself and the false]. I have varied this a little in the sense of the dialectical principle of the determined negation and have said, Falsum – the false thing – index sui et veri [The false is the sign of itself and the correct]. That means that the true thing determines the false thing, or via that which makes itself falsely known. And insofar as we are not allowed to cast the picture of utopia, insofar as we do not know what the correct thing would be, we know exactly, to be sure, what the false thing is.[27]

The fact that we seem to have given up on radical possibilities and are afraid to imagine utopian futures speaks not to the failure of utopia, but to the falsity of the ways in which we live our lives and think of our planet at the present time. The truth of the way that the world should be shows us the falseness of the way it is.

Something's missing – not this or that thing, easily located and thus introduced in a manner that resolves the quest for it once and for all. Something's missing: our ability to separate truth and falsity, and to catch a glimpse of a horizon that isn't merely the present we already know and find so troubled and wanting.

Notes

1. Ernst Bloch and Theodor Adorno, "Something's Missing: A Discussion between Ernst Bloch and Theodor W. Adorno on the Contradictions of Utopian Longing," in Ernst Bloch, *The Utopian Function of Art and Literature: Selected Essays*, trans. Jack Zipes and Frank Mecklenburg (Cambridge, MA: The MIT Press, 1998), 14.
2. Guy Debord, *Society of the Spectacle*, trans. Donald Nicholson-Smith (New York: Zones Books, 1994).

3. Slavoj Žižek, "Nobody has to be vile," *London Review of Books* 28, no. 7 (April 6, 2006): 10.

4. For an exception to this general trend in media coverage of Bill Gates's and Warren Buffett's "Giving Pledge," see "Negative Reaction to Charity Campaign: German Millionaires Criticize Gates' 'Giving Pledge,'" *Der Spiegel*, August 10, 2010. Available at: www.spiegel.de/international/germany/0,1518,710972,00.html (accessed November 8, 2010).

5. Paul Krugman, "The Curious Politics of Immigration," The Conscience of a Liberal Blog (*NY Times*), April 26, 2010. Available at: http://krugman.blogs.nytimes.com/2010/04/26/the-curious-politics-of-immigration/ (accessed November 8, 2010).

6. Nicholas Brown, "Hegel for Marxists (and Marxism for Everyone)," unpublished paper.

7. For a more detailed analysis, see Imre Szeman, "'Do No Evil': Google and Evil as a Political Category," *Topia: Canadian Journal of Cultural Studies* 18 (2007): 131–139.

8. Fredric Jameson has suggested that "the most radical demand to make on our own system . . . [is] the demand for full employment, universal full employment around the globe" (37). What such a demand reveals starkly is the shape and character of political and economic structures that render any such demand unrealizable. The possibility for all individuals to engage in productive social labor simply *cannot* happen because of the structural need for a reserve army of labor, which takes distinct forms in different parts of the world. Jameson's point here, as in much of his writing on utopia, is that because so basic a right cannot be realized, a political opening is possible: a demand for a "society structurally distinct from this one in every conceivable way, from the psychological to the sociological, from the cultural to the political" (37). Jameson, "The Politics of Utopia," *New Left Review* 25 (2004): 35–54.

9. Friedrich Nietzsche, "On Truth and Lying in an Extra-Moral Sense," *Friedrich Nietzsche on Rhetoric and Language*, ed. and trans. Sander L. Gilman, Carole Blair, and David J. Parent (New York: Oxford University Press, 1989), 251.

10. Bloch and Adorno, "Something's Missing," 1–17.

11. Ibid., 1.

12. Bloch in ibid., 3–4.

13. Adorno in ibid., 11.

14. Adorno in ibid., 13.
15. Ibid., 15.
16. Bloch in ibid., 7.
17. "Aber etwas fehlt," though translated as "But it won't quite do" and "But they won't quite do" in Bertolt Brecht, "The Rise and Fall of the City of Mahagonny," in *Bertolt Brecht: Collected Plays*, vol. 2, part 3, ed. John Willett and Ralph Mannheim (London: Eyre Methuen, 1979), 19. The title of Scene 8 is "Seek and ye shall not find."
18. Brecht, "The Rise and Fall of the City of Mahagonny," 20.
19. Theodor W. Adorno, "Mahagonny," in *The Weimar Republic Sourcebook*, ed. Anton Kaes, Martin Jay, and Edward Dimendberg (Berkeley, CA: University of California Press, 1994), 588. First published as "Mahagonny," *Musikblätter des Anbruch* 14 (February–March 1932): 12–15.
20. Brecht, "The Rise and Fall of the City of Mahagonny," 20.
21. Ibid., 63–64.
22. Lydia Goehr, "Hardboiled Disillusionment: *Mahagonny* as the Last Culinary Opera," *Cultural Critique* 68 (2008): 4–5.
23. Adorno, "Mahagonny," 589.
24. Adorno, "Mahagonny," 589.
25. Brecht, "The Rise and Fall of the City of Mahagonny," 24.
26. Adorno, "Mahagonny," 589.
27. Bloch and Adorno, "Something's Missing," 12.

Index

After Globalization, First Edition. Eric Cazdyn and Imre Szeman.
© 2011 Eric Cazdyn and Imre Szeman. Published 2011 by Blackwell Publishing Ltd.

Index

Index